P9-DHC-024

ON
ADOLESCENCE

On
Adolescence

A Psychoanalytic Interpretation

by Peter Blos

The Free Press, New York
Collier-Macmillan Limited, London

Copyright © 1962 by The Free Press of Glencoe, Inc.

Printed in the United States of America

All rights reserved. No part of this book may be reproduced or utilized in any form or by any means, electronic or mechanical, including photocopying, recording, or by any information storage and retrieval system, without permission in writing from the Publisher.

Collier-Macmillan Canada, Ltd., Toronto, Ontario

Library of Congress Catalog Card Number: 61–14110

First Free Press Paperback Edition 1966

I? I? What am I? "I am alone with the beating of my heart." I, hey I! What is I? "I is the lonely and the lost, always searching for . . . what?" Another I? An answering is it? No? But what then? There is more; the I is the way from the inner to the all, from the smallest of the self to the most of every people.

Now I look into myself and see the I of me, the weak and aimless thing which makes me. I is not strong and needs be, I needs to know direction, but has none. My I is not sure, there are too many wrongs and mixed truths within to know. I changes and does not know. I knows little reality and many dreams. What I am now is what will be used to build the later self. What I am is not what I want to be, although I am not sure what this is which I do not want.

But then what is I? My I is my answer to every all of every people. It is this which I have to give to the waiting world and from here comes all that is different.

I is to create.

—From a dramatic poem by John D., age 17.

114209

Preface

THERE COMES a time during one's study of a particular problem when the many observations and speculations that have accumulated before the inquiring mind make it an urgent task to establish organizing principles and a rank order of ideas. Because only by systematizing our findings can we put our observations and experience to use, and open the door to inquiry. These words express the mental climate in which this book came to life, after several decades of studying adolescents. All during these years I remained mindful of the words with which Freud brought the "Transformations in Puberty" to a close: "The starting-point and the final aim of the process . . . are clearly visible. The intermediate steps are still in many ways obscure to us. We shall have to leave more than one of them as an unsolved riddle." I have concentrated on the "intermediate steps"; they are described here as the phases of adolescence.

In concentrating on the "intermediate steps" I have arrived at the formulation of the five phases of the adolescent process. I am in consonance with the general trend in psychoanalytic theory when I attribute an increasingly weighty significance to the pregenital and preoedipal phases of drive and ego development. Over the years it has almost become commonplace to comment on the insufficiency of a theory of personality development which is based solely on libidinal progression. A much broader conception, which takes the entire psychological development into account has become an important part of psychoanalytic thinking. The recent expansion of ego psychology has also made us look at the latency period with new eyes; we have come to recognize that it is an essential preparatory transformation without which adolescence as a developmental phase cannot establish itself. Therefore this antecedent period receives explicit attention.

It should be said at the outset that this book concerns itself with the psychoanalytic theory of adolescence in its typical, or, shall we say, normal form. Neither psychopathology nor treatment of adolescents is considered herein, for a presentation of these subjects depends on the previous establishment of a unified theory of adolescence, which is precisely the task of this study. Whatever can be built on the theory as here offered must be left to future work.

It also should be made clear that I have restricted myself in this book to the kind of adolescent and to the kind of research of which I have firsthand knowledge. This is to say that my observations, my descriptions, and my conclusions are based on those adolescents of the Western world with whom psychoanalysts have become familiar. I have, of course, drawn liberally and appreciatively on the wealth of knowledge about adolescence that has been the result of psychoanalytic contributions; and in integrating these contributions with my own work I have paid due tribute to the respective authors. On the other hand, I have refrained from dipping into anthropological and sociological data because I did not intend to establish relevant connections between psychoanalysis and other disciplines. Nonetheless, environment and culture as intrinsic factors in personality formation have received special attention in a chapter exclusively devoted to this topic.

In the course of writing this book and of making use of my experiences with adolescents I have conscientiously tried to avoid two kinds of trouble which bedevil many of the writers in this field. On the one hand I have heeded William James' warning about the "psychologist's fallacy"—that is, "the confusion of his own standpoint with that of the mental fact about which he is making a report." The other precaution can best be expressed by humoring the problem; toward this end I shall quote a dialogue from Shakespeare's *Antony and Cleopatra*:

Lepidus: What manner o' thing is your crocodile?
Antony: It is shaped, sir, like itself, and it is as broad as it hath breadth; it is just so high as it is, and moves with its own organs; it lives by that which nourisheth it; and the elements once out of it, it transmigrates.
Lepidus: What colour is it of?
Antony: Of its own colour too.
Lepidus: 'Tis a strange serpent.

For critical reading of the manuscript I want to express my gratitude to Drs. Mary O'Neil Hawkins and Marjorie Harley. My special indebtedness, however, is to Dr. Andrée Royon who afforded me her enthusiasm when my ideas took shape and brought to bear on them the acuity of her mind as well as the wealth of her psychoanalytic knowledge; last but not least, she gave me the unsparing criticism of a true friend and colleague from the inception to the completion of this book. My everlasting indebtedness is to the many adolescents who over the years have assisted me in my endeavors to understand them.

PETER BLOS

Summer, 1961
Holderness, N.H.

Contents

ON
ADOLESCENCE

Introduction:
Puberty and Adolescence

AT NO TIME have observers of human development failed to recognize the momentous significance of the physical and psychological dimensions of puberty. Sexual maturation has always given this stage of growth a signal importance to which the personality transformations of this period were directly and causally related. However, not until the psychology of early childhood had been explored and systematized through psychoanalysis was it possible to understand puberty in its psychological aspects: it is to these aspects that we refer when we speak of *adolescence*. The elucidations of early childhood linked adolescence genetically to earlier periods of life; thus puberty was instated into a continuum of psychological development. We came to recognize adolescence as the terminal stage of the fourth phase of psychosexual development, the genital phase, which had been interrupted by the latency period.

The psychoanalytic knowledge of childhood was first derived by reconstruction from the analysis of adults and later confirmed and elaborated by child analysis and direct observation. What we have learned about adolescence is almost wholly the result of clinical studies of adolescents themselves. This source of information will undoubtedly be enriched and elaborated through memory and reconstruction of adolescence in the analysis of adults. It appears that certain psychic spheres and processes inaccessible to analysis during adolescence can more easily and succinctly be investigated in retrospect through the derivatives of the adolescent period analyzed at a later age. The reconstruction of adolescence in adult analysis has recently received explicit attention, and indeed is increasingly considered a requisite component of a total genetic reconstruction.

The biological event of puberty gives rise to a new drive and ego organization. In this process we recognize the developmental model of early childhood, wherein mental organizations were formed in association with physiological functions, thus establishing the erogenous zones of the body. The term puberty is used here to denote the physical manifestations of sexual maturation: e.g., prepuberty refers to the period just preceding the development of primary and secondary sex characters. The term adolescence is used to denote the psychological processes of adaptation to the condition of pubescence. Consequently, the phase of preadolescence, which makes its appearance at a given state of physical maturation, remains independent in its course: e.g., the phase of preadolescence can continue overly long, unaffected by the progression of physical maturation.

The fact remains that pubescent change or the state of sexual maturation influences the rise and decline of certain interests and attitudes; this has been borne out by statistical studies (Stone, et al. 1939). They have shown that "a greater proportion of postmenarchial as compared with premenarchial girls gave responses indicating heterosexual interests and interests in adornment and display of person; on the other hand, they revealed a disinterest in participation in games and activities requiring vigorous or strenuous activity; they engaged in or were interested in imaginative and day-dreaming activities." Such findings, of course, do not reveal intrinsic characteristics of the pubertal condition; however, they do demonstrate how sexual maturation initiates shifts and changes in the mental life of the pubescent child. The quality and content of these changes is immensely flexible; it is left to the sociologist to record and study their manifestations. It is the concern of this study to abstract from the manifest mental content those psychological processes which can be considered specific to the various phases of adolescence.

In the days of prepsychoanalytic psychology, puberty was considered the time of onset, physically and emotionally, of sexual development. The analytic insight into early childhood has corrected this view, and the onset of sexuality in early childhood has become an accepted fact. Freud (1905, b) described in broad outlines the phases of psychosexual development in the *Three Essays on the Theory of Sexuality,* and offered the first psychoanalytic concept of puberty: he applied the genetic principle to the period of puberty. As early as 1898, Freud has already stated that it is erroneous to suppose that the child's sexual life begins with the onset of puberty.

Psychoanalysis has always spoken of two prominent periods in the development of sexuality, namely, early childhood and puberty. Both phases emerge under the tutelage of physiological functions, such as nursing in infancy and genital maturation in puberty. Instinctual drives at the dawn of life enlist the perceptomotor apparatus for the reduction of tension. Consequently the child soon becomes inextricably interwoven with his environment, on which need gratification depends. The long duration of the child's dependency is what makes man human. In this process the development of memory, causality, conscience, and fantasy make thinking and conflict possible. Thus abundant alternative solutions to the pressures of instinctual drives make their appearance. The variability of the object of instinctual drives has always been described by psychoanalysis as almost infinite, while the aim has a far greater constancy. It is no surprise to see that the psychological representation of the environment, including attendant conflictual anxiety, soon stands in the way of any simple solution to drive-satisfaction; in other words, the total personality becomes gradually involved in the maintenance of a psychosomatic homeostasis.

During the period of growth—comprising roughly the first two decades of life—there is progressive personality differentiation and integration. Differentiating processes are effected by maturational stimulants simultaneously acting from within and from without in supplementary and complementary fashion, and are integrated in conformity with the maturational schedule of the body and of the psychic apparatuses. The capacity to assess, reconcile, and accommodate internal and external stimuli, benign and dangerous, enables the ego to live in relative harmony with drive, superego, and environment.

Let us return to the panorama of developmental peaks. Some of these deserve our special notice because later they will help us find our way in a more complicated terrain. We must keep in mind that the complex phenomena of adolescence are built on specific antecedents which reside in early childhood. If we can recognize the survival of these basic organizations in their derivative forms, we shall be able to discern psychic origins and to study the formation of psychic structures.

Infancy is governed by the pleasure-pain principle, which loses its supremacy as the infant's trust in the mother as the comforter of its physical or emotional distress grows stronger. This basic life situation is of lasting influence and is apt to be revived in critical situations during later years. The function of regulating anxiety is performed by the parents—particularly the mother—in the early years and is partly taken over by the child as fantasy life develops and soothing activities—sucking, stroking, masturbation, play, and body movement—progressively become subject to the child's volition. Thus the child relentlessly pursues new ways to master anxiety, ways in which play activities with fantasy content and psychological meaning move into the foreground of importance. The distinction of inside and outside reality, of me and not-me, signals the child's growing separation from the mother and a lessening of dependency. The differentiation takes a decisive turn at about two years of age, initiating the process of individuation; it ordinarily has achieved a degree of stability at about the age of three. Mobility, language, and social experiences widen the child's life space and bring to his awareness the desirability of being like others, most importantly, like the parent or sibling. This forward push into life fills the four- or five-year-old with the desire to take father's or mother's place or either one's alternately, indeed simultaneously. A logical consequence of the child's dependency on the adult makes him believe that taking the role of the parent of the same sex will afford him the desired attributes of the displaced parent, attributes which are so highly admired and envied by the young child. Reality renders the attainment of these wishes futile, however, and the child must settle reluctantly for the promise that the future will bring him the fulfillments he must forego at this stage. The child permanently preserves his aspirations and his defeats by making the parent a part of himself; therefore the superego has been defined as "the heir of the oedipus complex" (Freud, 1923, a).

The period intervening between the early bloom of infantile sexuality and pubescent genital sexuality is referred to as the latency period.

"Complete dependence on the parents ceases and identification begins to take the place of object-love" (A. Freud, 1936). Consequently, formal learning and group life attract more of the child's attention; social consciousness carries the child beyond the family confines, while family-centeredness continues to exert its influence. No new sexual aim arises during the years of about five to ten, namely from the end of early childhood to the beginning of puberty. These years constitute the latency period for which the lack of a new sexual aim is characteristic rather than the complete lack of sexual activity. There exists abundant evidence that all through middle childhood sexual activity or fantasy continue to exist in one form or another. The latency child acquires strength and competency in mastering both reality and instinct (sublimation) with the support of educational influences. These achievements are the fruit of the latency period; without their availability—or, to put it differently, without having passed through the latency period—the child will be defeated by puberty. The precondition for the adolescent process to evolve is a successful passage through the latency period.

The biphasic development of sexuality prolongs childhood and represents a uniquely human condition, which in great measure is responsible for man's cultural attainments. At the present time there is a tendency to prolong adolescence, due to the complexities of modern life. This of course cannot be without effect on the young individual and often overtaxes his adaptive potential.

Adolescence is most prominently characterized by physical changes, changes which are reflected in all facets of behavior. Not only is it true that adolescents of both sexes are deeply affected by the physical changes taking place in their own bodies—but on a more subtle and unconscious plane, the process of pubescence affects the development of their interests, their social behavior and the quality of their affective life. These patterns should not of course be regarded as the direct results of physiological factors, for no direct parallel can be established between adolescent changes occurring simultaneously in the anatomical, physiological, mental, and emotional development. Dispositions already existent before puberty will always affect the outcome.

There are, however, certain intrinsic features of the pubescent growth process which are relevant for an understanding of adolescent behavior and which therefore deserve our attention. Observers of adolescents have always been struck by the wide range in onset, duration, and termination of pubescence. A different tempo of physiological changes exists in different adolescents which is part of the individual's total growth pattern. Chronological age does not provide a valid criterion for physical maturation. Among the hundred boys studied by Stolz (1951) there are "ten who were two or more years retarded and an equal number who were two or more years accelerated in appropriate male structural and functional characteristics, described in terms of chronological age norms." Among girls a span of five years, from eleven to sixteen—with the mean menarchial age of 13.5 in the United States —constitutes the age range in which menarche occurs (Gallagher, 1960). Statistical studies have shown that the age of menarche has been slightly lowered during the last generation (Shuttleworth, 1938), and that the average height of the present generation of adolescent boys who have attained final stature is greater than that of their fathers. Not only is the individual variability of growth striking, but also the changes between generations have to be taken into account, since in adolescents there are always two generations significantly and crucially inter-twined.

Of course a certain stage of development prevails in each age group; and this majority, supported by outside influences, tends to set the stand-ard for physical appropriateness for the group. In relation to precocity and retardation, Stolz (1951) has noted that only in one or two cases of the hundred boys he studied was there "evidence that precocity contrib-uted to maladjustment, but eight of the ten retarded boys gave evidence of emotional insecurity." Generally, it can be said that those adolescents who enter pubescence early go through it rapidly, while the late matur-ing child progresses at a slower rate.

It is well known that girls begin their pubertal development and attain full growth at an earlier age than boys. "Girls gain in height at an accel-erating rate from nine to twelve years, whereas boys do so from eleven to fourteen years. This results in the fact that girls are taller than boys be-tween eleven and thirteen years" (Stuart, 1946). This difference in physical development between the sexes has an obvious significance for grouping children. Usually children are grouped in accordance with their chronological age level; consequently, children of the same age who are at different stages of physical development are put together in situa-tions which demand social and mental co-operation as well as competi-tion. The individual adolescent always lives within a group of age-mates who vary widely in physical development and in interests. This con-dition is responsible for the many forms of imitative and "as-if" behavior to which the adolescent resorts in order to keep within the expected pattern of conduct and to protect the social compatibility with the peer group to which he belongs.

In addition to the discrepancies in onset and duration of pubescence among a group of adolescents, the individual's own pattern of growth is not uniform throughout his body. Each organ system is affected by growth in a characteristic way; in terms of the total life span of the individual, each system consistently performs its function optimally. But during pubescence, extreme accelerations and retardations in the growth of particular organ systems produce an uneven distribution of growth within the total organism. Increase in body bulk may not be paralleled by a proportionate increase in breadth or in height; nor do primary and secondary sex characteristics develop at equal rates. This lack of uniformity in physical development, called *asymmetrical growth,* often puts extreme demands upon the physical and mental adaptivity of the individual. In this connection it has to be realized that growth often occurs as a sequence of sudden changes rather than as a gradual smooth progression. "The adolescent spurt of growth in height occurs during the tenth year in girls and during the thirteenth year in boys. The change from an accelerating to a decelerating rate occurs in the thirteenth year in girls and in the fifteenth year in boys" (Stuart, 1946). Growth spurts in relation to height, weight, musculature, and the development of primary and secondary sex characteristics may be accompanied by relevant emotional states. A change of one's body image, and a re-evaluation of the self in the light of new physical powers and sensations are two of the psychological consequences of the change in physical status. (These consequences are described below, in relation to the phases of adolescence.) And because the physical changes occurring during puberty are so marked and visible, the adolescent inevitably tends to compare his own bodily development with that of his contemporaries.

The majority of adolescents are concerned at one time or another with the normality of their physical status; the absence of clearcut age norms as far as adolescent physiology is concerned merely adds to their uncertainty. Physical differences among individuals of a comparable maturity level—and these differences are even greater in a group of the same age level—manifest themselves among girls in variations of the menstrual cycle and in breast development, among boys in variations of genital development, voice change, and facial hair. Such striking indications of

BRIDWELL LIBRARY
SOUTHERN METHODIST UNIVERSITY
DALLAS, TEXAS   75222

sexual maturation imbue physical growth with highly personal meanings.

Physical development, furthermore, does not always progress appropriately—it sometimes assumes features characteristic of the opposite sex. This seems to be less disturbing to girls than boys, perhaps because of the tendency among some groups of girls to prefer a boyish body build, a build also appreciated by boys. Boys are much more concerned (and so are their parents) when they manifest characteristics inappropriate to their sex. The development of the breast in boys (Grenlich, et al., 1942; Gallagher, 1960) tends to stimulate and accentuate bisexual fantasies and drives. The breast development is described by Stuart (1946) as "an elevation of the nipples in a slightly full areola. Occasionally, a mass of firm, sharply demarcated tissue several centimeters in diameter underlies this areola and gives the appearance of true breast development. This occurs about the time when dense, dark pubic hair is present at the base of the penis and when axillary hair is beginning to appear. This tissue disappears after a variable number of months, depending on its degree and development." In this connection it should also be mentioned that the preadolescent boy tends to adiposity of the lower torso which emphasizes feminine body contours. This condition normally disappears with accelerated growth in height.

Menarche is usually considered the sign that the girl has achieved sexual maturity. In fact this event really signals that the maturation of the reproductive organs is underway but is by no means complete. "It is now accepted that menstruation begins in most girls before their ovaries are capable of producing mature ova, and ovulation may take place before the uterus is mature enough to support normal gestation. This brings about a period of adolescent sterility" (Benedek, 1959, a). This period of post-menarchial sterility can last for a year or longer (Josselyn, 1954).

Pubescence is often marked by physical symptoms which make the afflicted adolescent acutely self-conscious of his changing body. Acne, a disfiguring skin condition, and various forms of dysmenorrhea are likely to interfere with the adolescent's desire to grow up. Obesity of different degrees and types, especially prevalent among girls, leads to experimentation with diets.

Often, the adolescent reacts to medical examination with self-conscious reluctance, which is prompted by the fear that the physician may discover inappropriate or abnormal developmental characteristics. Also,

the prospect of being examined is apt to intensify his masturbation conflicts, sexual fantasies, and the accompanying feelings of guilt.

One difficulty which arises in any discussion of adolescence stems
from the fact that there are many ways of completing the adolescent
process successfully, and thus achieving a stable ego and drive organization. Furthermore, the time span of this development is as relative as the
adaptive processes involved in the attainment of maturity are complex.
When ritualization and formalization relieve an individual from achieving his own resolution of the exigencies of growing up, no idiosyncratic
and personal adjustment has to be sought; little choice is open, and conflict is minimal. However, in cultures where tradition and custom exert
no unchallenged influence over the individual, the adolescent has to
achieve by personal resourcefulness the adaptation that institutionaliza-
tion does not offer him. On the other hand, this lack of institutionalized
patterning opens up the opportunity for individual development, for the
creation of a unique, highly original and personal variant on tradition.
The increase in psychological differentiation during adolescence is necessarily attended by an increase in psychic lability; this condition is reflected by adolescent emotional disturbances of varying seriousness and
crippling effects, transient or permanent.

It has been possible—with due allowance for some variability—to establish age norms of child development in early childhood. (In fact, the
younger the child, the narrower the variability.) A normative assessment
of adolescents must, however, be vague and incongruous. The high degree of plasticity so characteristic for adolescence works against this approach. It is true that there are sequential patterns of maturation in adolescence, but their relatedness to age is loose. Behavior at this age is a
complex phenomenon which is highly dependent on the individual life
history and on the milieu in which the adolescent grows up. However,
if we regard adolescence as a maturational period in which each individual has to work through the exigencies of his total life experiences in
order to arrive at a stable ego and drive organization, then any study of
adolescence must attempt to clarify those processes which lead to new
psychic formations or to psychic restructuring.

In many societies these new formations are conventionalized by traditional sanctions and taboos. The initiation rites which anthropologists
have so abundantly recorded are eloquent witnesses to the fact that at
puberty a profound reorganization of ego and libido positions occurs; and
some societies do provide models on which the adolescent can pattern his

personal resolution. By doing this, the society absorbs the maturational push of puberty into its organization and puts it to use for its own purposes. The designation of a new role and status offers the adolescent a self-image which is definite, reciprocal, and groupbound; at the same time, the societal assimilation of the maturing child is promoted. Without this kind of environmental complementation or reinforcement, the adolescent's self-image loses clarity and cohesiveness; consequently he requires constant restitutive and defensive operations to maintain it.

Forms of institutionalized status have changed through the ages and in different societies; they will not concern us in this study. We shall, in fact, restrict our investigations to Western culture, because only in this society have adolescents been studied with psychoanalytic methods. In contrast to many other cultures, modern Western society has progressively eliminated the ritualized or institutionalized assimilation of the adolescent. Religious remnants of such practices still exist; but they now have shrunk to historical, isolated relics out of step with the schedules of status change in all other areas of modern life.

There is still no societal agreement in Western culture as to the age at which an individual ceases to be a child, or ceases to be an adolescent and becomes an adult. The age definition of maturity has varied at different times, and it varies today in different localities. State laws differ considerably in defining the age of economic competence, as well as the age appropriate for obtaining a driver's license, getting married, and sustaining criminal liability. It is no wonder that under these contradictory and flexible societal conditions youth itself has created its own social forms and experiential patterns. The current "youth" or "peer cultures" are idiomatic expressions of adolescent needs. The adolescent has been forced, so to say, into a self-chosen and self-made way of life. All these efforts of youth are attempts to transform a biological event into a psychosocial experience.

Too little attention has been paid to the fact that adolescence, not only in spite of, but rather because of, its emotional turmoil, often affords spontaneous recovery from debilitating childhood influences, and offers the individual an opportunity to modify or rectify childhood exigencies which threatened to impede his progressive development. The regressive processes of adolescence permit the remodeling of defective or incomplete earlier developments; new identifications and counter-identifications play an important part in this. The profound upheaval associated with the emotional reorganization of adolescence thus harbors a beneficial potential: "The potentialities for formation of personality during latency and adolescence have been underrated in psychoanalytic writing" (Hartman, et al., 1946). Fenichel (1945) hinted at a similar concept: "Experience in puberty may solve conflicts or shift conflicts into a final direction; moreover, they may give older and oscillating constellations a final and definitive form." Erikson (1956) has suggested that we look at adolescence not as an affliction, but as a *"normative crisis, i.e.,* a normal phase of increased conflict characterized by a seeming fluctuation in ego strength, and yet also by a high growth potential. . . . What under prejudiced scrutiny may appear to be the onset of a neurosis, often is but an aggravated crisis which might prove to be self-liquidating and, in fact, contributive to the process of identity formation." One might add that the definitive settling of conflicts at the end of adolescence means either that they lose their disturbing quality because they have been characterologically stabilized, or they solidify into permanently debilitating symptoms or character disorders. We shall return to this complex process in the discussion of the terminal stage of adolescence.

Adolescence is here viewed as the sum total of all attempts at adjustment to the stage of puberty, to the new set of inner and outer—endogenous and exogenous—conditions which confront the individual. The urgent necessity to cope with the novel condition of puberty evokes all the modes of excitation, tension, gratification, and defense that ever played a role in previous years—that is, during the psychosexual development of infancy and early childhood. This infantile admixture is responsible for the bizarreness and the regressive character of adolescent behavior; it is the typical expression of the adolescent struggle to regain or to retain a psychic equilibrium which has been jolted by the crisis of puberty. The significant emotional needs and conflicts of early childhood must be recapitulated before new solutions with qualitatively different instinctual aims and ego interests can be found. This is why adolescence has been called a second edition of childhood; both periods have in common the fact that "a relatively strong id confronts a relatively weak ego" (A. Freud, 1936). It must be kept in mind that the pregenital phases of sexual organization are still at work trying to assert themselves; they interfere intermittently with the progress toward maturity.

The gradual advancement during adolescence toward the genital position and heterosexual orientation is only the continuation of a development which temporarily came to a standstill at the decline of the oedipal phase, a standstill which accentuates the biphasic sexual development in man.

We witness at adolescence a second step in individuation, the first one having occurred toward the end of the second year when the child experiences the fateful distinction between "self" and "non-self." A similar, yet far more complex, individuation experience occurs during adolescence, which leads in its final step to a sense of identity. Before the adolescent can consolidate this formation, he must pass through stages of self-consciousness and fragmented existence. The oppositional, rebellious, and resistive strivings, the stages of experimentation, the testing of the self by going to excess—all these have a positive usefulness in the process of self-definition. "This is not me" represents an important step in the achievement of individuation and in the establishment of autonomy; at an earlier age, it is condensed into a single word—"No!"

Adolescent individuation is accompanied by feelings of isolation, loneliness, and confusion. Individuation brings some of the dearest megalomaniacal dreams of childhood to an irrevocable end. They must now be relegated entirely to fantasy: their fulfillments can never again be considered seriously. The realization of the finality of the end of childhood, of the binding nature of commitments, of the definite limitation to individual existence itself—this realization creates a sense of urgency, fear, and panic. Consequently, many an adolescent tries to remain indefinitely in a transitional phase of development; this condition is called *prolonged adolescence.*

The adolescent's slow severance of the emotional ties to his family, his fearful or exhilarated entrance into the new life which beckons him, these experiences are among the profoundest in human existence. Only poets have been able to express adequately the quality of these feelings, their depth and scope. Sherwood Anderson has given a moving impression of the state of mind of an adolescent about to leave his home town, Winesburg, Ohio. His mother has just died; he is on his way to the big city where he must make a life for himself. The night before his departure he walks through the familiar streets of his town. Strange thoughts and feelings well up in him, arousing a desire for clarity, for awareness, for a link to past and future—briefly, he experiences that self-consciousness of existence which marks the entrance into adulthood.

George Willard, the Ohio village boy, was fast growing into manhood and new thoughts had been coming into his mind. All that day, amid the jam of people at the Fair, he had gone about feeling lonely. He was about to leave Winesburg to go away to some city where he hoped to get work on a city newspaper and he felt grown up. The mood that had taken possession of him was a thing known to men and unknown to boys. He felt old and a little tired. Memories awoke in him. To his mind his new sense of maturity set him apart, made him a half-tragic figure. He wanted someone to understand the feeling that had taken possession of him after his mother's death.

There is a time in the life of every boy when he for the first time takes the backward view of life. Perhaps that is the moment when he crosses the line into manhood. The boy is walking through the street of his town. He is thinking of the future and of the figure he will cut in the world. Ambitions and regrets awake within him. Suddenly something happens; he stops under a tree and waits as for a voice calling his name. Ghosts of old things creep into his consciousness; the voices outside of himself whisper a message concerning the limitations of life. From being quite sure of himself and his future he becomes not at all sure. If he be an imaginative boy a door is torn open and for the first time he looks out upon the world, seeing, as though they marched in procession before him, the countless figures of men who before his time have come out of nothingness into the world, lived their lives and again disappeared into nothingness. The sadness of sophistication has come to the boy. With a little gasp he sees himself as merely a leaf blown by the wind through the streets of his village. He knows that in spite of all the stout talk of his fellows he must live and die in uncertainty, a thing blown by the winds, a thing destined like corn to wilt in the sun. He shivers and looks eagerly about. The eighteen years he has lived seem but a moment, a breathing space in the long march of humanity. Already he hears death calling. With all his heart he wants to come close to some other human, touch someone with his hands, be touched by the hand of another. If he prefers that the other be a woman, that is because he believes that a woman will be gentle, that she will understand. He wants most of all, understanding.*

Anderson is describing the end of the adolescent process: childhood has receded into history, into memory; a new time perspective with a circumscribed past and a limited future sets life between birth and death. For the first time it becomes conceivable that one will age, as one's parents did and one's grandparents before them. The consciousness of one's age becomes suddenly different from that of childhood. George's mourning is like a symbol for the deep losses which adolescence entails. Alone and surrounded by man's eternal fear of abandonment and panic, the familiar and life-old need for human closeness awakens; love and under-

---

* Reprinted from Sherwood Anderson, *Winesburg, Ohio,* by permission of The Viking Press, Inc.

standing are expected to rekindle the trust in life, to blow away the fears of isolation and death. The limitless future of childhood shrinks to realistic proportions, to one of limited chances and goals; but, by the same token, the mastery of time and space and the conquest of helplessness afford a hitherto unknown promise of self-realization. This is the human condition of adolescence which the poet has laid bare.

II

Genetic
Considerations

THE FACT that adolescence constitutes one phase in the continuum of psychosexual development has always been implicit in psychoanalytic theory. The evolutional concept of psychoanalysis has opened the way to an understanding of those complex processes which during the adolescent period bring the instinctual vicissitudes of early childhood into harmony with the biological and social tasks thrust upon the individual during the second decade of his life. The years between early childhood and adolescence, the latency period, are of greatest preparatory importance for adolescence, because this period establishes new avenues for gratification and for mastery of the environment through the development of social competence and new physical and mental capabilities. Furthermore, latency development increases tension tolerance and makes an organized pursuit of learning possible; it also enlarges the conflict-free sphere of the ego, brings more stable and less ambivalent object relations into existence, and evolves workable and reliable methods for the maintenance of self-esteem. The outstanding characteristics of these methods are to be found in the areas of reality testing, defensive operations, and identifications. An increasing independence of the regulatory psychic functions from the environment, typical of this period, is usually considered an indication of ego strength.

In many ways, therefore, the child entering puberty is not the same as the one who entered the latency period. The instinctual urgencies of early childhood which decline during the latency years make themselves felt again at puberty. But the child whose ego development has relentlessly progressed during the intervening years of middle childhood has become resourceful enough to navigate successfully between the Scylla of instinct repression and the Charybdis of instinct gratification —or, to say it more simply, between progressive and regressive development (Bornstein, 1951; Buxbaum, 1951). The eventful passage through these straits is the story of adolescence.

Sexual maturation is the biological event which ushers in puberty: instinctual drives become intensified; new instinctual aims emerge only slowly and gradually, while infantile aims and objects of instinct gratification are pushed temporarily into the foreground. This process is brought to a conclusion when a sex-appropriate and ego-syntonic identity is established. The adolescent process which molds the personality in decisive and final ways can only be understood in terms of its antecedent history, the innate maturational push, and goal-oriented strivings, because these factors, in mutual interaction, effect the final personality formation. However, the uniqueness and the specificity of adolescent development is determined by preceding psychological organizations and by individual experiences during the prelatency years.

The genetic point of view with which adolescence is here approached makes it mandatory that we first turn our attention to early childhood. This does not mean recounting the total story of the psychological development of the child; it does entail a selective concentration on some aspects of drive and ego development, especially insofar as these influence the formation of masculinity and femininity. The stability of these formations, their irreversible, ego-syntonic fixity, eventually constitute the ground in which the sense of identity is anchored. The following discussion of early childhood is undertaken with the awareness that specific aspects of this period have genetically unique influences on the adolescent process. This approach makes adolescent behavioral phenomena tell something about their nature by revealing something of their history. Any organismic approach to behavior tends to establish a causative relevancy in three dimensions: the first is relative to the historical past of the organism, as a way to trace the sequential patterns of differentiation and integration; the second is relative to the adaptive processes in the present life situation of the individual; the third is concerned with the future, with directions, goals, anticipations with which the present is pregnant. "*Le présent est chargé du passé, et gros de l'avenir*" (Leibniz).

It goes without saying that the biological events of puberty push the problem of masculinity and femininity into a final position or into a final compromise formation. In fact, ego development during these years takes its cue from the drive organization that gains ascendancy or dominance during the successive phases of adolescence. Consequently, in order to understand the shifts of libido and aggression as well as the ego movements during adolescence, it is necessary to trace the development of masculinity and femininity through the different stages of psychosexual development and to investigate the influence of this development on the ego. This will be done here with particular emphasis on the different paths which the boy and girl follow in the formation of their respective masculine or feminine identity. We shall try to avoid misleading generalizations, mindful of Freud's (1931) remark: "We have, after all, long given up any expectation of a neat parallelism between male and female sexual development."

The special aspects of early development which are to be discussed were selected because they represent essential genetic antecedents which define the various phases of adolescence and instate them into a continuum of psychological development. The selective aspects of early development are subsequently viewed in terms of their dynamic and genetic correlations to the adolescent process. An individual adolescent case history—that of Judy—will be used to demonstrate the distinct interrelatedness that exists between early childhood and adolescent development.

1. Early Childhood and Adolescence

The infant is a totally dependent organism, who needs the caring and feeding mother for his survival. A mutuality of need-gratification which operates as a circular response between mother and child creates an interdependence, and this forms the basis for the infant's healthy physical and emotional growth. Because the first contact between mother and child centers around feeding, this experience becomes the prototype of later incorporative activity, physical or mental; attached to these processes are emotional qualities that have a remarkable endurance in the conscious and unconscious life of the human being.

The mainspring for the infant's activity lies in his physical needs and is organized in terms of the pleasure-pain principle. The feeding mother, the breast,* constitutes part of the child; only slowly is she experienced by him as an object, or rather a part-object. At this stage the mother—this summary expression of the impinging environment—is perceived as either a good or bad object and consequently not the identical object at all times. We therefore speak of a pre-ambivalent stage of object relation. This delineation is justified by the fact that the infant's positive and negative emotions, expressed by smiling or crying, are directed toward the identical person, who, however, at this early stage is not represented in the infant's mind by a cohesive and differentiated mental image. This state of affairs is consistent with the infant's exclusive self-experience, namely, his disposition to consider those physical and emotional states that are good (satiated, pleasant, soothing) as representing the self, while those that are bad (painful, tension-producing) as belonging to the non-self, to the external world. Protective barriers are erected against disorganizing stimuli; and these adaptive processes are the forerunners of certain mechanisms of defense. These first, dim reflections of a psychic structure lie within the confines of primary narcissism and are modeled on the oral schema, according to which that which is good (reduces tension, affords pleasure and satiation) is taken in, while that which is bad (increases tension, causes pain and frustration) is spit out. The archaic defenses which take their cue from this simple oral dichotomy are *introjection* and *projection*. These mechanisms are always readily invoked when the oral modality is employed in dealing with the environment or with conflicts in general.

With increasing awareness of the outside world, the infant elaborates a mental image of the comforting mother. This faculty enables the infant to avert tension—for short periods of time—by hallucinating the

---

* Following Winnicott (1953), the term breast ("A subjective phenomenon develops in the baby which we call the mother's breast.") is used here as a summary expression for "the whole technique of mothering."

return of the mother, or, generally, of the need-gratifying object. In this way a part of the instinctual drive is differentiated; and it eventually becomes the mediator between the drive and the environment, between the inner and outer world. The boundaries between these worlds are first drawn in terms of sensory, motor-affective experiences; consequently, the early ego is a body ego. The body ego receives reinforcement from another source. The infant's gradual loss of the "nipple," conjugated with the mother's decreasing gratification in "nursing," together lead to the infant's discovery of the gratification that can be derived from his own body, independent of the environment—by sucking, rocking, stroking, and so on. Autoerotism, which is a substitute gratification, thus introduces a self-regulatory approach to tension reduction. Nevertheless, the influx of object-derived gratification remains necessary for normal emotional development. A critical balance seems to exist between autoerotic and object-derived gratification; one extreme leads toward addiction and the other toward infantile dependency. Alice Balint (1939) lucidly stated this problem of infantile autoerotism, which at puberty comes to such a crucial impasse: "The overburdening of the auto-erotic function, however, soon leads to pathological phenomena: the auto-erotic activity degenerates into addiction. But, inversely, we may observe that an all too successful pedagogical suppression of auto-eroticism is followed by an overburdening of object-relations which usually appears as an abnormal dependence on and pathological clinging to the mother (or her representatives). On the other hand, a not too exaggerated inhibition of auto-eroticism reinforces the object attachments to the extent desirable for the educability of the child."

Toilet training marks a decisive forward step in ego development. The achievement of sphincter control produces a sense of mastery and a delineation of body boundaries—marked by the excretory orifices—which establishes for good a separation of the self and the outside world. This separation is greatly assisted by the fact that motility has developed in the meantime and has advanced to co-ordinated goal-directed movements; furthermore, locomotion has enabled the child to experience space and to grasp distant objects. The distance perceptors (eye, ear, nose) find a new dimension through the proximity perceptor (touch); the world of objects thus becomes palpable to the child. Although all objects still tend to be brought to the mouth, gradually they are used for playful pursuits, acquiring in the process tactile qualities. These achievements make the child more independent of the mother's nurturing attendance; yet by the same token they bring to the fore new aspects of dependency. The mother is no longer solely needed for instinct gratification (feeding, body comfort); but her presence is increasingly required for the novel purpose of instinct control. The fear of loss of love becomes the vehicle for the child's educability.

Anal compliance (toilet training) requires the complete surrender of a primitive instinctual gratification to external regulations relative to place, time, and manner. New defenses are erected, such as reaction formation and repression; these, however, can succeed only if they receive support and reinforcement from the environment. Praise and the fear of punishment play a powerful role in the domestication of the excretory sphincter. An innate opposition between drive discharge and drive control—and, in fact, the singular forcefulness of anal autonomy —is reflected in the innumerable difficulties, delays, relapses, and failures in the course of toilet training. The child's inner struggle can easily be discerned in his relationship to the parent, which at this stage has a highly ambivalent character. Aggressive manifestations break out with vigor and are usually met by an environment equally determined to control them. The child's impulsive aggressive behavior (biting, hitting, pushing) becomes subject to repression or modification by displacement and reaction formation. The deflection of drive energy is facilitated by the child's increasingly diversified interests and his locomotor independence. The fact remains, nonetheless, that the child now becomes aware that parental love and approval can only be secured by renouncing his aggressive, destructive drives and submitting his sphincters to the parental will. The training process is not without a specific bipolar orientation; and it is during the anal phase that the component instincts of sadism and masochism make their first and unmistakable appearance. In the helpless rage characteristic of the tantrum, both components are shortcircuited; soon, however, they find innumerable displacements of object and aim. Not only does the sadomasochistic balance become fateful for the total life of the individual, but more specifically, it also affects the development of masculinity and femininity.

During the first years the male-female polarity plays no psychological role in the child's mental life. Mother, father, and other adults are mainly experienced in terms of individual differences, in terms of the comfort or discomfort they provide in their respective relations with the child. It is of greatest consequence that children of both sexes experience the mother of early childhood not as a female, but as the active dispenser of comfort or frustration. "The role of the mother prior to sexual differentiation is not feminine but active" (Mack Brunswick, 1940). In relation to the mother the young child is essentially passive: he only receives, and all care is administered to him. The mother's delight in her child contributes to the child's feeling of well-being and constitutes a source of pleasure which early in life he endeavors—and learns how—to control. The child himself has no altruistic motive when he gives in return; instead he is merely trying to evoke, for his own good, the pleasurable reaction in the adult, foremost the mother. There is a long way to go from object dependency to object love. The former is concerned with self-preservation and governed by the pleasure-pain principle, and the mother's interests are felt by the child to be identical with his own (A. Balint, 1939); in the latter the partner's self-interest is acknowledged.

In the beginning of life the child is essentially passive in his libidinal strivings; but it must not be overlooked that he actively elicits responses from the environment, although the aim of this drive is a passive one. In fact, an essential line of demarcation lies between the child's early passivity in relation to an essentially active mother (environment), and the subsequent period when he begins to imitate his mother, and indeed identifies with her. The child enters a phase of active libidinal strivings toward the mother, the time of "Let me do it" and "Let me do it to you." Furthermore, by identifying with the mother the child acquires an increasing independence from her; in fact, her help and ministrations are progressively resented as interferences. The child now tends to do actively what he had passively experienced in the past. This fateful step from passivity to activity is alluded to by Mack Brunswick (1940): "One might state that a young child's inability to produce an adequate activity is one of the earliest abnormalities." The clinical importance of this statement is today firmly established. The bipolarity of active and passive is prephallic (Mack Brunswick, 1940). The attempt to overcome the basic passive position occupies the child for many years; and the reconciliation of both strivings significantly determines the development of masculinity and femininity. The ambiguity and fluctuation between the antithetical strivings of passivity and activity do not reach a final state of reconciliation and compromise until the terminal phase of adolescence, the phase of consolidation.

Most people, children as well as adults, react differently to male and female infants. By the selective acclaim—overt and covert—which the child's early random behavior evokes from the environment, especially the mother, certain aspects of behavior become qualitatively differentiated and preferentially developed. The role played by the so-called IRM factor (inner release mechanism) with reference to the differentiated responses of male and female infants and small children is still too uncertain to be used as a reliable explanatory concept. At any rate, we do observe that a gradual modulation of emphasis relative to male and female behavior and mental activity occurs at an early age. This modulation is induced by the selective responses of the environment which give rise to favored activities on all levels of mental and physical life. The differentiation lacks any novel psychosexual connotation until the child acknowledges the anatomical differences of male and female. This discovery and its psychological integration occur during the phallic phase, which is dominated by the child's conflicting triangular relationship to his parents, the oedipal constellation.

With the advent of the phallic phase the paths of psychosexual development which the boy and the girl follow become so rapidly and essentially divergent that it seems advisable to trace their development separately. This approach emphasizes the differences between male and female development which appear early in life; tracing their origins will highlight the later divergencies of adolescent personality development in the boy and in the girl.

All children have the same first love object, namely the mother. Anything and anybody interfering with the ready availability of the mother at the moment of need is considered by the child as an intrusion, and becomes gradually the target of the child's aggressive and hostile impulses; the rudiments of possessiveness and jealousy are recognizable early. For the boy, the mother continues through childhood to be the object of his affection; over the early years, it is only the *aim* of his drive that changes as the active component in his now masculine (phallic) strivings becomes ascendant. These strivings are expressed in well-known behavior, attitudes, interests, wishes and fantasies. At the genital phase the relationship between the sexes, the oedipal parents, becomes a matter of curiosity for all children, and the origin of babies a matter of speculation. This curiosity is always brought to an unsatisfactory and incomplete end by recourse to pregenital concepts and experiences. We shall see, in our discussion of preadolescence, that sexual enlightenment only obscures the persistence of infantile sexual theories.

When the child—boy or girl—takes cognizance of the genital, he
has at the outset no awareness of any sex difference. The child's ego-
morphic attitude makes him think others look like himself—they have
a mouth, eyes, hands, an anus, like his, and consequently must possess
the same genital. This phenomenon is a manifestation of primary narcissism. The recognition of sex difference is furthered during toilet training as soon as the different positions used for urination by boy and girl
are observed. This observation, however, is not carried to any definite
conclusion until the oedipal period; then it merges with fantasies, acquires meaning, and leads to conflictual and body-damage anxiety, all
indications that the child has become aware of the genital difference of
male and female, and that his psychosexual organization has progressed
to the phallic phase. This phase is dominated by an antithesis which is
no longer active-passive but phallic-castrated (Mack Brunswick, 1940;
Freud, 1923, b).

The organ which serves to discharge erotogenic (sexual) tension for
the boy at the phallic phase is the penis. But above and beyond that
fact, this organ also serves as a tension regulator for anxiety. Thus it
carries the autoerotic, soothing, and comforting function of the preceding erogenous zones, namely, the discharge function of excess excitation. This tension-regulatory mechanism of autoerotic genital activity
has a novel quality, however; for with the advent of the oedipal constellation, a genital (phallic) aim experienced in fantasy engenders
conflictual and inhibitory anxiety. It should be remembered that when
genital masturbatory activity in the boy in the phallic phase assumes a
degree of compulsiveness and resists all efforts at control ("habit disturbance"), it often takes this course as the only available countermeasure
against regression to infantile passivity. At puberty, masturbation is reactivated, and reassumes its primitive tension-regulatory function as well
as a defensive function against regression; its progressive function in
adolescence is discussed below.

The child's genital masturbation encounters far less environmental
tolerance than earlier oral autoerotic practices or undifferentiated hand-
body contacts which appear as transient tactile habits. The intolerance
may be due to the adult's unresolved masturbation conflicts; the fact
remains that the boy's phallic behavior appears to the adult closer to
sexuality than did the autoerotic oral behavior of earlier years. Whether
parents are intolerant or lenient about genital masturbation, the little
boy will renounce it in time. This renunciation is brought about by his

guilt feelings, engendered by incestuous fantasies, by his fear of retaliation and injury, and last but not least, by the narcissistic disenchantment derived from an acknowledgment of his physical immaturity. This last fact alone must necessarily bring all his wishes to naught.

No child ever acquires an exact concept of adult sexual relations—namely, those between his parents who serve as models for his identification in the respective roles. All phases of psychosexual organization contribute their experiences to the formulation of infantile sexual theories of this period. The child draws on his own physical experiences; consequently, his concept of sexual relations between the parents is determined by the prevalence of certain phases in his own libidinal life; we call such persistent drive dominances, *fixation points.* Consequently, each child forms an idiomatic theory of intercourse in which all the elements of pregenitality find a prominent place: sucking, biting, eating, urinating, defecating, beating, looking, touching, fondling, and so on. Looking at and touching the genitals appear to be specific for the phallic phase; penetration as a focal concept seems deferred until puberty (Mack Brunswick, 1940). An overlapping of all phases of psychosexual development must be kept in mind if one is to avoid the artificial and rigid simplicity of an itinerary and instead recognize the complex and—within limits—easily reversible development of the young child.

Let us now turn to a discussion of the little boy's triangular relationship, the oedipus complex, which develops between himself and his parents, and which proves to be of such profound significance for his later life. The boy's early active strivings in identification with the mother turn gradually but unmistakably into an emotional attachment which at a very early age acquires oedipal connotations. The father is considered an intruder; he is resented by the boy whose dependency on his mother makes her possible loss an ever threatening calamity. Signs of possessive jealousy make their appearance much earlier than anything analogous in the girl's life. The cause for this divergency and the disparate emotional development—and consequently the ego and superego development—of boy and girl lies in the fact that the love object (mother) for the boy remains the same during all the phases of his psychosexual development, while the girl has to abandon her first love object if her femininity is to develop normally.

The father from the outset plays a role different from that of the mother. In the first place, his own dedication to the child is never as complete as the mother's. He never exists as a part-object as distinctly as the mother does during the early mother-child relationship. "The child behaves towards the father more in accordance with reality because the archaic foundations of an original, natural identity of interests has never existed in its relation to the father. . . . Hence: love for the mother is originally a love without a sense of reality, while love and hate for the father—including the oedipus situation—is under the sway of reality" (A. Balint, 1939). The relationships between child and mother and between child and father do not simply depend on the behavior of father and mother, which is alterable at their discretion; the relationships are qualitatively different because their foundations are not the same. The little boy develops possessive love for the mother; admiration for and pride in his father. This admiration is strongly reinforced by his narcissism; indeed, the little boy's attachment to his father is based on a narcissistic object choice: "Father and myself are alike." Obviously, this attachment is also a source of ambivalence, of competition, comparison, and hostility; these emotions are particularly strong in the rivalry for the mother. Identification with the father—an essential step in the development of masculinity—is unavoidably accompanied by love for and rivalry with him. This is the triangular conflict situation summarized in the term, *oedipus complex.*

We must remember here the compound nature of the oedipal situation, and realize how fictitious the idea is of a pure oedipus complex. The theoretical schema is an abstraction: in life, active and passive, positive and negative positions intermingle. The significant difference is that one trend is either dominant or muted, manifest or latent, conscious or repressed, ego-syntonic or ego-alien. The various oedipal positions and the boy's resolutions of them are of special significance because these very same phenomena come to life again in adolescence.

The boy's earliest identification with the active mother is not abandoned totally until he has acknowledged the fact that the female lacks a penis, that the woman is castrated. With this discovery—dim, gradual, and often only partially accepted—the mother becomes devaluated; the shadow of disappointment falls on her image, and the boy's desire becomes mixed with fear at the thought of the mysterious physical difference from the norm—which for him, of course, is the male genital. This devaluating and defensively belittling attitude toward the female conceived during the phallic phase reappears in preadolescence, and often persists as a lifelong contemptuous attitude toward the female sex.

When the boy turns his sexual strivings toward the mother in the early dawn of the oedipal phase, his libidinal aim is a passive one, following the archaic mode of receptivity. The identification with the mother encourages the turning of libido toward the father, again with a passive aim; this is called the *passive* (negative) *oedipal position* of the boy. Fantasies of a passive nature—such as a wish for a baby from the father—play an important part in the boy's mental life during the early oedipal period. The identification with the mother, as has been mentioned, is destroyed by the boy's realization that being a female is identical with the loss of the penis. The narcissistic cathexis which this organ possesses forces the boy to abandon his identification with the mother and turn to an identification with the father. This step finally paves the way to his active, libidinal, and aggressive (masculine) turning toward the mother—which leads to the formation of his *active* (positive) *oedipal position*. This step has basic significance for the development of the boy's masculinity. Also as he directs his active libidinal urges toward the mother with increasing intensity, it is only to be expected that hostile and destructive wishes and fantasies will be aimed at the father. Jealousy and competition, love and hate are experienced by the little boy in the passionate pursuit of his desires.

The identification with the father indicates that a step in the boy's psychosexual development has been taken which confronts him with a fateful alternative in the resolution of his emotional dilemma. Three factors lead to the boy's abandonment of the active oedipal position: the fear of castration by the father; the love for the father; and the realization of his own physical immaturity. During this drawn-out struggle the boy's relationships to father and mother are highly ambivalent, mirroring the relative strengths of his active and passive strivings. Two modes for the resolution of the oedipus complex are open to the boy: 1) to identify with the father, to become like him in the future instead of replacing him or being like him at the present; or 2) to give up his active, competitive, and rivalrous strivings and return—at least partly—to submitting to the active (phallic) mother. The first mode strengthens the reality principle; the second reinstitutes the reign of the pleasure principle. Submission to the phallic mother constitutes a regression which becomes a critical challenge at puberty, when the boy's maleness reaches physical maturity.

It must be re-emphasized that the processes which are being described here separately are in reality not so distinct. An active and a passive oedipus complex are not as mutually exclusive as oil and water; they do blend in various degrees. Furthermore, repression permits a component to survive in the unconscious when its aim and object cannot be renounced; and in middle childhood and especially in adolescence this component can be recognized in its derivative manifestations.

The normal resolution of the boy's oedipus complex leads to masculine identification (formation of superego and ego ideal), and by establishing a massive repression of oedipal wishes, a temporary settlement of the phallic drive is effected. The consolidation of the latency period can therefore take place: because now aim-inhibited drive energy is available for sublimation, and an infinite multitude of organized pursuits permits a vigorous progress in ego development and a firm entrenchment of the reality principle. I will discuss in Chapter III those aspects of latency which are preconditional for the unfolding of the adolescent process.

The oedipal situation of the girl makes it clear that the female development, by virtue of its early history, is bound to involve tasks and resolutions which are different from those of the boy. Nonetheless, we must not overlook the fact that all children have identical fundamental life experiences on which all that follows is erected. Consequently, the inherent problems of polarity and of mutual envy which exist between the sexes give rise to a sense of relative incompleteness. In this human condition we can recognize the forces which at times attract the sexes passionately to each other and at other times drive them forcibly apart. Let us now consider the vicissitudes pertinent to the emotional development of the girl.

As has been indicated above, the divergence between the psychosexual development of boy and girl appears early in the phallic phase. Before then the girl has more or less shared with the boy the passive position in relation to the mother or her representatives; and with the development of motility and locomotion, they both enter into an increasingly active phase with the emphasis on autonomy and mastery of the object world. The active trend is more marked in the boy than in the girl; but in this matter, sibling position and environmental stimulation and commendation appear to exert a strong modifying influence. The sum total of these influences is not without consequence for the girl's future task, namely, her need to renounce both the active and later the phallic position, an extended task which is only brought to completion at adolescence.

The fact that the girl's first love belongs to the mother predestines the mother always to be considered a refuge in times of stress. This is particularly evident when the mother's love is experienced as lacking, dangerous, or antagonistic and is sought for frantically throughout the rest of the girl's life. Parenthetically, the search for the preoedipal mother is a typical constellation in the etiology of female delinquency (see Chapter VII, page 236). The girl's early love for the mother is highly ambivalent, a characteristic quality it never loses; in fact, whenever regression brings this early relationship to life again, we find that an excess of primitive ambivalence is always characteristic of it. The early identification with the active mother leads the girl into an initial *active* (negative) *oedipal position*, typical for female development. When the girl turns her love needs to the father the danger always exists that her passive striving toward him will reawaken the early oral modality, and that a return to the primal passivity will preclude her successful advancement to femininity. This impasse is often dramatically displayed during the adolescent years. Whenever an unduly strong attachment to the father marks the girl's oedipal situation, unquestionably the precursor of this emotion is always an unduly deep and persistent attachment to the mother of the preoedipal years. That is, a strong father attachment follows a strong mother attachment: "The great dependence on the father in women merely takes over the heritage of an equally great attachment to the mother" (Freud, 1931).

The two-phasic development, active-passive, which marks the girl's oedipal development implies not only a shift in instinctual aim, but a change of the love object from mother to father. Nothing analogous exists in the development of the boy. Could this essentially female aspect of development be responsible for the fact that women—indeed, even adolescent girls—possess an intuitive grasp of male emotionality far more profound than men usually show for the emotionality of women? In any event, it has to be noted that the girl does not renounce her active (phallic) position for long. The girl's penis envy, more broadly conceived as woman's "masculinity complex," has to be thought of as a secondary formation (Deutsch, 1944). Indeed, this complex operates as a defense or resistance against primal passivity; it cannot be given up until, through identification with the oedipal mother, the avenue toward feminine passivity is opened.

The girl's turning with a passive aim to the oedipal love object, the father—the *passive* or *positive oedipal position*—is rather late when compared to the boy's active or positive oedipal position. The active trend of female development is never as deeply repressed as the boy's corresponding antithetical trend of passivity. His repression is most forcefully established during his active oedipal position. It must be realized that the female's legitimate—biological and social—outlets for her active strivings are numerous, and are essential to her life as woman and mother, while passivity is anathema to the boy and represents the negation of his masculine identity. His "wish for a child" is far more deeply repressed than the girl's "wish for a penis," a fact which is well known from analytical work with children, adolescents, and adults. There is a corollary in personality development to the fact that the female possesses both an active (clitoris) and a passive-receptive (vagina) sexual organ, while the male lacks equivalently bipolar anatomical and erogenous structures.

During the period of the genital organization of the libido, the phallic phase, the girl does not yet fully acknowledge the anatomical difference between boy and girl. The girl behaves as if she possessed a penis; her imitation of boyish behavior, for example, characterizes the phallic component of this period in her life. In this period lie the origins of the tomboy who in later years is the unrelenting defender of the phallic position, often indeed the only acceptable way of life to the young adolescent girl. Normally, the girl's sense of reality leads her to acknowledge the fact that she does not have a penis; but for some time the girl continues to act as if this were not true. What the little boy (perhaps a brother) does out of exuberance and pride, the little girl may imitate out of stubbornness and spite—only to feel ridiculous and self-conscious. The reverse is equally true, but with a difference: the boy's imitation of a girl is early in life discouraged by severe social taboos. A tomboy remains respectable for a long time; a sissy never ceases to be despicable.

The antithetical positions of phallic-castrated gradually establish themselves in the girl's mind and cause a variety of reactions. The obvious first target for the expression of her disappointment is the mother, who has not given her daughter what she has given the boy. The weaning trauma, the loss of the nipple, and the feeling of body-part loss associated with sphincter control, all reappear; they are the forerunners of subsequent castration anxiety. Investigations of body differences, sexual curiosity about the parents, the arrival of a sibling, the observation of menstruation and pregnancy, and so on, finally make the girl realize that the mother shares her deficiency. This insight allows the girl to compare herself with the mother; as a consequence, she devaluates the mother and turns to the father. Here again, narcissistic libido contributes its share to the choice of the love object. Thus, possession of the phallus is eventually conceded to the love object: this renunciation gives rise to passive wishes and the desire to be possessed.

We see, then, that the very fact—namely, the recognition of castration—which in the boy brings on the destruction of the oedipus complex, in the girl brings the oedipus complex into existence (Freud, 1924, b; Mack Brunswick, 1940). No force or circumstance similar to the one which makes the boy renounce his oedipal wishes exists in the situation of the girl: only the limitations of physical immaturity, incestuous guilt feelings, and the persistent narcissistic injury experienced in masturbatory activity combine to bring about a decline of her oedipal fantasies and facilitate her entrance into the latency period. The resolution of the girl's oedipus complex does not come about until her adolescence (Mack Brunswick, 1940); or perhaps later, with the birth of a child; or perhaps never at all, in any complete fashion.

As we can readily see, the timetables for these crucial conflicts and their resolution differ to such an extent for the two sexes that generalizations which refer to both distort intrinsic facts. Therefore, it must be emphasized again that schematic description cannot be literally and rigidly applied to life. For example, the girl's passive (positive) oedipal situation does not vitiate the fact that she continues to regard the mother as the comfort-providing and protecting person in her life: the mother continues—in Greenacre's (1948) words—to be the "food giver and body warmer." The active and the passive oedipus complex of the girl intermingle and persist with changing emphasis.

The renunciation of oedipal wishes in conjunction with the decline or the repression of masturbation, both normally accomplished between the ages of five and seven, lead the girl to an increasing dependency on the mother and an identification with her. This identification is different from the early one with the active mother; it includes the mother's roles as mother and wife, and her relationship with and attitude toward the husband-father. It also takes cognizance of the mother's social role in home and community. The normal course is now to renounce the oedipal father while identifying with the oedipal mother; but the girl may achieve a deviate outcome of this phase by a split in her ego. In this case, she resorts to a regressive solution; in consonance with the oral mode she incorporates the father (Sachs, 1929) and makes him part of herself, while at the same time she continues to live in anxious and stubborn dependency on the preoedipal mother. By incorporating the father, she gives up the love object in the outer world, but preserves its existence permanently by merging with it, by establishing an identity which blurs the dichotomy of the oedipal subject and object. We shall later investigate the consequences of this regressive resolution of the oedipus complex on the pubertal girl's body-image and her sense of reality. At any rate, this constellation comes to an impasse during early adolescence, when the girl has to come to terms with her bisexuality. Much of what appears to be an adolescent conflictual problem is seen, on closer inspection, to be the result of early structural ego defects and malformations.

The progression by which the girl ascends from her primitive passive oral dependency to passive genital receptivity requires a massive repression of infantile, pregenital sexuality which historically is bound up with the primary mother-child relationship. The fact that the boy continues to elaborate his psychosexual progression in relation to the same person, namely, the mother, relieves him from this massive repression of pregenitality. "One of the greatest differences between the sexes is the enormous extent to which infantile sexuality is repressed in the girl. Except in profound neurotic states no man resorts to any similar repression of his infantile sexuality" (Mack Brunswick, 1940). This quantitative difference in repression throws light on the striking behavioral variations of the preadolescent boy and girl.

Since the oedipus complex for the girl is a "secondary formation" (Freud, 1924, b), she must evolve psychic means for removing the first (archaic) love object and defending against the regressive pull; these means are entirely different from those the boy employs to cope with the same problem. The major task for the boy is to renounce his early passivity; for the girl, it is to abandon her first love object. A parallel struggle, the same for both boy and girl, is to achieve object constancy, to overcome ambivalence and thus make the progression to stable (postambivalent) relationships possible. These major tasks involve crucial foci in psychic integration and differentiation, foci which engender potential developmental failures caused either by the traumatic or by the excessively gratificatory nature of experiences in early childhood. Both these extremes create fixation points which appear with full force during adolescence; indeed, these fixation points are responsible for the structuring of the adolescent crisis. Fixation points as they relate specifically to the different phases of adolescence will be discussed later in the context of the adolescent process and in relation to the idiosyncratic and highly personal meanings behind the façade of sameness or similarity which adolescents show to the observer.

In addition to exploring the instinctual development of the young child, we must also trace the faculty which maintains the homeostatic balance of the psychic apparatus. This faculty, located in the ego, takes its cues from the progressive maturation of the body, its function and structure. In this sense, it can be comprehended as a regulatory system, which acquires controlling (timing and channeling) influence over increasingly complex instinctual drives, over consciousness, over perception, over cognition, and over action. Thus, the ego protects the integrity of the personality on the respective level to which it has progressed. The ego mediates between drive and outer world, ideally affording the individual a maximum of gratification with a minimum of anxiety. Censoring and inhibiting ego influences, which eventually become consolidated in a disparate institution, the superego, appear early in the mental life of the child.

At this point some remarks about ego development in early childhood are in order; I shall emphasize those aspects relevant for adolescence. The ego emerges from the id, and is separated from it when the infant recognizes that oral satiation is dependent on the presence of a separate object, the "breast." The first ego boundary is thus a body boundary; this boundary is reinforced by perception and memory, both of which give rise to a psychic representation of the environment and of the interaction (experience) with it. "The rudiments of the ego take their patterns from the environmental conditions which have left their imprint on the infant's mind by way of his early pleasure-pain experiences, the conditions themselves becoming internalized in the ego structure" (A. Freud, 1954). It has already been mentioned that the earliest mechanism dealing with the outside world is in terms of the pleasure-pain principle and follows the oral mode; it consists of either "taking in" (introjection) or "spitting out" (projection). The former is the forerunner of identification (secondary), while the latter foreshadows repression. Both identification and repression are put into operation only after the reality principle has established itself and ambivalence has at least partially been overcome. The timing of this operation depends on the maturation of perception, locomotion, and language development, in particular. A failure in early identificatory processes, and an unduly long and intensive dependence on the mother—generally speaking, on the environment—for the maintenance of identity and a sense of reality render the child extremely vulnerable in establishing ego autonomy. Such a child has to be eternally "fed" and reassured for his anxiety to be kept within tolerable bounds.

With the advent of toilet training the fear of loss of love becomes accentuated and anxiety is controlled by magic thought; from this mode of control derives the mechanism of undoing so closely related to compulsive behavior. The most radical endeavor to cope with the coprophilic drive and the related component instincts is manifested in the "turning into the opposite" or in the mechanism of reaction formation. This endeavor brings to life the affects of compassion and disgust, and establishes a firm hold on reality and social norms. In addition, it serves as a safe assurance of parental love through identification with their wishes. A source for the feeling of well-being and contentment similar to that of being loved is discovered—pleasing the internalized parent by doing as told. Keen interest in the world of objects increases during these years; intellectual inquisitiveness and curiosity reaches the infantile peak; and the power of observation sharpens the child's wit. Play blossoms forth in imaginative richness and is attended to with the earnestness of work. In play the child binds anxiety by repetition, and masters anxiety by gradually assimilating the impact of traumatic or conflictual experiences which crowd the days and nights of his life.

When the child is in firm possession of sphincter control, of coordinated motility, of language, of perception, and is capable of cognitive functions, a sense of pride and an exuberance emerge which mark the child's temper. This mood, however, is destined to be clouded over by his oedipal strivings and by the awareness of his immaturity. The child under the sway of the reality principle finds only temporary relief in the oedipal attachment; recognizing the alternatives which confront him, he rescues his integrity by identification and by firmly consolidating a psychic institution, the superego, which adds a third source of anxiety— the others being the id and the outside world—with which henceforth he has to reckon.

The superego of the boy and of the girl develops differently. The fact that the oedipus complex of the girl is not resolved until adolescence differentiates her development startlingly from the boy's, whose oedipal wishes become subject to a more massive repression at the beginning of the latency period. The superego, "the heir of the oedipus complex," is consequently more rigid and exacting in the boy than in the girl. Due to the massive repression of oedipal libido the boy possesses a more reality-oriented turn of mind, a clearer and more independent body image; in contrast, the girl never achieves this simplicity and directness of repression. The boy's clearer body image is, of course, also a reflection of the physical fact that his genital is exposed and open to sensory accessibility, both visual and tactile; since the female genital is invaginated, she is permitted less direct observational concreteness (Freud, 1925; Greenacre, 1948). Sensations of the clitoris in conjunction with those of touch must serve as the indicators from which the girl assembles the mental image of her genital. These conditions and their psychological consequences in terms of the development of interests, talents, bodily skills, and learning propensities will be discussed in terms of adolescent phenomena.

Once more I shall highlight a basic difference in the early emotional development of boy and girl. The boy represses most radically his oedipal strivings, with the consequence that he acquires a severe superego. The girl, in contrast, represses most forcefully her pregenital strivings, with the result that genitality asserts itself rapidly and unequivocally as soon as instinctual tensions begin to rise at the onset of puberty. One reason for the more massive repression of the boy in entering latency is certainly his radical renunciation of passivity; there is nothing of equal urgency in the girl's renunciation of the active position.

The psychosexual development which was disrupted by the oedipal impasse is taken up again and continued at puberty. "In the earlier phases" as stated by Freud (1938, b), "the separate component instincts set about their pursuit of pleasure independently of one another; in the phallic phase there are the first signs of an organization which subordinates the other trends to the primacy of the genitals and signifies the beginning of a co-ordination of the general pursuit of pleasure into the sexual function. The complete organization is not attained until puberty, in a fourth, or genital phase."

How these major events representative of all aspects of the unfolding instinctual life and of ego development during early childhood, exert their distinct influences on the adolescent process is the topic to which we shall now turn our attention.

2. *Adolescence and Early Childhood: Judy*

It is fairly easy to describe the significant developmental phases of early childhood which have a particular bearing on the adolescent process. However, it is a staggering and most complex undertaking to try to systematize those typical and generalized connections and congruities which exist between adolescence and early childhood. An attempt at delineating the developmental phases of the adolescent period—that is, at outlining a theory of adolescence—will be made later on. At this point, I shall use an inductive approach to the problem and demonstrate in the life history of a single individual how the transformations at puberty are significantly determined by the experiences of early childhood and how they proceed in idiosyncratic fashion within the typical phenomenology of an adolescent milieu.

The interrelatedness between adolescence and early childhood will be illustrated by the history of an individual adolescent, a girl named Judy. Her passage through adolescence will be viewed here in the continuum of her psychological development; that is, the particular crisis of adolescence proper, as it took shape in Judy's life, will be related to the crucial experiences which shaped her early personality development. More specifically, an attempt will be made to trace her adolescent conflicts as well as her adaptive accomplishments and failures in her early childhood.

With her entrance into puberty a change came over Judy. Her family and teachers noticed how troubled and worried she was. When this state of affairs did not improve after several years, at the age of fourteen she was finally brought to the attention of a child guidance clinic.

It should be made clear at the outset that the course of therapy will not concern us as such in the presentation of this case. However, the by-products of therapy—the illumination of the dynamic and genetic aspects of Judy's personality formation—represent valuable data which can be used for the reconstruction of her total development. No doubt this girl's history contains unusual features; but this is true for any history in the realm of personal experiences. In Judy's case the circumstances of her sibling constellation offered concrete, if rare, situational data which allowed a clear view of emerging emotional patterns, the study of which is our main objective. In this sense, then, her case offered advantages because of the clarity of reconstruction possible; therefore, it was chosen regardless of its apparent unusualness. The essential facets of Judy's adolescent development will be recounted as they presented themselves during the three years of her contact with the clinic. After this report, I shall discuss the specific life constellation in Judy's early childhood by tracing and isolating the specific trauma which foreshadowed a specific crisis in Judy's adolescence.

A. Judy's Adolescence

Judy presented herself as unhappy and angry. A skin condition (acne) disfigured her face, and Judy made matters worse by constantly picking and tearing at herself. She felt ugly; and she stayed at home where she spent endless hours of the day and night reading. She fought with her mother at the slightest provocation, accusing her of not having any understanding, and of not even trying to understand her daughter.

Judy was a triplet; the other two children were boys to whom, so Judy felt, the mother gave generously of her interest and affection. Judy had always felt close to a brother six years older; he never acknowledged her sisterly yearnings, but he remained the most important family member in terms of Judy's emotional development. Judy resented being a triplet; sharing had been her lot from the beginning of life. With the onset of puberty she was possessed by feelings of rage and despair alternating with remorse and depressed moods. Headaches made her afraid she might have an illness of the brain. Thoughts of death and suicide filled her fantasy life; she imagined scenes eloquent with remorse and grief for the mourners, foremost of whom were her parents.

Judy suffered under the realization that she did not love her parents; at times she even disliked them, and she knew that this was not right. Such sentiments, Judy reasoned, were contrary to the Ten Commandments, and it was sinful for her to harbor them. Her first words at her first meeting with the therapist were: "You know what my trouble is? I don't like my mother." Starting with the beginning of puberty, age ten, these feelings had haunted and tortured Judy's life; they had gained momentum until she had become afraid of being overwhelmed by her inner rage and sense of despair. Any friendship with her peers or any kindliness shown by an adult turned quickly into a disappointment for her owing to the magnitude of her emotional needs. Judy first showed people the ugliest side of herself; rarely and then only for brief moments would she let others see how friendly, sweet, and generous she actually could be, and indeed wished to be.

Her inner turmoil had never prevented Judy from doing her school work conscientiously; in fact, she always did extremely well in school. Only during her early teens did her studies become so important to her that they caused intense worries. She could not sleep well before the day of an examination, always fearing that she would falter in the contest on the academic battlefield. She never—or very rarely—failed to pass with high marks. Judy acted as if her life depended on succeeding in her school work, and she was determined to go to college despite her family's disinterest and discouragement. Judy indignantly brushed the argument aside that sisters should renounce a college career in favor of brothers. She branded her parents selfish when they argued that a good daughter starts to earn money as soon as she can, and continues to work until she gets married. Judy knew that her family's income was marginal, and that at times of crisis welfare assistance was the degrading alternative to outright poverty. True, the family was hard pressed economically; but beyond that, it was the mother's fear of losing her daughter that made her antagonistic to the idea of Judy's higher education. She told her daughter quite frankly that as a college graduate she would surely marry out of her class, and then she would look down on her parents or even ignore them. At other times, the mother in her irrational way argued aloud (this was customary in the family) by saying, "Let your brother Charlie have college all to himself, please; he never was good in anything, and it will make up for things." No wonder Judy felt that her mother was resentful of her and was annoyed that she did better in school than the boys. Judy was convinced that her mother stifled her ambitions and belittled her achievements in order to have some of the glory of public recognition for her less successful sons.

Judy considered a higher education her due; she was the brightest child in the family, and had often been called "gifted" and "genius" by her teachers—much to the disdain of her mother, who openly made fun of such compliments. Judy was proud of her intelligence, and flung it into her brothers' faces when the mother was present. In the family she was called the "know-all" with "uppity airs"; but nobody could deny her academic success. But although this success was useful for staking out her claim in the world, it was useless as a source of enjoyment or satisfaction; quite the contrary, it became a source of constant anxiety. Most remarkable was Judy's unswerving determination over the years to become a nurse and eventually to become a teacher of nurses. She never deviated from this occupational choice nor doubted for a moment its absolute correctness.

Judy's misery at not having close friends was intense. What she wanted most was a good and close girlfriend. Any sign of friendship offered by a girl filled her with such intense feelings that she became wildly demanding and possessive. She soon aroused such a turmoil of emotions that her potential friend had to withdraw. Then Judy felt deserted, alone, full of envy and jealousy. She became self-conscious of being an "outsider." Girls walked in pairs and she walked singly behind them. "I like to walk in the middle," was the way Judy expressed her sense of exclusion. The same thing happened in camp where eleven girls shared one bunk; she thought of herself as "the eleventh," "the odd one," "the extra member." Whenever she saw people together, the "outsider" idea repeated itself in monotonous sameness. At times it seemed best to Judy to avoid people; then she would neither be envious of them nor mean to them. Burying herself in books protected her against an overwhelming anger she felt rising within herself in social situations; her temper frightened her, and she took refuge in social isolation.

During these periods of isolation Judy became depressed and brooding. A painful feeling of separateness overcame her at home, and she desperately wished her mother would be her friend. In tears she once related to the therapist that her mother had again failed to understand her when she had wanted to confide in her. She had told her mother that a certain girl she knew had a mother to whom she could tell everything, just as if she were a sister. Judy too wished she had someone like that. The mother replied, "You can tell me everything." Judy answered, "I cannot trust you," whereupon the mother slapped her face. "That was a lot of understanding!" Judy commented bitterly. Such incidents, however, did not lessen the strong bond between them. Judy often turned to her mother for help and craved her love and understanding inordinately; at other times she turned against her, blaming her for all her own miseries. To ask that the therapist be her mother's therapist too was an unusual request for an adolescent girl; but Judy felt that any situation which tended to enhance their union was desirable. Needless to say, the hopes woven into these situations were destined always to crumble.

The contradictory desires which Judy felt toward her mother resulted in unending battles between them. Judy complained that her mother treated her like a child; nevertheless, she gave in to her demands. On one occasion Judy accused her mother of telling her how to spend her money ("She tells me how to think and what to be!"), only to blame her simultaneously for not being interested in anything she did, felt, or wished. Nothing was given to her, she complained; what she has learned she got all from books.

In this connection Judy's preparation for menstruation is particularly telling. Her mother had told her about menstruation when Judy was about ten years old. According to Judy's recollection, the mother told her that "Soon something is going to happen every month." Judy anxiously asked what it was that would happen, but the only reply she received was a vague hint: "You'll see, something will happen, something physical." This imprecision frightened her and she would stand in front of the mirror, look at herself, and wonder what would happen to her. She expected something terrible. "Would I get a freckle on my nose or a lump on my back every month?" When she was eleven years old she woke up one morning and found the sheet bloodstained. She was frightened, but tried to ignore it—only to return from school with blood on her legs, her slip, and her skirt. She ran to her mother screaming, "Mommy, I am dying, I am dying, I'm bleeding to death." Her mother's only response was, "Now you are a woman." Judy pleaded with her mother to explain, but her mother only reiterated that one day when she was older, she would understand. About a year later, Judy turned to a cousin for information and finally everything was explained to her. However, she was still confused when she tried to think about marriage, masturbation, or homosexuality. "The only thing which helps me out of my confusion is books." Early in puberty Judy was frightened by sex; she told of an incident at her uncle's house when she was babysitting for her cousin, and the uncle had asked her to undress in front of him. Judy added, "Of course, I didn't," and continued her account by describing how the uncle had touched her "all over." She could not imagine what his intentions were; she only knew that she could not stand his touching her much longer. "I nearly went out of my mind," she added, and concluded the telling of this episode with the enigmatic remark, "My father, he never touches me."

Judy's emotional sensitivity had a physical corrollary—an intense reaction to body contact. She felt repulsed by her mother's demonstrations of affection, and shrank from any physical closeness to another person. On the other hand, for years Judy had been afraid of being alone, and she still shared a bed with her mother; strangely enough, she had never made any attempt to get a bed of her own. The arrangement of sleeping with her mother was only vaguely based on necessity because on weekends when the father—who worked during the night—was at home, Judy had to sleep in the livingroom. Only reluctantly did she surrender her place in the parental bed. When the family finally moved to a larger apartment where Judy had a room of her own, the sleeping habit still remained unchanged and for a long time was not mentioned to the therapist by either mother or daughter. When Judy finally admitted the "secret," she was embarrassed and blushed profusely. Judy eventually began to complain that the sleeping arrangement was unsatisfactory; but no expressed intention to alter it ever effected any change. In restless sleep Judy often slapped her mother or spread her arms over her face, muttering angry words which were incomprehensible to the mother. Judy never had any recollection of these nocturnal scenes, but she was told about them by the mother.

Finally, by the purchase of her own bed, Judy established a physical separation from her mother; this step also signaled the acceptance of her conflicts as her own and beyond resolution by maternal protection and gratification. Not until then could she resist her mother's and her own desires for closeness which came to such perfect fulfillment when they had a heart to heart talk after having gone to bed. After she began to sleep alone, her sleep continued to be disturbed: she related nightmares which frightened her, dreams about death, always death due to murder. Judy was most afraid of being alone—of being alone now and being alone in the future. The thoughts which frightened her can be summed up in a sentence: "Maybe no one will love me and maybe I will not love anybody." Beset by such doubts she felt mean and selfish; wouldn't it have been better if a person like herself were not alive? She could never quite rid herself of the thought that her unhappiness was brought on by her own doing; a sense of guilt weighed heavily on her mind. In day-dreams of suicide she saw herself floating down the river; for a while people would write letters and then they would all forget that she had ever lived.

These gloomy moods were in contrast to her bright moments, which she experienced especially when she was with friends. On such—indeed rare—occasions she could be silly, playful, and carefree. One night that she spent with a girlfriend was full of fun. Both girls, then thirteen years old, were acting giddy and letting themselves be carried away by their fantasies. They imagined they were living in Buckingham Palace; dressed in beautiful gowns, they busied themselves with rearranging and properly furnishing the palace, and paraded around the room giving orders to their servants, laughing at their own silliness. In favorite day-dreams Judy recreated her family life into a mixture of present and future, in which her mother and her triplet brothers appeared, while her father was never included; this fact struck her as strange. Judy's gay moods were shortlived; sadness took hold of her easily. If she heard about sick or dying strangers, or if she saw a dead dog lying in the street, tears welled up, and she would cry quietly to herself.

In an effort to become a better person Judy turned away from the superficiality of modern life to a search for deeper meanings in human existence. She didn't know whether these meanings were to be found in religion or in the loyalty to one's convictions and ideas; and she tried them both without ever being satisfied with her dedication. When Judy changed to a new high school her mother complained about the poor condition of the building, but Judy enthusiastically praised the school, declaring clean walls and tiled corridors to be unimportant. How stupid of her mother, she said, to notice only the appearance of things and to ignore what really mattered, namely the substance, the thought, the atmosphere, the people. Such sophistry got Judy into many arguments, and gave her the reputation of being a snob.

Judy never felt at ease with boys outside the family. She felt unloved and unlovable. She was convinced that they would not like her because she was not pretty. Her girlfriends were pretty and their conquests filled her with envy. Judy was always the onlooker, the outsider. The game of love which the adolescent girls around her seemed to play so adroitly remained a mystifying puzzle to Judy. For a while she treated boys and girls alike and eradicated the inequalities which gave rise to her anxiety. Many events indicated clearly that Judy was frightened by her own desires and by the strength of her emotions. At camp she blacked out once after a dance at which she had felt happy and gay. A year later, again at camp, she was seized by a strange feeling while walking with a boy along a pond; she suddenly became afraid that he would push her into the water. Rape fantasies and physical violence were at odds with her desire for tender love. Musing over the pond scene with the therapist, Judy admitted she wished she had been kissed by the boy, since she had never been kissed in her life. But, she added, the "other part of sex" still frightened her. "How can you know," she asked in exasperation, "that you are in love?" For her, the danger always loomed large that she would be carried away by sexual desires without being in love. If only her mother had introduced her to sex more gently and less cruelly, Judy thought, everything would have turned out differently for her.

Judy's social life was a constant reminder to her that she was not as good as others; that was why, she thought, she was not able to attract boys. She went to school dances, to "Y" parties, to club meetings, to political gatherings, only to walk away with her craving for friendship and love unfulfilled. Her own inadequacy, a streak of meanness, and unkindly feelings—so Judy reasoned—were responsible for her social defeats. At these times Judy always returned to the idea that there might be something wrong with her physically, maybe a brain tumor which an operation could remove. She was never convinced of the validity of this fear; but a vague sense of uncertainty about her bodily intactness remained with her for several of her adolescent years.

Judy spent much of her time at home in unending arguments with the family. She demonstrated her boredom to everybody and alternately blamed herself or her mother for the fact that she was condemned to look at the four walls of her room. During all this time, Judy rarely spoke of her father; she felt she hardly knew him and remembered little about him. Once, while thinking about him during an interview, Judy became quiet for a few minutes. Her lower lip began to quiver; tears came to her eyes; and she said, "I must have had a father when I was a child because I have a father now. He must have been there, but I can't remember him. Where was he? Why wasn't he there? Didn't he care?" Her father, she added sarcastically, loved only his stomach. In tears, she revealed her deepest fear—that she could not be loved.

The depressed moods which Judy recurrently experienced during her adolescence lifted spontaneously and gave way to a period of brighter and more playful temper. One such moment came when Judy fell in love. She first met Billy casually, and secretly continued a relationship with him from a distance. From her window she watched him as he went to and from work, as he rode on his bicycle, or walked over to the store. She felt like a peeping Tom while she did this, and called herself a "spy." Finally, she met him again and they went out together; it all ended when the boy moved out of town shortly after. Judy had no hesitation in telling the therapist that she dreamed about him at night and thought about him during the day. A fad in vogue among the girls at school at this time fitted well into Judy's need to daydream and at the same time made her part of the group of peers who engaged in this pastime. The fad consisted in making up stories about a "paper-doll boyfriend,"—that is, a boyfriend who did not exist but who was created by the girl in order for her to be able to tell other people about him. This allowed a girl to talk about a boyfriend without having one and at the same time without lying, since the other girls knew it was make-believe. At times fact and fiction got blurred—as for instance, the entire group, Judy included, worked itself into an excited and giddy state over the en-

gagement of one of the girls before they all sobered up to the realization
that it was, after all, only a "paper-doll engagement." Judy at this time
was sixteen years old; she thought of herself as being pretty childish,
nevertheless she enjoyed this silly game of make-believe for the few
weeks during which it was in vogue. Shortly after this episode of shared
daydreams, Judy attached herself to a man teacher whose criticism and
praise darkened or brightened her day. She talked about him with true
affection and trust, and she summed up this new experience by saying,
"All I know is that I like him." She added, "My father never smiled the
way he does; I could never go to my father but I can go to Mr. X; *he* is
interested—*he* pays attention."

When Judy was fifteen her older brother, twenty-one, got married,
and Judy was a bridesmaid at the wedding. She became a real "member
of the wedding," as absorbed in the event as if she were the bride-to-be.
She was ecstatically happy about her dress and she gave herself over to
fantasies of love and happiness. Her emotional state went from ecstasy
to erotic excitement; she could not help but giggle and blush, and think
of wedding gowns and finery. At this time she became particularly loath
to be alone. In speaking of this, she revealed that in fact she experienced
transient claustrophobic anxiety; she desperately needed the presence of
others to protect her against the temptation to masturbate. When in a
state of sexual excitement she panicked from fear that her impulses
would break through the barrier of rigid control. Judy had always loved
her older brother as though he were a mixture of brother and father. No
wonder that his marriage stirred up incestuous wishes which were
sanctified by her altruistic surrender—that is, by her devoted love for her
future sister-in-law. Her wish for a baby was barely disguised, and it
came to awareness as soon as her sister-in-law's pregnancy was announced during the first year of marriage. As soon as the baby was born,
Judy declared that the only one she got along with was her brother's
baby. She loved that baby, and said that some day she would like to have
a baby like it. At this time Judy was sixteen years old.

Only gradually did Judy turn her heterosexual feelings toward people outside the family; for a while she went out with her triplet brother
Charlie, who had no girlfriend at the time. Whenever Judy did show
signs of affectionate feelings for a boy and an attachment seemed about
to develop, the mother would voice objections of one sort or another in
order to devaluate her daughter's choice. Judy became aware of her
mother's jealousy and possessiveness, but in order to free herself from

them, she had to renounce her own dependency needs and acknowledge her sexual wishes. For some time tender love and sexual love were kept apart. When she felt sexually attracted by a boy, she avoided him, but "spied" on him from the distance. She then saw herself, rather consciously, in a prostitute image, "slinking around a telephone pole with a beret pulled over one eye in the half-lit evening dusk." She added, with affected cynicism, "After all, this generation has been brought up in the era of Pat X"—a reference to a call girl who figured in a sensational trial of prostitution in New York society. These poses of the "floogie-ish and glittery prostitute" which encompassed all of Judy's forbidden sexual fantasies gave way without transition to romantic love in the classroom, at the beach, and on the dance floor. Devoted longing and affectionate feelings for various boys reached a sudden climax and disappeared as suddenly as they had arisen; anxiety always intervened.

Regardless of defeats and disappointments, Judy's desire to love relentlessly propelled her into new episodes with boys. The various stages of this development were passed through slowly, forward thrusts alternating with standstills and regressions. Not until the age of seventeen did Judy reach the point in her emotional development at which she acknowledged the rudiments of an extrafamilial, heterosexual orientation. She gradually accepted her sexual impulses more directly, the more confident she grew about being able to control her instinctual drives. The two basic fears which Judy had so clearly recognized early in her adolescence—the fear of loss of control and the fear of not being able to love—proved to be two sides of the same coin.

B. THE RECONSTRUCTION OF A DEVELOPMENTAL CONTINUUM

Let us now turn to a consideration of Judy's earlier life, to see how a genetic appraisal can help us to an appreciation of some of those factors in Judy's early life which to a large extent determined her adolescent development. In establishing a continuum in her development, we will trace the modifications of significant emotional patterns of early childhood—modifications influenced by extraneous factors, such as family configuration and transactional prototypes established among family members. Simultaneously, we will have to consider the formative effects of intrinsic factors, such as constitutional endowment and maturation. The interplay of these various components produces early in life a basic regulatory approach to the maintenance of optimal well-being. This regulatory approach later undergoes many modifications which are brought about by the advances of the ego and also by the particular ways in which the pregenital stages of psychosexual development have been liquidated. Our attention will be focused not only on the precursors of adolescent conflict, but also on the adaptive processes and their germinal antecedents in early life.

It has already been mentioned that Judy was the one girl of a triplet birth, and that she had one older brother, six years her senior. The parents had not planned the second pregnancy; in fact, they did not wish to have any more children since they could barely provide for the first, since the father had never managed to achieve stable and adequate employment. The new pregnancy was tolerated by the mother, who was resigned to it. The father, on the contrary, and despite all practical arguments, was happy to see his family grow larger. In the seventh month of pregnancy the mother was told that she would have triplets; she was shocked and angry, but the father was proud and happy about the news. This difference in the parental attitudes continued to persist: the mother felt trapped by her children, defeated and sucked dry; the father maintained a positive and warm attitude toward them, and felt interested in and optimistic about their development—without, however, contributing a share of effort and responsibility in accordance with the needs of a large family. He liked having a family; but he kept this treasured possession at arm's length in order to live his life in his own way, stubbornly holding out against the emotional and material demands which his wife and his children made on him.

The delivery was normal; it was a full-term birth. Judy was the firstborn. From the start Judy showed the greatest vitality of the three and made the least demands on the mother. This fact is of particular importance, since the two boys were a constant cause of worry to the mother. Judy and her brother Ben each had a birthweight of four pounds, fourteen ounces, but both boys fell behind Judy in weight gain. And their eating as well as their sleeping habits never acquired the dependability of their sister's, who soon was more competent, more independent, and generally more mature than her brothers. The mother described Judy as a "lively, quick, and good-natured" infant, while she could only use words of woe and pity to describe her infant boys. Judy walked at nine months, Ben at fifteen months, and Charlie at twenty-four months. Judy started talking at about one year; her brothers followed, with Charlie always trailing way behind. Judy's toilet training was accomplished early and with such ease that her mother had no recollection as to dates and details of her behavior. In contrast, she had plenty of exact recollections when it came to discussing the boys. The same held true for the triplets' health; while the boys needed constant attention, Judy never presented a health problem in her early childhood. Not until pre-puberty did Judy's health arouse concern, first in relation to her skin (acne), and soon after in relation to her headaches.

During all the years of early childhood Judy was always—at least in the eyes of the mother—the norm or the "yardstick" by which the children's progress was measured. No doubt Judy's development was the most satisfactory of the three infants. However, to the mother it was an act of injustice that the boys should be sickly and weak while the girl was healthy and strong.

Judy was the first-born; in learning too she was always ahead. This characteristic became more marked as soon as the infant stage was passed. Because Judy progressed well, she received the least attention from the mother, and consequently Judy was deprived of mothering early in life. She seemed content with the care she received, while the boys always demanded more. As long as the babies could be satisfied with bottles and physical care they were all treated the same way; however, the boys required more specialized feeding and care than Judy did. The mother recalled that she never saw the infants as individuals, but only as three babies needing the bottle. Difficulties arose when the babies could not be pacified any longer by feeding, but demanded different handling according to their individual needs.

In trying to secure her mother's love, Judy soon took her cue from her environment, that is, from the response her advanced development elicited; consequently, she came to rely on her achievements for the maintenance of her dependency needs. Judy started early to please the mother with her accomplishments and with a show of apparent inde-pendence. Thus, in order to secure the mother's love, Judy had to sur-render prematurely gratifications in which she saw her brothers indulged for an inordinately long time. Circumstances, maturational pace, and spe-cial endowment contributed their respective shares to this child's early personality organization, in which an outstanding tolerance for frustra-tion and a tendency to compliance as an effort to master anxiety are noticeable. Judy's satisfactory development as an infant set the level of expectation from the start, and seemingly she found it easy to fit into the image which the environment had contrived. She became what others wanted her to be; she received acceptance and praise in return, but she forfeited a sense of worth and wholeness, the lack of which was so apparent during her adolescence.

Judy thus became a model child. She had to keep up her progress in order to please her parents, particularly her mother. Needless to say, her drive for achievement received powerful reinforcement from her agressive and retaliatory impulses. Judy could outdo and outshine her brothers, and consequently she could soon qualify to become mother's little helper. Judy's advanced development turned her into a kind of older sister who had to watch and help her brothers. For years she was the leader, the protector, and, in fact, the little nursemaid of her brothers. "I helped everybody [meaning her brothers] and nobody helped me" were Judy's angry and resentful words when she later thought back to her childhood years. Judy's yearning for love, her sense of loneliness, her boundless jealousy and emotional greed all had their roots in these early years.

During the preoedipal period Judy identified with the active mother; she helped her in bringing up the children. By this identification, Judy escaped from oral dependency, but she acquired early a profound sense of guilt: her motherliness barely covered her hostile impulse toward her brothers, and her insatiable oral needs in relation to her mother. In order to maintain the separateness from the mother and yet be close to her, the child became like her; she incorporated the mother's demands and expectations, which she then fulfilled with a vengeance. Around this hostile identification the child's emotional life emerged in a more integrated and lasting pattern: high self-expectations going hand-in-hand with low self-esteem. The child strove to be good, but she always fell short of the ideal; in this she was similar to the mother, who possessed all goodness but never became the unselfish and bountiful mother whom Judy desired. Judy's self-blame is an echo of her blame of the mother, who abandoned her for the sake of her brothers and *her* self-interest.

Judy was described by her mother as a "wonderful, jolly good baby" until the age of five. At this time she became disappointed in her father, who related to the children in his own friendly way whenever he himself needed companionship, and who hardly noticed the desire of his children to be loved by him. Judy turned her affection from the father to the older brother, who became, in these years, a father-substitute for the little girl. This switch of oedipal strivings from the father to the older brother was presaged by the close relationship which existed between the mother and her oldest son, a relationship which made this boy the unquestionably preferred male in the family. The older brother, in fact, assumed in many ways a paternal role in relation to Judy. The then preadolescent boy showed no open affection for his little sister; but he expressed his interest in her through telling her how to behave and by reprimanding her whenever she made mistakes. The extent to which the brother had become the representative of the oedipal father was dramatically displayed by Judy's emotional involvement in his marriage when she was fifteen. The magnitude of Judy's disappointment in the oedipal father can be fathomed by her adolescent emotional outcry when she remembered how her father had deserted her in her childhood at a time when she had needed him most.

With the close of the oedipal phase, around the age of five, a change came over Judy: once again she repeated the earlier pattern of compensating for a disappointment by becoming self-sufficient and competent. However, she overcompensated, and turned snobbish and sullen; traits which became more marked with the firmer establishment of the latency period. Judy felt superior to the rest of the family, and thought she deserved a special life of her own. The outline of the family romance is discernible in Judy's haughty attitude, and it emerged again in adolescence when with her friend she playacted living in Buckingham Palace.

An earlier fantasy should be mentioned here because it lingered on until adolescence, namely, the fantasy that "we were really quadruplets, two boys and two girls; one girl had died in childbirth and I was alone." The search for completeness remained a search for the lost twin sister. In this fantasy is entombed the child's early loss of mothering as well as restitution for the genital incompleteness which she had experienced vis-à-vis her brothers. Judy always needed a girlfriend whom she could admire and possess; but just this need brought about the loss of the girlfriend she so desperately desired.

The consequences of the oedipal disappointment were, in Judy's case, easily discernible: she gave herself over to learning in which she succeeded very well. Her brothers were left far behind while she forged ahead with an unbending intellectual competitiveness and ambition. Secondly, Judy's sexual feelings underwent a massive repression and created an emotional impoverishment which did not reach a critical stage until puberty. The seduction scene with the uncle seems to have been a prepuberty trauma, following the model described by Greenacre (1950). "These traumata were provoked by the victims, and were compulsive repetitions of preoedipal conflicts influencing the intensity of the oedipal phase and subsequent severity and deformation of the super-ego." Another conclusion of Greenacre's paper is borne out in Judy's case, namely, "the utilization of the trauma as a masochistic justification for a defense against sexuality." The skin sensitivity which played such an outstanding part in Judy's seduction experience hints at an early body contact disturbance in infancy. The uncle's request for her to undress reflects both her own wish for sexual stimulation by fondling, and simultaneously an affirmation of the sexual danger which the male represents. This incident was followed by an avoidance of any situation which might arouse sexual feelings. When Judy eventually found herself alone with a boy she feared being attacked by him; obviously, she feared her own loss of control. To an impasse of this kind she reacted with nausea and vomiting. We recognize in these transient symptoms an ingestive lability which seems to extend back into the period of oral ambivalence. When Judy was away at camp during her early adolescence she would get hunger sensations or an upset stomach. She would call home and ask for food but would steadfastly turn down the mother's anxious suggestion that she come home.

Judy's personality organization took shape around a triad of constellations: 1) an oral insatiability which predisposed her to depressive moods; 2) a dependency and an ambivalent object relationship which paved the way to a hostile identification which allowed her to maintain contact with the loved and hated object; 3) aggressive, rivalrous impulses which were inhibited and turned against the self; a permanent feeling of guilt prevailed. This characteristic pattern of dealing with drive, superego, and environment was more or less complete at the time the child entered the latency period. It remained intact until puberty disturbed the existing balance and upset the precarious calm of the preceding years. However, the effort which carried Judy through the latency period must not be underrated; she resisted with stubborn determination a return to maternal dependency and conceded to her brothers the world of childish pleasures while she set out to pursue those avenues of gratification (school success) which were open to her outside the narrow confines of the family. Judy turned her whole energy to learning; and we recognize in her ego ideal the outcome of her conflicting tendencies. She wanted to become a nurse and a teacher of nurses. This vocational aspiration, which she preserved with unusual pertinacity, represents a sublimation of her own need to be nursed by the mother as well as the child's early identification with the active mother; furthermore, we recognize Judy's way of mastering frustration and counteracting the regressive pull by turning what she passively desired into something she actively performed. Her vocational choice was thus based on a focal childhood trauma; it offered within the matrix of social conformity and prestige an organized activity by which the mastery of the trauma could be articulated as a life task.

Her too extensive use of the defense mechanism of reversal interfered with Judy's development of femininity; the passive position remained attached to the infantile dependency on the mother and only tentatively was it abandoned during the oedipal phase. When at puberty the instinctual drives became intensified, the girl literally returned to the mother and shared the bed with her. The secrecy around this arrangement, and the details of sleeping habits described above leave no doubt that this clinging to the mother was but a continuation of preoedipal wishes which had never been given up. It is of interest to note that Judy's capacity to separate—at the start only physically—from her mother was effected by her positive relationship to the therapist, a young, understanding, and attractive woman. The girl found in her an ego ideal, a sister rather than a mother. The therapist, being less exacting and more tolerant than Judy's superego, permitted the girl to experience her as unselfish, without exploitative motives. At times Judy even wore a sweater the same color as that worn by the therapist; she had indeed found her twin sister. In her dress she was strongly influenced by her relationship to the therapist. She began to appreciate feminine clothes, which was an obvious change, since in her home sloppy and unkempt looks were customary. This transference helped her to move from a demanding dependency to a sharing one. Thus she assimilated an idealized alter ego in a relationship which was lifted from the realm of fantasy to an experience in reality. During the process, Judy's sense of completeness and worthiness emerged; simultaneously, her aggressive competitiveness subsided, and her hostile identification receded. Sexual fantasies moved into the foreground, and she developed crushes on male teachers whom she idealized.

The progressive detachment from the preoedipal mother led to a revival of abandoned oedipal wishes. Heterosexual object finding became commensurate with and ceased to be antagonistic to academic success. Sexual fantasies and sensations were acknowledged as ego syntonic with no overriding of the self-protective barrier of her physical and emotional self. A fear of the power of her emotions was still evident in Judy's behavior; but her interests, activities, and experiences clearly indicated that a decisive turn toward femininity had occurred, and with it, Judy entered the phase of late adolescence.

III

Phases
of Adolescence

PASSAGE through the adolescent period proceeds neither at an even rate nor in a straight line. Indeed, the goals and attainments of mental life which characterize the various phases of the adolescent period are often contradictory in direction and qualitatively heterogeneous; this is to say, that progression, digression, and regression are alternately in evidence, as they always are during phases which transiently involve antagonistic aims. Defensive and adaptive mechanisms intertwine, and the duration of any of the phases cannot be fixed by any time schedule or age reference. This extraordinary elasticity of psychological movement, which underlies the spectacular diversity of the adolescent period, cannot be stressed too much. However, the fact remains that an orderly sequence of psychological development does exist, and it can be described in terms of more or less distinct phases.

The adolescent may rush through these various phases, or he may

elaborate any one of them in endless variations; but he cannot altogether sidestep the essential psychic transformations of the various
phases. Their elaboration by processes of differentiation over an extended period of time results in a complex personality structure; a hasty
passage through adolescence usually produces an imprint on the adult
which is best described as primitivization. Neither of these two developments should be confused with levels of maturity; rather they are evidence of degrees of complexity and differentiation. Both the innate
forward push, and the growth potential of adolescent personality development aim relentlessly at integrating the novel maturational attainment
of puberty and the older, accustomed modes of equilibrium maintenance.
By this process of integration a continuity in the experience of the ego
is preserved which facilitates the emergence of a stable sense of self—or,
a sense of identity.

1. The Latency Period, An Introduction

The specific importance of the latency period for the successful approach, entrance, and passage of adolescence has been mentioned. The
latency period furnishes the child with the equipment, in terms of ego
development, which prepares him for the encounter with the drive incre-
ment of puberty. The child, in other words, is made ready for the task
of dispersing the energic influx onto all levels of personality functioning
which were elaborated during the latency period. Consequently, he is
able to divert instinctual energy into differentiated psychic structures
and into manifold activities of psychosocial dimensions, instead of having to experience it solely as an increase in sexual and aggressive tension. Freud (1905, b) referred to abortive latency as a "spontaneous
sexual precocity" which is due to the fact that the latency period did not
successfully establish itself; therefore, he thought, the "sexual inhibitions" which constitute an essential component of the latency period
have not been adequately acquired, thus "occasioning sexual manifestations which, owing on the one hand to the sexual inhibitions being incomplete and on the other hand to the genital system being undevel-
oped, are bound to be in the nature of perversions."

The literal interpretation of the term *latency period* to mean that
these years are devoid of sexual urges—that is, that sexuality is latent—
has long ago been superseded by an acknowledgment of clinical evidence that sexual feelings expressed in masturbatory, voyeuristic, ex-

hibitionistic, and sadomasochistic activities do not cease to exist during the latency period (Alpert, 1941; Bornstein, 1951). However, no new instinctual aim appears at this stage. What does change in the latency period is the growing control of the ego and superego over the instinctual life. Fenichel (1945, b) referred to this: "During the latency period the instinctual demands themselves have not changed much; but the ego has." Sexual activity during the latency period is relegated to the role of a transient regulator of tension; this function is superseded by the emergence of a variety of ego activities, sublimatory, adaptive, and defensive in nature. This shift is substantially promoted by the fact that "object relations are given up and are replaced by identifications" (Freud, 1924, b). The shift in cathexis from an outer to an inner object may well be called an essential criterion of the latency period. Freud (1905, b) made special reference to this fact, which, however, was overshadowed by the more general concept that "sexual inhibition" is the outstanding indicator of the latency period. He stated: "From time to time [during the latency period] a fragmentary manifestation of sexuality which has evaded sublimation may break through; or some sexual activity may persist through the whole duration of the latency period until the sexual instinct emerges with greater intensity at puberty. Due to the latency development the direct expression of, for example, sexual and dependency needs, decreases since they became amalgamated with more complex, alloplastic endeavors, or are kept in abeyance by defenses of which the obsessive-compulsive ones are typical for this period."

The dependency on parental assurance for feelings of worth and significance is progressively replaced during the latency period by a sense of self-esteem derived from achievements and mastery which earn objective and social approbation. The child's own inner resourcefulness thus joins the parent as the regulator of his self-esteem. With the superego in ascendancy, the child thus becomes better able to maintain his narcissistic balance more or less independently. The widening scope of his social, intellectual, and motor proficiencies in turn allows him a vast array of resources, all of which help him to keep his narcissistic balance within a narrower range than was possible in early childhood. A greater stability in affect and mood is in evidence.

Concomitantly with these developments, ego functions acquire an increasing resistivity to regression; and significant ego activities, such as perception, learning, memory, and thinking become more firmly consolidated in the conflict-free sphere of the ego. It follows that instinctual tension fluctuations therefore do not threaten the intactness of ego functions, as they were able to do in prelatency years. The establishment of stable identifications makes the child more independent of object relations and their undulating intensity and quality; ambivalence declines markedly, especially during the latter part of the latency period (Bornstein, 1951). The consequence of more stringent inner controls becomes apparent in the emergence of behavior and by attitudes which are motivated by logic and oriented toward values. This general development brings higher mental functions into autonomous play and reduces decisively the use of the body as an expressive instrument of inner life. From this point of view, latency can be described in terms of the "reduction of the expressive use of the whole body, increase in capacity for verbal expression in isolation from motor activity" (Kris, 1939). Language itself undergoes a change; the conjunction "because" is used with greater proficiency (Werner, 1940). Furthermore, language is more and more used to veil; as is indicated by the use of allegory, comparison, and simile, in contrast with the usage of the younger child, whose language expresses without circumlocutions his emotions and wishes. Ella Sharpe (Sharpe, 1940) has shown that the use of the metaphor stands out in the latency period and in adolescence; this particular figure of speech "evolves alongside the control of the bodily orifices. Emotions which originally accompanied bodily discharge find substitute channels and materials." A gain in artistic self-expression compensates for the loss of unself-conscious bodily spontaneity.

An advancement of social awareness in the latency child goes hand in hand with his separation of rational thinking and fantasy, with his separation of public-world and private-world behavior—in short, with a novel, keenly-felt differentiation. In this differentiation the child readily seizes on normative social institutions, such as education, school, and playground, for a valuative model which will promote his integrative behavior.

Boys and girls show significant difference in their latency development. Regression to the pregenital level as a defense at the beginning of latency seems more typical for the boy than for the girl. The boy's regressive proclivity foreshadows his preadolescent development. The fact that the boy abandons the oedipal phase more stringently and definitely than the girl renders the early part of his latency period extremely difficult. The girl, in contrast, enters this period with less conflict. Indeed, she preserves with a sense of freedom some of the phallic features of her preoedipal past. Greenacre (1950, a) expressed the opinion that "some degree of bisexual identification probably occurs in most girls at some time during the latency period, unless the girl remains almost exclusively under the domination of prolonged oedipal strivings." The girl enters a more conflictual time during the later years of her latency years when a breakthrough of her instinctual drives is imminent and her superego proves inadequate to stem the onrushing tide of prepuberty.

The general characteristics of latency which I have summarized have been described in detail in several psychoanalytic studies of the latency period (Fries, 1958), some with special reference to choice of books (Peller, 1958; Friedlander, 1942); to wit (Wolfenstein, 1955); and to play (Peller, 1954).

A prerequisite for entering the adolescent phase of drive organization is the consolidation of the latency period; otherwise the pubescent child experiences a simple intensification of prelatency strivings and exhibits infantile behavior of arrested rather than regressive nature. In analytic work with adolescents—mainly young adolescents—whose latency period has never been satisfactorily established, we are accustomed to preface or intersperse the analytic work with educational interventions in order to bring about some essential latency attainments.

In one case, a well-developed ten-year-old boy who showed learning difficulties, social inadequacy, and bizarre thinking, abruptly at the age of ten expressed a desire to sleep in his mother's bed and keep his father away from her. Demands for embraces and kisses alternated with wishes to be picked up by the mother like a child or to be allowed to sit on her lap. The mother had the tendency to yield to the child's wishes. It seemed essential at the very beginning of the child's analysis to help the mother develop a resistance to her son's sexual advances and to teach her how to frustrate him while offering substitute gratifications. The fact that the mother restrained him actively from the realization of his oedipal wishes influenced the child's reaction in a decisive way: he reacted to the mother's prohibitions with repression of his oedipal wishes and a show of resignation. He became compulsively preoccupied with schoolwork, filling workbook after workbook, checking his answers incessantly. This compulsive behavior served as a defense against anal retaliatory urges directed at the frustrating mother; these urges were acted out in relation to the mothers of his schoolmates. After his regressive behavior was worked through, oedipal material appeared in the analysis and castration anxiety became prominent through denial, projection, and confused thinking. The boy's interest turned to castration themes derived mainly from the Bible: the killing of a male lamb at Passover; the Lord who "will smite all the first-born in the land of Egypt"; Herod's slaying of the little children of Bethlehem. It is believed that without the use of preparatory educational methods at the outset of the analysis the treatment of this boy would have been seriously jeopardized.

The attainments of the latency period which might well represent the essential precondition for an advance to adolescence can be summarized as follows: Intelligence must have developed through a sharp delineation between primary and secondary process thinking, and through the employment of judgment, generalization, and logic; social understanding, empathy, and altruistic feelings must have acquired considerable stability; physical stature must allow independence and mastery of the environment; ego functions must have acquired ever greater resistivity to regression and to disintegration under the impact of minor, that is, everyday, critical situations; the synthesizing capacity of the ego must have become effective and complex; and finally, the ego must be sufficiently able to defend its integrity with progressively less assistance from the outside world. These latency achievements have to yield to the pubertal increase in drive energy. If the novel condition of puberty only reinforces latency achievements which were carried out under the influence of sexual repression, then, as Anna Freud (1936) remarked, "the character of the individual during the latency period will declare itself for good and all." Emotional immaturity will be the lasting outcome, as it always is when a task specific for one phase is circumvented by falling back on or holding on to the attainments of the preceding developmental phase.

2. Preadolescence

During the preadolescent phase a quantitative increase of instinctual pressure leads to an indiscriminate cathexis of all those libidinal and aggressive modes of gratification which have served the child well during the early years of his life. Neither a new love object nor a new instinctual aim can yet be discerned at this phase. Any experience can become sexually stimulating—even those thoughts, fantasies, and activities which are devoid of any obvious erotic connotation. For example, the stimuli to which the preadolescent boy reacts with an erection are nonspecific; it is not necessarily an erotic stimulus which causes genital excitation, for it can be provoked by anger, fear, shock, or general excitement. First emissions in the waking state are often due to affective states such as these, rather than to specifically erotic stimulation. Among the physically more mature boys, competitive situations like wrestling have been reported to result in spontaneous emissions. This state of affairs in the boy entering pubescence testifies to the function of the genital as a nonspecific discharge organ of tension; this is characteristic of childhood up to the time of adolescence proper, when the organ gradually acquires exclusive sensitivity to heterosexual stimuli.

The resurgence of pregenital urges is not uniformly manifested among boys and girls because each sex copes with the pubertal drive increase in a different way. Erikson (1951) has described the striking differences in play constructions of preadolescents. It becomes apparent from his material that the theme of maleness and femaleness leads to different play configurations in boy and girl. It is the preoccupation (unconscious and preconscious) with the sexual organs, their function, intactness, and protection, and not the relationship theme of love and its fulfillment which stands out in the play construction of the preadolescent. Erikson comments: "The most significant sex differences in the use of play space, then, add up to the following picture: in the boys, the outstanding variables are height and downfall and motion and its channelization or arrest (policeman); in girls, static interiors which are open, simply inclosed or blocked and intruded upon."

In general terms, it can be said that a *quantitative* increase in drive characterizes preadolescence, and that this condition leads to a more or less extended resurgence of pregenitality (A. Freud, 1936). This innovation brings the latency period to an end; the child becomes more difficult to reach, to teach, and to control. Whatever education has accomplished over the previous years in terms of instinct control and social conformity seems now doomed to disintegration.

Gesell (1956) reports that girls at the age of ten are given to "smutty jokes, usually related to the buttocks rather than to sex," while boys prefer "dirty jokes, especially about elimination"; he states that girls grasp with greater clarity the separation between the eliminative and the reproductive systems, but that they still show a tendency to confuse the two. Sexual curiosity in boys and girls shifts from anatomy and content to function and process. They know where babies come from, but they are mystified about how this relates to their own bodies. Among girls open curiosity is replaced by whisperings and secrecy; and to share a secret the content of which is usually of an undisguised sexual nature remains a form of intimacy and conspiracy during this phase. This situation differs from the latency period when merely to have a secret as such —about any topic—is the source of delight and excitement.

The following vignette from the analysis of a preadolescent boy with a learning disability due to defective instinct control illustrates how the revival of pregenital impulses undergoes gradual suppression and transformation before sublimation is re-established.

A boy of twelve who struggled with an upsurge of pregenitality and who had repeatedly provoked painful encounters with home and school authorities finally was able to use institutional safeguards (school and church) to help him in instinct control and to protect him against anxiety and guilt. He came to consider the anal jokes and words which had gotten him into trouble as sinful, and he reminded himself of the punishment which could follow his sinning, namely, expulsion from school and condemnation by God. He referred to an imaginary boy who was expelled from school (of course, he was talking about himself) for having told the following joke: "Mrs. Hershey put her nuts into her chocolate." According to the boy's explanation, "nuts" has three meanings: eating, being crazy, and penis; chocolate refers to the cloaca. But now, the youngster assured the analyst, he no longer thinks of such dirty jokes or laughs about a "stinking ass hole"; now he makes up funny nonsense words or sentences. Just thinking of this makes him burst into laughter. He offers an example: "George Washingmachine went on a bicycle down the Missislappy and signed the declaration of indigestion." A disguise, but indeed a thin one; for the excited fun derived from the nonsense and expressed in the gay laughter betrays the unconscious meaning. The boy was now able openly to recruit an audience for his "jokes," and thus procured relief from the guilt which stems from the objectionable impulse (Blos, 1941). After a time of almost compulsive invention or recitation of "cleansed" jokes, this boy progressively abandoned his counterphobic courage and concentrated on his school subjects with great vigor.

Direct instinct gratification ordinarily meets a disapproving superego. In this conflict the ego resorts to many well-known solutions: defenses like repression, reaction formation, displacement, and others are reinstated or reinforced. This allows the child to develop skills and interests which carry peer approval and peer prestige, and to indulge in the many overcompensatory actions, in compulsive behavior and obsessional thoughts in order to bind anxiety. Typical for this age is the collector's single-minded interest which concentrates on stamps, coins, matchbook covers, campaign buttons, or on other objects which lend themselves to this form of activity. One novel solution in the service of instinct gratification appears during preadolescence: socialization of guilt. This new device to circumvent the superego conflict stems from the social maturation achieved during latency development; the child uses it to unburden his guilt onto the group in general, or more specifically onto the leader as the instigator of acts of transgression. The socialization of guilt temporarily renders autoplastic defenses at least to some degree dispensable. The phenomenon of shared or projected guilt feelings is one reason for the increasing significance of group or gang affiliation during this stage.

Naturally, all these defenses are not always commensurate to the onslaught of instinctual demands; fears, phobias, and nervous habits may appear as transitory symptoms. Developmental and descriptive psychology refers to the *tensional outlets* of this stage: frequent stomach- and head-aches, nail biting, drawing in the lips, stuttering, muttering, hand-to-mouth behaviors, hair twirling, fiddling with things; a few children still suck their thumbs (Gesell, 1956).

Two typical modes of preadolescent behavior in boys and girls throw light on the central conflict of the two sexes at this stage. The boy behaves hostilely toward girls, he belittles them, and tries to avoid them; in their company he brags, boasts, and teases, he shows off and exaggerates. In essence, he denies his anxiety rather than attempts to establish a relationship. The castration anxiety which brought the oedipal phase to its decline reappears and forces the boy into the exclusive company of his own sex. In the girl this phase is characterized by a "thrust of activity," during which playacting and tomboyishness reach their height (Deutsch, 1944). In this demonstrative denial of femininity may be discerned the unresolved childhood conflict of penis envy, the central conflict of the preadolescent girl, a conflict which finds a dramatic temporary suspension while phallic fantasies have their last fling before femininity asserts itself.

A girl of seventeen described her preadolescence as follows: "The transition that I underwent at the age of eleven, when I was as social as a five-year-old and wanted to be as social as a fourteen-year-old, was accompanied by a series of factors. Of these probably the most important and the most difficult for me to explain was my own maturation. I gradually broke away from my brother's code, that he held until sixteen, of the inferiority of girls. I changed from tagging after gangs of boys, who would not accept me, to joining groups of girls, who would. Here was where the Girl Scouts became a guiding force in my life. I would do my good deed proudly each day. The scout leader was a breezy woman I admired, as she so directly contrasted with the fussy school teachers and my parents."

Another study (More, 1953) recorded a girl's wishes at different age levels of "the person I would like to be" when grown up. These self-images projected into the future throw light on the convergence of ego interests and psychosexual developments. At age eleven one girl wanted to be a WAVE—"wear a uniform and look like my mother." In addition, she "would like to fly airplanes and learn to fly." At age twelve she wanted to be a nurse, because a nurse "helps people and dresses neatly." At age sixteen she wanted to be a model or a stenographer "be 5'6" and weigh 120 pounds." Nostalgically, she adds here: "I wanted to join the WAVES but I can't, so I guess I will have to be satisfied with the other jobs. This was my secret ambition."

It is a well known fact that preadolescence involves totally different psychological developments in boy and girl. The dissimilarities between the sexes is striking; descriptive psychology has paid extensive attention to this period and has accumulated a mass of relevant observational data. The boy takes a circuitous route toward a genital orientation via pregenital drive cathexis; in contrast, the girl turns far more readily and forcefully toward the other sex.

Only with reference to the boy is it correct to say that the quantitative increase of the instinctual drive during preadolescence leads to an indiscriminate cathexis of pregenitality. In fact, the resurgence of pregenitality marks the termination of latency for the male. At this time boys show an increase in diffuse motility (restlessness, fidgetiness), and in oral greediness, sadistic activities, anal activities (expressed in coprophilic pleasures, "dirty" language, a disregard for cleanliness, a fascination with odors, the skillful production of onomatopoetic noises), and phallic, exhibitionistic games. An eleven-year-old boy who started analysis at ten illustrated these developments aptly by saying, "My favorite word now is 'crap.' The older I get the dirtier I become." At age fourteen the same boy made the following retrospective comparison: "At eleven my mind was only on filth, now it is on sex. There is a great difference."

We are here reminded of Dostoevsky's remarks about boys of this age; one cannot help but notice the constancy of place and age of preadolescent characteristics. In *The Brothers Karamazov* we find this passage: "There are 'certain' words and conversations unhappily impossible to eradicate in schools. Boys pure in mind and heart, almost children, are fond of talking in school among themselves of things, pictures, and images of which even soldiers would sometimes hesitate to speak. More than that, much that soldiers have no knowledge or conception of is familiar to quite young children of our intellectual and higher classes. There is no moral depravity, no real corrupt inner cynicism in it, but there is the appearance of it, and it is often looked upon among them as something refined, subtle, daring and worthy of imitation."

The fantasies of preadolescent boys are usually well protected; more freely communicated are the ego-syntonic thoughts of grandiosity and smuttiness. One well-protected fantasy, preserved from an early age of about five years and used again at the age of eleven to arouse genital stimulation, was revealed in installments by a boy in analysis. He did not reveal the accompanying sexual sensation until two years later, when he spontaneously corrected his earlier denial. The fantasy was this: "I always thought girls are wound up with a key which was stuck into the side of their thighs. When they were wound up they were very tall; boys in proportion were only one inch high. The boys climbed up the legs of these tall girls, got under their skirt and into their underwear. In there were hammocks hanging down from nowhere. The boys climbed into the hammocks. I always called this to myself 'riding the girl.'" Thus, the word *riding* acquired a very special, erotically tinged, and slightly embarrassing connotation.

This daydream, as is usually the case, was elaborated at preadolescence and fused with current events. In the case of this boy, it took the form of a fantasy in which girls at school captured his best friend and stripped him. The theme of killing, subduing, humiliating, and exploiting the giant, *i.e.*, phallic female (the archaic mother imago) returned in endless variations. The inequity in the imagined battles between boys and girls highlighted, in this case, the fear of the female as well as the boy's own aggressive impulse against the mother's body, especially the breasts, which he referred to as "those protruding masses," or, derogatorily, as "the teats" or "their upper sex organs." He felt that he was restrained from wrestling or being rough with girls as a way of curbing his destructive urges directed against their breasts. Girls, so he reasoned, are protected because "they need those things." One of his tirades against girls went like this: "Girls are supposed to be so feeble. It's all a farce. Why open the door for them? They can do it. In fact, they are often stronger than boys. All on account of the babies they are protected. One baby at a time. A man can make a million of them in no time. But, no, man can be sacrificed in war and be killed." He wished to hit a girl's breast when he felt he was not being allowed to touch it. He knew the stage of breast development of each girl in his class. Typically, these fantasies and strivings were counteracted by his affirmation, "I'm glad I'm a boy"; in collective defensiveness, he banded together with his pals.

The above material is quoted as further clinical support for the theoretical model of preadolescence; an interpretation of the material permits the delineation of the typical preadolescent conflict of the boy as one of fear and envy of the female. The identificatory tendency with the phallic mother tends to alleviate the castration anxiety in relation to her; normally a defensive organization is built up against this tendency. We are reminded here of Bettelheim's (1954) thesis that pubertal initiation rites serve the purpose for the boy of resolving his envy of the female. In essence, then, a bisexual identification has to be resolved (Mead, 1958). Bettelheim (1954) offers clinical material which demonstrates "that certain initiation rites originate in the adolescent's attempts to integrate his envy of the other sex or to adjust to the social role prescribed for his sex and give up pregenital, childish gratifications."

At the stage of preadolescence, the boy has to renounce again, and now definitively, his wish for a baby (breast, passivity) and, more or less, complete the task of the oedipal period (Mack-Brunswick, 1940). In a gifted man, this wish may find fulfillment in creative work; and whenever such men seek treatment because their creative activity has ceased to function, they reveal a typical drive organization which Jacobson (1950) described in her paper "The Wish for a Child in Boys." With regard to these patients, Jacobson says that "their creative activity regularly shows intensely cathexed unconscious feminine reproductive fantasies." Van der Leeuw (1958) stressed the boy's normal envy of the preoedipal mother and the importance for progressive development which lies in its resolution, namely the relinquishment of the "preoedipal wish to be pregnant and bear children like mother." Van der Leeuw continues: "The obstacles to be overcome are the feelings of rage, jealousy, rivalry, and above all of impotence and helplessness and the destructive aggression which accompany these experiences. In early childhood childbearing is experienced as achievement, power and competition with the mother. It represents being active like mother. It is an identification with the active producing mother." Fixation on the preadolescent level renders this phase a lasting drive organization; in cases of such fixation, the phase of preadolescence has miscarried due to an insurmountable castration fear in relation to the archaic mother which is resolved by an identification with the phallic woman.

How does the preadolescent boy regard the girl of this age? Certainly, the preadolescent girl does not show the same features as the boy; she is either a tomboy or a young aggressive female. To the preadolescent boy she appears as Diana, the young goddess of the hunt, who displays her charms while she runs through the wilderness with a pack of hounds. I use this mythological reference here in order to emphasize the defensive aspect of the boy's pregenital drive cathexis, namely his avoidance of the castrating woman, the archaic mother. My knowledge of the fantasies, play activities, dreams, and symptomatic behavior of preadolescent boys has made me conclude that castration anxiety in relation to the phallic mother is not only a universal occurrence of male preadolescence, but can be considered its central theme. This recurrent observation may possibly be due to the fact that I see in analysis so many young adolescent boys with passive strivings who come from families with strong and domineering mothers; and this consideration certainly requires careful scrutiny. The conclusions mentioned above will now be illustrated by some examples from the analyses of preadolescent boys.

In several dreams of an eleven-year-old boy who was obese, submissive, inhibited, and compulsive, there repeatedly appeared a naked woman; her lower body part was not well remembered and vaguely seen, and her breast, observed in its proper place, had penislike qualities, either as an erectile or urinary organ. The dreams of this boy were always prompted by his experiences in a co-educational school where the competition between boys and girls offered him endless proof of the girls' malice, foul play, and predatory viciousness. When the reassurance provided by compulsive masturbation was interpreted in terms of the preadolescent impasse described above, a sleep disturbance developed with the prevalent fear that his mother might kill him during the night.

A fourteen-year-old boy who was still in the preadolescent phase and presented a severe psychogenic learning disability reported recurrent dreams in which he was chased by an ape in the jungle, or in which a monster looked into his room at night through the half-open door. Although petrified, the boy decided in his dream that he would kill the monster. These dreams came ever closer to the actuality of the boy's life when his aggression against and fear of his mother reached a new climax. This event coincided with his asking the therapist for information about sex, of which he claimed to be totally ignorant; during these talks the boy suddenly exclaimed, "Of course! the gorilla is mommie." The ape-monster represented the phallic, castrating preoedipal mother. The father was seen as benign and submissive; he represented no threat.

A third boy, still in protracted preadolescence at the age of fourteen, whose emphatic disinterest in girls had become the theme of analytic investigation, recognized his suppressed curiosity and attraction but also his deadly fear of the female. He justified the concealment of his feelings and the show of indifference and hostility by saying, "Girls are out to kill you but you aren't allowed to touch them; they are so delicate." He felt that no self-assertion was permissible and that final submission to the attack would be the only possible outcome of the encounter.

Grete Bibring (1953) has described the course of a development in which the boy reaches the positive oedipal phase without the help of a prohibiting father through a regression to the preoedipal mother. However, in his attachment to her he experiences oedipal anxieties; this mother, the seductress, becomes the witch in the matriarchal family setting: preoedipal frustrations and oedipal threats all become concentrated in one and the same figure.

The castration anxiety which brought the oedipal phase of the boy to its decline reappears with the onset of puberty. Pubertal castration anxiety of the male is in its initial stage related to the active, the powerful, the procreative mother. A second stage which is typical for adolescence proper will be described later. At preadolescence we observe that passive strivings are overcompensated and the defense against them is powerfully reinforced by sexual maturation (A. Freud, 1936). The typical stage of male preadolescence, before a successful turn toward masculinity is effected, receives its characteristic quality from the employment of the homosexual defense against castration anxiety. It is precisely this defensive solution of the boy underlying his typical group behavior which descriptive psychology has labeled the "gang stage."* Psychoanalytic psychology refers to it as the "homosexual stage" of preadolescence.

This stage must be set off from a later, transient, and more or less elaborated homosexual phase of early adolescence when a member of

_____
* Not to be confused with the gang of the older adolescent boy.

the same sex is taken as a love object under the influence of the ego ideal. In the preadolescent homosexual phase of the boy a turn to the same sex is an avoidance maneuver; in the second homosexual phase— which more deserves the name—a narcissistic object choice has declared itself. Erotically-tinged intense friendships are well-known manifestations of this later stage.

The dissimilarity in male and female preadolescent behavior is foreshadowed by the massive repression of pregenitality which the girl had to establish before she could move into the oedipal phase; in fact, this repression is a prerequisite for the normal development of femininity. As the girl turns away from her mother due to the narcissistic disappointment in her as the castrated woman, she represses also those instinctual drives which were intimately related to the mother's care and bodily ministrations, namely the total scope of pregenitality. Mack-Brunswick (1940) in her classical paper, "The Preoedipal Phase of the Libido Development," states: "One of the greatest differences between the sexes is the enormous extent to which infantile sexuality is repressed in the girl. Except in profound neurotic states no man resorts to any similar repression of his infantile sexuality."

The girl who cannot maintain the repression of her pregenitality encounters difficulties in her development. Consequently, the young adolescent girl normally exaggerates her heterosexual desires and attaches herself to boys often in frantic succession. "Paradoxically," Helene Deutsch (1944) remarks, "the girl's mother relation is more persistent, and often more intense and dangerous, than the boy's. The inhibition she encounters when she turns toward reality (in prepuberty) brings her back to her mother for a period marked by heightened and more infantile love demands."

In considering the dissimilarity between male and female preadolescence it is necessary to remember that the oedipal conflict in the girl is not brought to such an abrupt and fateful termination as is the boy's. Freud (1931) stated, "The girl remains in the Oedipal situation for an indefinite period; she only abandons it late in life, and then incompletely." Consequently, the girl struggles with object relations more intensely during her adolescence; in fact, the prolonged and painful severance from the mother constitutes the major task of this period. "A prepubertal attempt at liberation from the mother that has failed or was too weak can inhibit future psychologic growth and leave a definitely infantile imprint on the woman's entire personality" (Deutsch, 1944).

The preadolescent boy struggles with castration anxiety (fear and wish) in relation to the archaic mother and accordingly turns away from the opposite sex; the girl, on the other hand, defends herself against the regressive pull to the preoedipal mother by a forceful and decisive turn toward heterosexuality. In this role the preadolescent girl cannot be called "feminine," since she so obviously is the aggressor and the seducer in the game of pseudolove; indeed, the phallic quality of her sexuality is prominent at this stage and affords her for a brief period an unusual sense of adequacy and completeness. The fact that the average girl between the ages of eleven to thirteen is taller than the average boy of the same age only accentuates this situation. Benedek (1956, a) refers to endocrine findings: "Before the procreative function matures, before ovulation sets in with relative regularity, the estrogen phase is dominant, as if to facilitate the developmental tasks of adolescence, namely, to establish emotional relations with the male sex." Helene Deutsch (1944) has referred to "prepuberty" of the girl as "the period of greatest freedom from infantile sexuality." This condition is normally accompanied by a forceful "turn to reality" (Deutsch) which, in my opinion, serves to counteract the resurgence of infantile strivings, i.e., of pregenitality.

The conflict specific for the phase of female preadolescence reveals its defensive nature particularly well in cases in which a progressive development has not been sustained. Female delinquency, for example, offers the opportunity par excellence to study the preadolescent drive organization in the girl. We are familiar with the fact that in "prepuberty of girls, the attachment to the mother represents a greater danger than the attachment to the father" (Deutsch, 1944). In female delinquency, which, broadly speaking, represents sexual acting-out behavior, the fixation on the preoedipal mother plays a most decisive role. In fact, female delinquency is often precipitated by the strong regressive pull to the preoedipal mother and the panic which this surrender invokes. Careful scrutiny reveals that the girl's turn to heterosexual acting out, which appears to represent the recrudescence of oedipal wishes, proves really to be related to earlier fixation points lying in the pregenital phases of psychosexual development; frustration or overstimulation or both had been experienced. The pseudoheterosexuality of the delinquent girl serves as a defense against the regressive pull to the preoedipal mother, a pull which is frantically resisted because it would mean remaining attached to a homosexual object, and thus fatally rupturing the development of femininity. A fourteen-year-old girl when asked why she needed ten boy friends at once, answered with righteous indignation: "I have to do this; if I didn't have so many boy friends they would say I am a lesbian." The "they" in this statement is the projection of those instinctual urges the girl endeavors so vehemently to contradict by her exhibitionistic behavior.

A rupture in the girl's progressive emotional development caused by the advent of puberty constitutes a more serious threat to her personality integration than does any similar break for the boy. The following case abstract illustrates a typical delinquent breakdown of the female preadolescent drive organization, and reveals the crucial nature of the emotional task which the girl must accomplish before she can enter the more advanced stages of adolescence. Nancy, whose case is described in Chapter VII at greater length, is a good illustration of female preadolescence and its vicissitudes.

Nancy, age thirteen, was a sex delinquent. She had indiscriminate sexual relations with teenage boys, tormenting her mother with the tales of her exploits. She had experienced feelings of loneliness since childhood, and blamed her mother for her unhappiness. Nancy believed that her mother had never wanted her, and she made incessant and unreasonable demands on her. Nancy was obsessed by the wish for a baby; all her sexual fantasies pointed to the "mother-baby" theme and basically to an overwhelming oral greed. She had a dream in which she had sexual relations with teenage boys; in the dream she had 365 babies, one a day for a year from one boy, whom she shot after this was accomplished.

The sexual acting out gradually ceased after Nancy developed a friendship with a young, promiscuous, married, pregnant woman of twenty who had three children. In friendship with this girlfriend-mother, Nancy both found the gratification of her oral and maternal needs and was protected against homosexual surrender. She played mother to the children, and took care of them while their mother walked the streets. From this friendship Nancy emerged at fifteen as a narcissistic and rather prudish person. She developed an interest in acting and began to pursue the necessary training; but she failed to progress to genuine heterosexual object finding.

In summary, we can say that in normal female development the phase of preadolescent drive organization is dominated by a defense against the regressive pull to the preoedipal mother. This struggle is reflected in the many conflicts which arise between mother and daughter during this period. A progression to adolescence proper in the girl is marked by the emergence of oedipal feelings which are first displaced and finally extinguished by an "irreversible process of displacement," aptly designated by Anny Katan (1937) as "object removal."

Having defined the preadolescent drive organization in terms of preoedipal positions, let us consider the first analysis of an adolescent girl, namely Dora (Freud, 1905). Dora was sixteen when she first visited Freud and eighteen when she started treatment. The material of the case history, which we will review here, refers to the preadolescent drive organization of the girl. Her preoedipal mother fixation proved to be of pathogenic intensity and represented an insurmountable obstacle in the path of progressive adolescent development.

At the end of the chapter, "The Clinical Picture," Freud introduces an element which he confesses "can only serve to obscure and efface the outlines of the fine poetic conflict which we have been able to ascribe to Dora. For behind Dora's supervalent train of thought which was concerned with her father's relations to Frau K., there lay a feeling of jealousy which had that lady as its *object*—a feeling, that is, which could only be based upon an affection on Dora's part for one of her own sex." We could paraphrase the end of this sentence by saying: which could only be based upon an affection on the girl's part for her mother. Freud describes Dora's relationships to her governess, to her girl cousin, and to Frau K. which had a "greater pathogenic effect" than the oedipal situation which "she tried to use as a screen" for the deeper trauma of having been sacrificed by her intimate friend, Frau K., "without a moment's hesitation so that her relations with her father might not be disturbed." Freud concludes "that Dora's supervalent train of thought, which was concerned with her father's relations with Frau K., was designed not only for the purpose of suppressing her love for Herr K., which had once been conscious, but also to conceal her love for Frau K., which was in a deeper sense unconscious." We are familiar with the fact that oedipal strivings are louder and are more conspicuous in adolescence than the preoedipal fixations which, however, are usually of more profound pathogenic import. In the case of Dora the analysis came to an end "before it could throw any light on this side of her mental life."

Again and again, adolescents convey to us that they desperately need a foothold on the oedipal level—a sex-appropriate position—before earlier fixations can become accessible to analytic investigation. In this connection a reference to a young, passive adolescent boy seems relevant.

During three years of analysis, from the age of eleven to thirteen, he stubbornly maintained an image of his "milk-toast" father as the strong and important man in the family. The powerful father served this boy as a defense against preoedipal castration anxiety. The boy never permitted himself to criticize, doubt, or question the analyst: in his eyes the analyst was always right. He would not allow himself to look at the clock for fear of insulting the analyst. The analysis of the transference brought to light the boy's fears of the analyst: fear of retaliation and injury. The analysis of this oedipal castration anxiety opened the way to the far more disturbing anxieties felt in relation to the preoedipal mother; the uncovering of the earlier fixations resulted in a realistic if disappointing re-evaluation of the father. This case indicates that the maintenance of an "illusory oedipal" situation masks a strong preoedipal fixation.

The definition of preadolescence which I have suggested on the basis of instinctual organization does not at first seem to coincide with the subdivisions elaborated by Helene Deutsch (1944) with reference to the girl. She refers to the opening phase of adolescence as prepuberty (ages ten to twelve) which is the "prerevolutionary" era when the girl experiences the "greatest freedom from infantile sexuality." At this stage the girl shows a decisive "turn toward reality" and an "intensive process of adaptation to reality" which is characterized by a "thrust of activity." "Playacting" and "tomboyishness" testify to her "renunciation of infantile phantasy"; her "interest shifts from anatomical differences to physiological processes." The aegis under which these developments occur is in short the "liberation from the mother."

This formulation fits well into the model which I have described; however, I suspect that the girls' "thrust of activity" which precedes the increase of passivity constitutes an attempt to master actively what she has experienced passively while in the care of the nurturing mother; instead of taking the preoedipal mother as love object, the girl identifies temporarily with her active phallic image. The girl's transient phallic illusion gives this period an exalted vital tenor which does not lack a danger of fixation.

This phase appears with great clarity in the analysis of those girls who are "horse-crazy" during their preadolescent years. The analysis of their dreams indicates that the horse is appropriated by the girl as a phallic equivalent and treated with devoted, loving care; as *pars pro toto* it stands for the oedipal father. The love for the horse is narcissistic, in contradistinction, for example, to the girl's love for her dog, which is maternal and companionable. Such transitional devotion to horses at preadolescence may well constitute a normal stage in female development; but where it hampers libidinal progression, it represents a fixation at this level.

The force with which the girl turns away from infantile fantasy and sexuality is proportionate to the strength of the regressive pull in the direction of the primal love object, the mother. Should she surrender, act out the regression by displacement, or return to the early preoedipal fixation point, a deviate adolescent development will follow.

3. On Adolescent Object Choice

The state of mind and body which is generally associated with adolescence (both early adolescence and adolescence proper) has a distinctly different quality from the preadolescent phase. The difference shows itself in a far wider and richer emotional life, in a turn to a more goal-directed orientation aiming at growing up, in a relentless attempt at self-definition in answer to the question, "Who am I?" The problem of object relations moves into the foreground as a central theme and its variations color the entire psychological development of the two subsequent phases. What differentiates this period from the phase of preadolescence is therefore the shift from a merely quantitative drive increase to the emergence of a distinctly new drive quality. An abandonment of the preadolescent regressive position is noticeable. Pregenitality loses increasingly the role of a satiatory function, by becoming relegated to an initiatory activity—mentally and physically—it gives rise to a new drive component, namely forepleasure. This shift in drive organization eventually gives genitality a place of prime order. This hierarchical organization of drives and its definitive and irreversible character represents an innovation which decisively influences ego development. The ego, so to say, takes its cue from shifts in instinctual organization and elaborates in its own structure a hierarchical organization of ego functions and of defensive patterns. Both assume at the close of adolescence an irreversible fixity, called *character*; this firmer structure, which emerges from these phases—and is indeed built on attainments of the latency period—will not be complete until the phase of postadolescence.

While the differentiation between preadolescence and the two phases which follow is fairly clear, some justification is necessary for present-ing "early adolescence" and "adolescence proper" as two separate entities. On strictly observational grounds this division is justified, because after preadolescence a period of repeated attempts at separation from primary love objects becomes noticeable. At early adolescence an upsurge of close idealizing friendships with members of the same sex commonly occurs; a low point in sustained interests and creativity is apparent, and a clumsy groping for new—not merely oppositional—values emerges; in short, a transitional phase possessing its own characteristics exists before adoles-cence asserts itself in full bloom.

During adolescence proper, a decisive turn toward heterosexuality and the final and irreversible renunciation of the incestuous object occurs; A. Katan (1937) has suggested calling this process "object removal." Cer-tain types of defenses, such as intellectualization and asceticism, belong to the phase of adolescence proper. In general, a tendency toward inner experience and toward self-discovery becomes noticeable; hence the reli-gious experience, and the discovery of beauty in all its possible manifesta-tions. We recognize that this development is a form of sublimation of the child's love for the idealized parent and a consequence of the final renunciation of early love objects. The feeling of "being in love," and a concern with philosophical, political, and social problems are typical of adolescence proper. The decisive break with childhood's way of life occurs in this phase; to the years of late adolescence is left the task of testing these new and momentous achievements, and building them into the continuance of a total life experience.

In setting up the two phases of early adolescence and adolescence proper, I am in agreement with Helene Deutsch (1944) who divides the adolescence of the girl into "early puberty" and "puberty and adoles-cence." In the latter phase, which she also calls "advanced puberty," heterosexual tendencies are characteristic. I emphasize the characteristic which unifies both, namely, object relinquishment and object finding, i.e., the definitive turn toward separation from the family and the grad-ual hierarchical arrangement of drive components and ego functions. An increasing social self-awareness with attendant anxiety and guilt is an essential ingredient of both these phases.

Naturally, any division of phases remains an abstraction; there is no such neat compartmentalization in actual development. The value of this kind of formulation about phases lies in the fact that it focuses our attention on orderly developmental sequences; the phases also make it easier to see the essential psychological modifications and tasks which characterize each phase, as they roughly follow the epigenetic principle of development. Transitions are vague and slow, and beset with oscillating movements; larger or smaller remnants of a seemingly completed phase of adolescent development nevertheless persist for a longer or shorter time during subsequent phases. These irregularities are apt to blur the developmental schedule if it is applied too narrowly and too literally.

A profound reorganization of the emotional life takes place during early adolescence and adolescence proper, with attendant and well-recognized states of chaos. The elaboration of characteristic defenses, often extreme as well as transient, safeguards the integrity of the ego. Certain defensive maneuvers of adolescence ultimately prove to be of adaptive value, and consequently facilitate the integration of realistic inclinations, talents, faculties, and ambitions; there is no doubt that the stable assemblage of such manifold trends constitutes a prerequisite for adult membership in society.

The pivotal problem of early adolescence and adolescence proper resides in a series of predicaments over object relations. The solution of the problem depends on the many variations this theme undergoes over the years; these ultimately determine the genuine or spurious attainment of adulthood. Some of the variations hark back to childhood. We have only to remember that the child's need to be loved fuses only gradually with the need to love; the need to receive only slowly arouses its counterpart, the need to give; and the need to be "done to" is more or less forcefully reversed into the need to "do to others." The passive role of being controlled is gradually and partially replaced by the child's urge for active control of the outside world. This polarity of active and passive aims re-emerges as a crucial issue during adolescence. The ambivalence so characteristic of adolescence encompasses not only the love-hate alternative, but manifests itself with even greater poignancy in the polarity of active and passive instinctual aims. This is equally true for both boy and girl. The rebellion against the superego in male adolescence often represents active opposition against passive feminine tendencies which once were an essential part of the boy's oedipal relationship to his father. Freud (1915) formulated this problem in relation to adolescence as follows: "Not until completion of development at the time of puberty does the polarity of sexuality coincide with male and female. In maleness is concentrated subject, activity, and the possession of a penis; femaleness carries on the object, and passivity. The vagina becomes valued henceforth as an asylum for the penis; it comes into the inheritance of the mother's womb."

Before a reconciliation and mature balance is reached the extreme positions of all active or all passive, or more often an oscillation between both usually mark adolescent behavior for some time. The earliest passive dependency on the mother possesses an undeniable attraction for the adolescent of either sex. It should be noted that boys often transfer the need for passive dependency to the father; in this case, the boy enters a homosexual drive constellation which may be either transient or lasting. The more strongly this passive need is felt—for instance, by an overindulged or by a severely deprived child—the stronger becomes the defense against it by rebellious and hostile actions and fantasies; paranoid ideas are not infrequent. This conflict, obviously, can lead to a surrender to passive strivings, to a demanding, clinging attitude, or to the renunciation of the instinctual drives. This last condition resembles very closely the position of the latency period. Most often a blending of all these attempts at stabilizing the active-passive polarity is the rule.

This theme of conflict reflects the modification of drives and the attempt to bring them into harmony with the ego, the ego ideal, the superego, and the somatic condition of puberty. Autoerotic gratification must eventually lead to object related gratification. The drive polarity of active-passive is exercised in relation to the ego, to the object, and to the outside world. This state of affairs accounts in great measure for adolescent object choice, as well as for the fluctuating patterns of adolescent mood swings, behavioral changes, and shifts in the capacity of reality testing. These instabilities and incongruities have often been described and indeed have been singled out as the significant general characteristics of adolescence; and this is, indeed, correct for the phases of early adolescence and adolescence proper. Polarities like the following, it is well-known, appear in one and the same individual: submission and rebellion, delicate sensitivity and emotional coarseness, gregariousness and withdrawal into solitude, altruism and egotism, boundless optimism and dejected hopelessness, intense attachments and sudden faithlessness, lofty ideals and petty argumentativeness, idealism and materialism, dedication and indifference, impulse acceptance and impulse rejection, voracious appetite, excessive indulgence and cruel self-negation (asceticism), physical exuberance and inert sluggishness. These oscillating patterns of behavior reflect psychological changes which progress neither in a straight line nor at an even pace. The problems of ambivalence, narcissism, and fixation play significant roles; their implications will be discussed below.

Early adolescence and adolescence proper must accomplish the renunciation of the primary love objects, the parents, as sexual objects; siblings and parent substitutes have to be included in this process of renunciation. These phases, then, are concerned essentially with object relinquishment and object finding, and these processes reverberate in the ego to produce cathectic shifts which influence both the existing object representations and self-representation. Consequently, the sense of self or sense of identity acquires a heretofore unknown lability.

During early adolescence and adolescence proper the drive turns toward genitality, the libidinous objects change from the preoedipal and oedipal to the nonincestuous, heterosexual object. The ego safeguards its integrity through defensive operations; some of these are ego restricting and require countercathectic energy for their maintenance, while others prove to be adaptive, and to allow aim-inhibited (sublimatory) drive discharge; these become the permanent regulators of self-esteem.

4. Early Adolescence

Pubertal maturation normally forces the boy out of his preadolescent defensive self-sufficiency and pregenital drive cathexis; the girl is equally pushed toward the development of her femininity. Before she can take this step she has to abandon her newly-won preadolescent identity as the amazon, often masquerading as the vamp, which for a time has safeguarded her against the regression to the preoedipal mother. Both boy and girl now turn more forcefully to the libidinous extrafamiliar object; that is to say, the genuine process of separation from early object ties has begun. This process moves through various stages until, ultimately and ideally, mature object relations are established. The distinctive character of early adolescence resides in the decathexis of the incestuous love objects; as a consequence, free-floating object libido clamors for new accommodations.

Before we follow this train of thought, we must discuss some of the consequences of the decathexis typical for this phase. The process as a whole can be described in terms of inter- and intrasystemic dynamics. First of all, the superego, an agency of control, whose functions are to inhibit and regulate self-esteem, decreases in efficacy; this leaves the ego without the simple and compelling directives of conscience. The ego can no longer depend on the authority of the superego, its own efforts to mediate between drives and outer world are fumbling and inefficient. In fact, the superego now becomes a more open adversary, so that essentially the ego is left weak, isolated, and inadequate in face of a three-pronged emergency (A. Freud, 1936). The weakening of the superego is a function of its constituent origin, namely, the internalization of the parent at the settlement of the oedipal conflict; for at the time when the young adolescent withdraws from the parents, *pari passu*, the decathexis encompasses also their object representations and their internalized moral equivalents which reside in the superego.

By this age values, standards, and moral laws have acquired an appreciable independence from parental authority, they have become ego-syntonic, and they operate partly within the ego. Nevertheless during early adolescence self-control threatens to break down and in extreme cases delinquency takes over. Actions of this kind, which vary in degree of intensity, are usually related to the search for a love object; they also offer escape from loneliness, isolation, and the depressed moods which accompany the cathectic shifts. The case of Nancy (See Chapter VII) well illustrates this course of early adolescent development underlying delinquent behavior. Normally, acting out is forestalled by a recourse to fantasy, to autoeroticism, to ego alterations—for instance, a deflection of the object libido onto the self, which is to say, by a recourse to narcissism.

The withdrawal of object cathexis and the widening gap between ego and superego result in an impoverishment of the ego; this is experienced by the adolescent as a feeling of void, an inner turmoil which can be directed, in the search for relief, toward any mitigating opportunity which the environment may offer. The intensity of withdrawal from early object ties is determined not only by the rising and ebbing rhythms of instinctual tension, but also by the ego's capacity to ward off conflictual anxiety. Some children do not experience any conflict in relation to their parents; they either have repressed the sexual drive, or else their drive endowment is low and therefore the ego possesses the capacity to master it. This last idea is still too untested to serve as a reliable explanatory concept; one is, on the other hand, impressed by the small degree to which pubertal maturation in and by itself affects the emotional agitation of adolescence. Whenever direct and parallel reactions are observed, close scrutiny will reveal that a psychological condition exists which shares the responsibility for the acute, intense upset. The same holds true for environmental conditions if they range within normal limits. Both pubertal changes and environmental conditions can initiate or intensify adolescent reactions but they cannot exclusively create them. These ideas are fully developed in Chapter VI.

Let us return to the initial idea that in early adolescence a decathexis of the familiar love objects occurs with a consequent search for new objects. The young adolescent turns to "the friend." In fact, the friend acquires a heretofore unknown importance and significance for both boy and girl. The object choice of early adolescence follows the narcissistic model. At this age friendship is different from the preadolescent companion-in-adventure among boys or the secret-sharing whispering partner among girls; of course, they both do not suddenly cease to exist.

The boy now forms friendships which demand an idealization of the friend; some characteristic in the other is admired and loved because it constitutes a quality which the subject himself would like to possess, and in the friendship he possesses it by proxy. This choice follows Freud's (1914) model: "Whoever possesses the qualities without which the ego cannot achieve its ideal, he is the one who will be loved." Freud explained that this stage in the expanding love life of the individual leads to the formation of the ego ideal and thus internalizes an object relationship which otherwise would have led to homosexuality, latent or manifest. Fixation on the phase of early adolescence does follow this course.

The ego ideal as a psychic formation within the ego not only removes the superego from its unchallenged position which it had held until now; it also absorbs narcissistic and homosexual libido. Freud's remarks (1914) which are relevant to this discussion are as follows: "In this way large amounts of an essentially homosexual kind [of libido] are drawn into the formation of the narcissistic ego ideal and find outlet and satisfaction in maintaining it." He continues: "The ego ideal has imposed severe conditions upon the satisfaction of libido through objects; for it causes some of them to be rejected by means of its censor, as being incompatible. When no such ideal has been formed, the sexual trend in question makes its appearance unchanged in the personality in the form of a perversion. To be their own ideal once more, in regard to sexual no less than other trends, as they were in childhood—this is what people strive to attain as their happiness." The new distribution of libido thus enhances the progression to heterosexual object finding, and serves to maintain stable relationships.

The ego ideal which the friend represents may yield under the sexual urge and lead into a stage of homosexuality with voyeurism, exhibitionism, and mutual masturbation (latent or manifest). Essentially, masturbation fantasies counteract castration anxiety. The sadomasochistic heterosexual themes of such fantasies easily become disturbing, and relief is found in the turning to a homosexual object choice. In these fantasies, the friend, as a comrade in arms, often participates in heterosexual orgies and battles. The erotic feelings which frequently accompany early adolescent friendships constitute a partial explanation of the sudden disruption of these attachments. Other contributing factors which bring these friendships to a sudden end lie in the inevitable frustration which a continued, exclusive friendship is bound to entail: the idealized friend shrinks to ordinary proportions whenever the ego ideal has established itself independently from the object in the outer world.

It seems that in the boy's ego ideal formation, a process is repeated which once before, at the decline of the oedipal period, consolidated the superego through identification with the father. In both instances a controlling agency is established which gives life a new direction and meaning; simultaneously, this agency is also able to regulate the maintenance of self-esteem (narcissistic balance). The megalomania of the young child is shattered by the undeniably privileged position and power of the parent; its remnants are taken over by the superego, which thus partakes in the "magnificence" of the parent. In early adolescence, the megalomania of childhood that allowed the child a sense of perfection so long as he was part of the parent is now taken over by the ego ideal. "As always where the libido is concerned, man has here again shown himself incapable of giving up a satisfaction he had once enjoyed. He is not willing to forego the narcissistic perfection of his childhood, and when, as he grows up, he is disturbed by the admonitions of others and by the awakening of his own critical judgment, so that he can no longer retain that perfection, he seeks to recover it in the new form of the ego ideal. What he projects before him as his ideal is the substitute for the lost narcissism of his childhood in which he was his own ideal" (Freud, 1914).

The typical early adolescent friendship of the boy in which idealization and eroticism blend into a unique feeling has been classically described in *Tonio Kröger*, a short story by Thomas Mann (1914). The story opens with Tonio waiting after school for his friend Hans Hansen; they had planned to go for a walk together. Tonio is deeply wounded when he notices that Hans had almost forgotten their engagement, but he forgives him readily as soon as he sees his friend's remorse. In this mood they set out on their walk.*

. . . Tonio did not speak. He suffered. His rather oblique brows were drawn together in a frown, his lips were rounded to a whistle, he gazed into space with his head on one side. Posture and manner were habitual.

Suddenly Hans shoved his arm into Tonio's, with a sideways look—he knew very well what the trouble was. And Tonio, though he was silent for the next few steps, felt his heart soften.

"I hadn't forgotten, you see, Tonio," Hans said, gazing at the pavement, "I only thought it wouldn't come off today because it was so wet and windy. But I don't mind that at all, and it's jolly of you to have waited. I thought you had gone home, and I was cross. . . ."

. . . The truth was, Tonio loved Hans Hansen, and had already suffered much on his account. He who loves the more is the inferior and must suffer; in this hard and simple fact his fourteen-year-old soul had already been instructed by life; and he was so organized that he received such experiences consciously, wrote them down as it were inwardly, and even, in a certain way, took pleasure in them, though without ever letting them mould his conduct, indeed, or drawing any practical advantage from them. Being what he was, he found this knowledge far more important and far more interesting than the sort they made him learn in school; yes, during his lesson hours in the vaulted Gothic classrooms he was mainly occupied in feeling his way about among these intuitions of his and penetrating them. The process gave him the same kind of satisfaction as that he felt when he moved about in his room with his violin—for he played the violin—and made the tones, brought out as softly as ever he knew how, mingle with the splashing of the fountain that leaped and danced down there in the garden beneath the branches of the old walnut tree. . . .

. . . As he wasted his time at home, was slow and absent-minded at school, and always had bad marks from the masters, he was in the habit of bringing home pitifully poor reports, which troubled and angered his father, a tall, fastidiously dressed man, with thoughtful blue eyes, and always a wild flower in his buttonhole. But for his mother, she cared nothing about the reports—Tonio's beautiful black-haired mother, whose name was Consuelo, and who was so absolutely different from the other ladies in the town, because father had brought her long ago from some place far down on the map.

Tonio loved his dark, fiery mother, who played the piano and mandolin so wonderfully, and he was glad his doubtful standing among men did not distress her. Though at the same time he found his father's annoyance a more dignified and respectable attitude and despite his scoldings understood him very well, whereas his mother's blithe indifference always seemed just

* Reprinted from "Tonio Kröger," in *Stories of Three Decades* by Thomas Mann, by permission of Alfred A. Knopf, Inc. Copyright 1936 by Alfred A. Knopf, Inc.

a little wanton. His thoughts at times would run something like this: "It is true enough that I am what I am and will not and cannot alter: heedless, self-willed, with my mind on things nobody else thinks of. And so it is right they should scold and punish me and not smother things all up with kisses and music. After all, we are not gypsies living in a green wagon; we're respectable people, the family of Consul Kröger." And not seldom he would think: "Why is it I am different, why do I fight everything, why am I at odds with the masters and like a stranger among the other boys? The good scholars, and the solid majority—they don't find the masters funny, they don't write verses, their thoughts are all about things that people do think about and can talk about out loud. How regular and comfortable they must feel, knowing that everybody knows just where they stand! It must be nice! But what is the matter with me, and what will be the end of it all?"

These thoughts about himself and his relation to life played an important part in Tonio's love for Hans Hansen. He loved him in the first place because he was handsome; but in the next because he was in every respect his own opposite and foil. Hans Hansen was a capital scholar, and a jolly chap to boot, who was head at drill, rode and swam to perfection, and lived in the sunshine of popularity. The masters were almost tender with him, they called him Hans and were partial to him in every way; the other pupils curried favour with him; even grown people stopped him on the street, twitched the shock of hair beneath his Danish sailor cap, and said: "Ah, here you are, Hans Hansen, with your pretty blond hair! Still head of the school? Remember me to your father and mother, that's a fine lad!"

Such was Hans Hansen; and ever since Tonio Kröger had known him, from the very minute he set eyes on him, he had burned inwardly with a heavy, envious longing. "Who else has blue eyes like yours, or lives in such friendliness and harmony with all the world? You are always spending your time with some right and proper occupation. When you have done your prep you take your riding-lesson, or make things with a fret-saw; even in the holidays, at the seashore, you row and sail and swim all the time, while I wander off somewhere and lie down in the sand and stare at the strange and mysterious changes that whisk over the face of the sea. And all that is why your eyes are so clear. To be like you . . ."

He made no attempt to be like Hans Hansen, and perhaps hardly even seriously wanted to. What he did ardently, painfully want was that just as he was, Hans Hansen should love him; and he wooed Hans Hansen in his own way, deeply, lingeringly, devotedly, with a melancholy that gnawed and burned more terribly than all the sudden passion one might have expected from his exotic looks.

And he wooed not in vain. Hans respected Tonio's superior power of putting certain difficult matters into words; moreover, he felt the lively presence of an uncommonly strong and tender feeling for himself; he was grateful for it, and his response gave Tonio much happiness—though also many pangs of jealousy and disillusion over his futile efforts to establish a communion of spirit between them. For the queer thing was that Tonio,

who after all envied Hans Hansen for being what he was, still kept on trying to draw him over to his own side; though of course he could succeed in
this at most only at moments and superficially. . . .

The walk had come to an end: Tonio had tried in vain to engage
Hans in a close communion of the poetic ideas which aroused such overwhelming feelings in him. They parted and Tonio walked back home
alone. . . .

. . . Tonio passed under the squat old city gate, along by the harbour,
and up the steep, wet, windy, gabled street to his parents' house. His heart
beat richly: longing was awake in it, and a gentle envy; a faint contempt,
and no little innocent bliss. . . .

The friendship between Tonio and Hans shows clearly how the friend
represents the missing perfections of the self. In Tonio's case the friendship reflects Tonio's conflict in the identification with his mother and
his father, or, rather, his failure to integrate them both. Hans is the boy
his father would have loved to call his son; but renouncing his dreaming
self would have meant renouncing his beloved mother. His ego ideal,
which perpetuates his envy of his father and the things for which he
stands, now is expressed in a positive proclamation, and enters Tonio's
life in a decisive way. A compromise formation is attempted: "I love in
Hans what father stands for in life."

Only adolescence proper can show how this newly-created ego-ideal
will influence heterosexual object choice; and only late adolescence can
show how the state of inner disunity will be resolved. We will discuss
Tonio again later, since Mann presents the psychological sequence of
focal events in his life as an adolescent boy and young man.

The tender feelings of the boy for his father, and indeed his tendency to submit to his father's wishes, values, and prescriptions represent
a conflictual constellation for the young adolescent. It finds a resolution
in a summary opposition to the father, or it can be expressed in the aim-
inhibited gratification of shared interests and chummy comradeship.
Should the father have played an important maternal role by tending the
physical needs of the young child, the adolescent's tender and passive
strivings toward him will be powerfully reinforced. In this connection I
shall report the dream of an early adolescent boy.

George was in analysis because he was effeminate, anxious, suffered
from insomnia and encountered difficulties in learning and concentration. He had had one dream repeatedly during the previous year; it was

accompanied by anxiety. "It is like an image on a movie screen. There are shapes which simultaneously have different shapes and qualities. Like an object being huge, endless, enormous, and also as thin as a wire; or smooth and soft, and also jagged and hard. Everything changes in rapid transition and there is a soundtrack; I discovered that only last night: the voice is Dad's. It is soft and melodious and also harsh and sharp and loud." The associations led to the memory of his father, who sang him to sleep from the time he was three until he was six; already at that age he could not fall asleep. "When Dad sang to me it always helped and put me to sleep." The moving shapes reminiscent of Lewin's dream screen (breast) became fused in George's dream with the father's soothing voice. The melodious stream of the song induced sleep just as being nursed had done earlier. Indeed, the nursing situation is the model of the sleep-inducing experience; the tender love for the father offered his oral craving an object which inevitably led to homosexual tendencies in early adolescence, and in fact, unduly delayed the progression to adolescence proper.

Let us now turn to the girl in early adolescence. She shows no narrow parallelism to the boy's development. Certainly, friendship plays an equally important part in her life. The lack of a girlfriend can throw her into longing despair, and the loss of a friend can precipitate depression and complete loss of interest in life. Helene Deutsch (1944) refers to several occasions on which she has "observed onsets of psychosis in girls who had lost their friends and could not find compensation in their mothers."

One typical form of idealization among girls is the "crush." This idealized and eroticized attachment extends to both men and women; only in relation to women does it appear in its unadulterated form. The objects chosen possess some partial similarity or striking dissimilarity to the parent. The *Diary of a Young Girl* (Hug-Hellmuth, 1919) contains the description of a crush which is as commonplace today as when it was recorded by the diarist. At age eleven the young girl of this diary was overwhelmed by the implications of menstruation ("streams of blood"), intercourse, and fascinating speculations about the maturing male and female bodies, including those about the equivalent of menstruation in the boy. Her salvation from anxiety and excitement came through a crush on a "beautiful woman" whom she secretly called "Gold-Fairy."

The thought of this woman filled the girl with the bliss of innocent childhood. When she finally found out the age of her beloved she wrote in her diary: "36—a lovely number. I like it so much. I don't really know why but when I hear anyone say that number it sounds to me like a squirrel, jumping in the woods."

The object of the crush is loved passively, with the aim of getting a handout of attention or affection or of being overwhelmed by all kinds of eroticized or sexualized approaches. This development continues into adolescence proper. The masochistic and passive quality of the crush is an intermediary stage between the phallic position of preadolescence and the progression to femininity. It is in fact the intermediate bisexual stage of female early adolescence which Helene Deutsch (1944) has described in its typical form for the girl of this age. "The presence of a strongly bisexual tendency shortly before the conflicts of adolescence . . . is less repressed in girls than in boys. In this period of their life girls are quite willing to stress their masculinity, while the boy is ashamed of his femininity and denies it." (Tonio Kröger illustrates this last point.)

The girl, then, is much more consciously occupied by the idea: "Am I a boy or a girl?" Often girls maintain the belief that they can decide either way; the result is that they reserve certain feeling and ego states for some occasions, and at others switch to a bisexual emphasis. Girls at this stage experience a strange vagueness in the sense of time and space, and imagine memories of events which their family tells them never happened or never happened in a particular way. This vagueness of reality and ego perception is a concomitant feature of the bisexual ambiguity. The theme of bisexuality in the girl is most intriguingly told by Virginia Woolf in *Orlando,* in which the main character is transfigured from man to woman.

To illustrate the bisexual stage of the girl, I will quote here a tape-recorded excerpt from an interview with an adolescent girl, aged fifteen. In the conversation with the interviewer Betty deals with her fantasy life, in which the bisexual position finds eloquent expression (Blos, 1941).

Interviewer. Do you dream much?
Betty. Last night I got to bed at nine-fifteen and I had curlers on my hair. I should have stayed up about a half an hour but I always dream . . . taking everything in general, I dream of fishes, and . . . spooks . . . and cars and everything. I stay up till about ten o'clock and I can't get to sleep.

I. You mean just pictures in your mind.

B. Yes. Of myself and different people, everything in general.

I. What kind of pictures?

B. Oh, first of a girl just like Jane and then of a man like a girl and then of a girl that's turned into a girl that's another girl. It's all mixed up but mostly I'm a girl dressed like a boy. I don't know why.

I. Have you had that picture much, for many years?

B. Yes, you see, at first, when I was young I was a girl who was dressed like a boy, and nobody knew I was a girl. Then I was a girl dressed like a boy, but only a certain few people knew I was a girl; finally I was a girl dressed like a boy and then half of the time I was a girl. I remember when I came a great distance I'd turn into a boy and I should have turned into a girl, and I spent the whole night deciding.

I. Which did you decide?

B. I decided to be a girl dressed like a boy and that I should let everybody know I was a girl and only on certain occasions . . .

I. When was that?

B. That must have been last year or the year before last, and this year, once, I was a girl that was dressed as a boy, and see, I thought I had to be true to my sex and be dressed like a boy, and then I designed it all so it should be that I was a girl that was dressed like a boy. I don't know why.

I. And is that a story you've kept since you were a little girl?

B. Yes, since I was about four.

I. Sort of an imaginary thing that becomes a plot.

B. Everybody I like comes into it and has a place.

I. Does it put you to sleep, too, sometimes?

B. I go off to sleep in the middle of it, I think.

I. What were you in the dream after you made this decision?

B. I was a girl.

I. You were a girl?

B. Yes. . . .

I. That you wouldn't become a boy for a while, you decided to be a girl?

B. Oh do you mean *that?* I thought you meant the other decision.

I. What other decision?

B. Oh, the part when I changed the girl to a boy.

I. You decided in this picture that you were going to be a girl, you didn't wear boys' clothes, but you, yourself, were a girl, that was a year and a half ago?

B. Yes.

I. Well, what did you decide the other night? After you and Jane had made this resolution? [Referring to a resolution not to go out with boys for two years.]

B. Oh—

I. You were still a girl?

B. I was still a girl.

I. But do you always end up a girl?

B. Well, sometimes I leave and they still think I'm a boy, sometimes I end up that way.

I. Well, which do you mostly end up?

B. A girl.

I. Have you changed anything in the plot since Jane and you made this resolution?

B. Well, I haven't ended it yet.

I. I see, you're just going to let it go on and see how it comes out.

B. Well, at the moment, I was grown up just like a boy and then somebody found out that I was a girl and then I dressed like a girl but I was with all these boys and now I'm still a girl with the boys.

I. I see, that's where you are now. You're going to continue the story and see where it goes.

B. I don't know what's going to happen now.

I. Well, it sounds very interesting.

B. Every time I see a movie, it goes queer. . . .

I. Why?

B. I don't know, I get queer ideas from the movies.

I. What kind?

B. I mean if I see. . .if somebody says something darling, I think of the words and I have to put it in.

I. Then you have to be the girl, is that it?

B. No, not the girl in the movies. Then I have to say something that's very adorable, or somebody else has to say it to me.

I. Yes, in your picture.

B. Yes, if I see a plot that's very nice, I take the plot and I fix it all up.

I. And you put a person in the plot?

B. Yes, and a couple of other people, but I mean the people's faces and situations are slightly different.

I. Yes, well, what kind of a plot, for instance?

B. Oh, I don't know, I don't know how to explain it, but. . .let's see. . . did you see *Lives of a Bengal Lancer?*

I. Yes.

B. Well, do you remember when he says that line. . .I forget it, but I was crazy about that so I put that in, I got the whole Bengal Lancers mixed in some places.

I. And were you the boy in the movie?

B. Yes, I was the cute one (not the one who got killed, because I didn't like him), so I was him, and Jane was somebody else—she wasn't either of those, but she was somebody else. She was another person there that wasn't in it. I don't remember who he was. . .who was he?. . .the person who got killed was somebody, maybe it was Mabel that I don't like at all.

I. When you were little, would you rather have been a boy than a girl?

B. Yes. When I was a very little child, I wanted to be a boy.

I. Why? Do you remember?

B. I wanted to be a boy. . .I don't know. . .Now I like to be a girl because I like. . .because I hate the way boys dress. I think it's terrible, but I don't know why I wanted to be a boy, I think it's because I'm much more used to boys, because I mean if I like a boy, I'm absolutely hopeless. It so happens it hasn't happened yet but I have a couple of friends who are crazy about boys but it doesn't do them any good, because they can't ask a boy to go any place or anything. If you were a boy it would simplify that.

The bisexual position of the girl in early adolescence is closely related to the problem of narcissism. In early adolescence the narcissistic object choice is prevalent; while during adolescence proper narcissistic defenses gain in scope. The illusory penis is maintained as a psychic reality in order to protect the girl against narcissistic depletion; and equality with boys is still a question of life and death. Bisexual self-representation with more or less vague perception of the body finds an expression in all sorts of activities, interests, preoccupations, and daydreams. This condition continues to exist until the girl deflects onto her whole body that part of the narcissistic libido which was attached to the bisexual body image, and seeks completion not within herself but in heterosexual love. How the turn is made which leads from the early adolescent bisexual position to the next phase of heterosexual orientation will occupy us later. The changes in the girl who is passing from preadolescence into adolescence proper were described in a longitudinal clinical study (Blos, 1941), from which I shall quote some pertinent observations.

Despite Lois' complete knowledge of the facts of sex, her transition from the boyish rowdyism of twelve and thirteen to her "sickly sentimentalism" of fifteen and sixteen was exceedingly difficult, painful, distasteful. Having always boasted to herself of her immunity to such stupid sensations—having been proud of her superior self-sufficiency—she despised herself for her first thrill at the sight of and nearness to a boy. She was disgusted with her strange interest in her heretofore unimportant body and appearance after this thrill. And when she found herself craving attention, envying other girls, their beauty and attractiveness, she was at the same time repulsed by it; her scorn for herself knew no bounds. She became morbid and despondent, lost all confidence in herself, suffered an acute disintegration which continued to an almost drastic extent—then, fortunately, took a new hold on life, faced facts intelligently and courageously and built up a whole new outlook, but not without passing through a sort of defiant, vulgar stage. During this latter stage she seemed to delight in playing on words such as fornication, adultery, illegitimacy, passion, etc. The vulgar, defiant stage seems to have passed and Lois is now satisfied to be the woman she is and can make of herself. During the "vulgar" stage Lois boasted to her friends of having many "affairs."

The decline of the bisexual tendency marks the entrance into adolescence proper. At the early adolescent stage the girl demonstrates a remarkable facility for living by proxy, *i.e.*, to effect temporary identifications as trial actions. The danger does exist, however, that this propensity will lead to acting out, to premature sexual intercourse for which the girl is in no way prepared. These experiences usually have a traumatic effect, favor regressive development, and lead to a deviate form of adolescence. Friendships, crushes, fantasy life, intellectual interests, athletic activities, and preoccupation with grooming in general, all protect the girl against precocious—that is, defensive heterosexual—activity. However, the girl's ultimate safeguard for her normal passage through this phase is the emotional availability of the parent, particularly the mother or a mother substitute.

5. Adolescence Proper

Puberty has relentlessly pushed the young adolescent forward. His search for object relations, or, conversely, his active avoidance of them, illuminates the psychological developments which are taking place during this phase.

During adolescence proper, this search for object relations assumes new aspects, different from those prevalent during the preadolescent and early adolescent phases. Heterosexual object finding, made possible by the abandonment of the narcissistic and bisexual positions, characterizes the psychological development of adolescence proper. More precisely, we should speak of a gradual affirmation of the sex-appropriate drive moving into ascendancy and bringing increasingly conflictual anxiety to bear on the ego. Defensive and adaptive mechanisms, in all their complex variety, come into the foreground of mental life. The unfolding complexity of mental processes during this phase makes a comprehensive presentation by which all major facets can be taken in at one glance impossible; it becomes increasingly necessary to break up the mounting complexities of mental development into component aspects and to pay more attention to the enormous variability of development.

The tenor of adolescence proper, often referred to as middle adolescence, is one of imminent finality and decisive turns; compared with the earlier phases the emotional life is more intense, deeper, and has greater scope. The adolescent breaks away for good from infantile love objects—after having played earlier preludes to this theme many times and in many keys. Oedipal wishes and their attending conflicts come to life again. The finality of this inner break with the past shakes the adolescent's emotional life to the center; by the same token, this break opens up to him unknown horizons, raises hopes, and generates fears.

The phase of adolescence which we are now about to explore corresponds to the second act of the classical drama: the *dramatis personae* have all become intricately and irrevocably entangled; the spectator has come to realize that there can be no return to the expectancies and propitious events of the opening scene; and he recognizes that the conflicts will relentlessly drive forward to a climactic final settlement. After the second act events have taken a decisive turn; but as yet the specific outcome is unknown, and only the last act of the drama can enlighten us about it. Similarly, during adolescence proper, inner conflicts have reached a point of irrevocable entanglement but the outcome of the turmoil is not predictable. We cannot help but have hunches, and we can prognosticate as often correctly as not; but only late adolescence will tell us whether we have correctly foreseen the outcome. Helene Deutsch (1944) summarizes her opinion on this problem by saying, "Only subsequent developments can show whether pathological phenomena are involved in such cases or merely intensified difficulties of adolescence." Prediction studies would help us to understand and evaluate the nonpathological aspects of this stage in development during which the personality normally shows many apparently pathognomic features. Research in adolescence might be stimulated by the prediction studies which have been conducted on infancy and early childhood (M. Kris, 1957), as well as from Anna Freud's critique (A. Freud, 1958) of this research.

During adolescence proper, the adolescent gradually turns to heterosexual love, and I shall now discuss the inner changes which are essential, indeed preconditional, for the advance to heterosexuality. This development involves many disparate processes, and it is their integration which essentially advances emotional maturation. Adolescents of this phase who rush into heterosexual activity do not, by virtue of this experience, acquire the preconditions for heterosexual love, and as one scrutinizes teenage marriage, one realizes how slowly the capacity for mature heterosexual love develops. From a psychoanalytic point of view the major issues reside in the nature of the cathectic shifts related to inner objects and to the self, rather than merely in behavioral phenomena (such as, for instance, holding a job or having sexual relations) as relevant indices of psychological change or progression.

The withdrawal of cathexis from the parents, or rather from their object representations in the ego, results in a deflection of cathectic energy on the self. In the boy, as we have seen, this change leads to a narcissistic object choice based on an ego ideal; we may discern in this libidinal constellation the newly-attempted resolution of reactivated remnants of the positive and negative oedipus complex. In the girl we observed a perseverance in the bisexual position with an attending overvaluation of the phallic component. A serious arrestment in drive development appears if this component is not conceded in due time to the heterosexual love object. This is to say that sexual identity formation becomes the ultimate achievement of adolescent drive differentiation during this phase.

An increase in narcissism is observable in both sexes. This fact should be emphasized because it results in a variety of ego states which are characteristic for adolescence proper. The increase precedes the consolidation of heterosexual love; or, to be exact, it is closely interwoven with the ongoing process of nonincestuous object finding. One can easily observe how adolescents abandon their aggrandizing self-sufficiency and autoerotic activities as soon as, for example, the boy experiences tender feelings for a girl. The shift of cathexis from the self to the new object alters the libidinal economy, so that gratification is now sought from the object rather than from the self. As a fifteen-year-old boy expressed it: "As soon as I have a girl in mind, I don't have to eat like a pig or masturbate all the time." Protection against disappointment, rejection, and failure in the game of love is, needless to say, assured by all forms of narcissistic aggrandizement. In addition, this state allows mental preoccupation with ideas which lead to inventive solutions or useful mental constructs, which, however, derive their fascination from displaced aim-inhibited drives—e.g., intellectualization. Sandy, an adolescent boy of fourteen, extremely timid and afraid of rejection, decided to ask a girl to go out with him. At this time Sandy reported in his analysis that he spent several hours a day thinking about his "controlling the earth." Two inventions, he says, are necessary: "an energy producer and a matter duplicator" (that is to say, a hold on the male and female principle). With those inventions, he says, he could control the earth. The analyst remarked, "including Jane." Sandy answered, "When I dialed Jane's number last night I kept on thinking of the monetary control of a world system. I stammered when she answered the phone, but I made it appear to be an act."

The narcissistic quality of the adolescent's personality is well known. The withdrawal of object cathexis leads to an overvaluation of the self, to heightened self-perception at the expense of reality testing, to an extreme touchiness and self-absorption, and generally, to self-centeredness and self-aggrandizement. The adolescent's withdrawal of cathexis from the object world can lead to narcissistic withdrawal and loss of reality testing; these were first described by Bernfeld (1923), who also pointed out the similarity of this state to that of an incipient psychosis. The impoverishment of the ego is due to two sources: 1) the repression of the instinctual drives; and 2) the incapacity to extend object libido to infantile love objects as well as to accept the emotions they extend. The latter source can also be viewed as a resistance against regression.

Narcissistic defenses, so characteristic for adolescence, are occasioned by the inability to give up the gratifying parent on whose omnipotence the child came to depend rather than developing his own faculties; such a child upon entering early adolescence finds himself totally unable to face his disillusionment about himself for his actual and limited attainment in reality. This condition in its typical form will be described in Chapter VII; it is the central problem of the pathological impasse of prolonged adolescence. A distinction must be made among narcissistic object choice, narcissistic defenses, and the narcissistic transitory stage which normally precedes heterosexual object finding. This transitory stage, which we shall now discuss at some length, is the consequence of the decathexis of the internalized parent, or, to be more exact, of its object representations. This results in primitive transient, identificatory processes which serve narcissistic as well as object-related needs.

The estrangement which the adolescent experiences in relation to the familiar objects of his childhood is a further consequence of the "delibidinization of the outside world" (A. Freud, 1936). The defusion of the instincts in relation to object representations influences the manifest behavior of the adolescent to his parents or their substitutes through projective-introjective mechanisms. The "good" and "bad" introjects become confused with the present parents and their actual conduct. The decathexis of the object representations removes them as a source of libidinal gratification; consequently, an object hunger can be observed in the adolescent, an avaricious desire which leads to constantly changing, superficial attachments and identifications. Object relations at this stage lead automatically to transient identifications, and this prevents object libido from being totally drained by deflection onto the self. The object hunger of this phase can assume overwhelming proportions; any object, real or imaginary, may serve as a hold on the object world. The identity of the real object of this hunger, however, is denied; it is the parent of the same sex. Identification, positive or negative, with the parent of the same sex has to be achieved before heterosexual love can exist. The new objects are not only screens against old introjects but are also attempts to neutralize the "bad" introjects with new "good" introjects (Greenson, 1954). This concept throws light on the economic function of the "crush." Hunger sensations and the tendency to gorge food are only in part conditioned by the physical growth needs of the adolescent; they can be observed to fluctuate significantly with the rise and decline of primitive object hunger, that is, the incorporative function. I have observed in several adolescents of this phase that hunger sensations or the need for food decreased startlingly at the time a meaningful and gratifying heterosexual object entered their life. The significant role orality plays in the separation process, which involves intensified oral cravings, also explains the frequency of depressed moods in adolescence as a "transient regression to the oral-incorporative (alimentary) phase of development" (Benedek, 1956, a).

The narcissistic stage is not only a delaying or holding action caused by reluctance to renounce definitively the early love objects, quite to the contrary, it also represents a positive stage in the disengagement process. While previously the parent was overvalued, considered with awe, and not realistically assessed, he now becomes undervalued and is seen to have the shabby proportions of a fallen idol. The narcissistic self-inflation shows up in the adolescent's arrogance and rebelliousness, in his defiance of rules, and in his flouting of the parent's authority. Once the source of narcissistic gratification derived from parental love has ceased to flow, the ego becomes invested with narcissistic libido which is withdrawn from the internalized parent. The ultimate result of this cathectic shift must be that the ego develops the capacity to secure on the basis of realistic achievement that amount of narcissistic supply which is essential for the maintenance of self-esteem. Thus we see that the narcissistic stage operates in the service of progressive development, and is usually intermingled with the slow ascendancy of heterosexual object finding.

"Where the formation of the ego is involved, the narcissism . . . is a progressive trait . . . insofar as the libido development is in question, this narcissism is, on the contrary, obstructive and regressive" (Deutsch, 1944). This stage of transitory narcissism turns into an ominous disruption of progressive development only when the narcissism is structured into a defensive holding operation and so inhibits rather than promotes the disengagement process. The process of separation and its facilitation are what give the narcissistic stage its positive and progressive quality. As to the regression carried out under these auspices, Nietzsche's aphorism comes to mind: "They say he is going backwards, indeed, he is, because he attempts to take a big jump." One might also speak of a "regression in the service of the ego" which normally takes place at this particular juncture of adolescent development.

The narcissistic isolation of the adolescent is counteracted in many ways, all of which aim at maintaining his hold on object relations and on firm ego boundaries. Both holds are constantly imperiled, and the threat of such loss entails anxiety and panic; it also initiates regressive restitutive processes which range from mild depersonalization feelings to psychotic states. An in-between territory in which the pull of narcissistic regression is counteracted by object-related ideation and keen perception of instinctual drives exists in the extraordinarily rich fantasy life and daydreaming of the adolescent. These fantasies implement the cathectic shifts by "trial action" as it were, and help the adolescent to assimilate in small doses the affective experiences toward which his progressive development is moving. Fantasy life and creativity at this stage are at a peak; artistic and ideational expression make it possible to communicate highly personal experiences which as such become a vehicle for social participation. The narcissistic component remains obvious; and indeed, narcissistic gratification derived from such creations is legitimate. Private fantasies can be compared to "trial action" because more often than not they are preparatory functions for initiating interpersonal transactions.

The following passage from a short story by George Barker (1951) expresses well the unique feelings of the adolescent who is in transit through this in-between territory:

Those exquisitely melancholy afternoons of my adolescence when I used to walk with the abstraction of a somnambulist through the damp avenues of Richmond Park, thinking that life would never happen to me, wondering why the banked fires of my anticipations, burning in my belly worse than raw alcohol, seemed not to show to strangers as I wandered in the gardens. And often it appeared to me, the frustration, in the disguise of an hallucination: looking between the trees that dripped with hanging mist I sometimes saw classical statues take on an instant of life, turning their naked beauty towards me; or I heard a voice speak out of a bush: "Everything will be answered if you will only not look around." And I have stood waiting, not daring to look behind me, expecting a hand on my shoulder that would tender an apotheosis or an assignation—but there was only the gust of wind and the page of newspaper blowing breezily up and past me like a dirty interjection. Or a bicyclist flashed by, offering possibility until he reached me and decamping with it when he had passed. For I was suffering from a simple but devastating propensity: I was hoping to live.

It is interesting to note how this description, doubtlessly autobiographical, emphasizes the heightened keenness of the sense organs, the eye and ear especially. A cathectic shift endows the sense organs with a perceptive hyperacuity which derives its special content and quality from projection: internal events are now experienced as outer perceptions, and their quality often approximates hallucinations. It must be remembered that eye, ear, and touch play an outstanding role in the establishment of early object relations at a time when differentiation between "I" and "non-I" is nonexistent, but is being introduced by introjective and projective processes. Does this adolescent sensory hypercathexis aid the ego to hold on to the object world which he is constantly in danger of losing? Indeed, is it not this very propensity to project internal processes and experience them as outer reality that gives adolescence its characteristic feature of pseudo-psychotic functioning? Feelings of estrangement, of unreality, and of depersonalization threaten to disrupt the continuity of ego feeling; and although these are extreme conditions, the fact remains that the adolescent does experience the outer world with a unique sensory quality which he thinks is not shared by others: "Nobody ever felt the way I do." "Nobody sees the world the way I do." Mother Nature becomes a personal respondent to the adolescent; the beauty of nature is discovered and exalted emotional states are experienced.

This hypersensitivity is particularly present in relation to the overwhelming yearnings of love. A sixteen-year-old boy describes his first experience of tender love with a particular reference to tactile sensations: "It is an amorphous emotion—it can turn into anything—walking barefoot in the grass, walking in the wind with my eyes closed and saying, Eileen. It is just loving to love somebody. When it rains I keep the window open and soak in the air. If there is a spring bounce in the air I feel exuberant—I live entirely with the change of the weather now."

The normal role of fantasies and hallucinatory experiences during adolescence has been described by Landauer (1935). "Perception constitutes the taking-in of the outer reality which normally is preserved as love-and-hate-object; the adolescent driven by the need for love returns to the infantile mode of incorporating objects by destruction in order to reproduce them in hallucinations, or (in less flagrant form) in fantasies, as an outer reality which is now identical with his ego; this phenomenon is part of adolescent solipsism."

It should be said that the discovery of nature and beauty is representative for a particular social and educational group, which roughly coincides with the middle and upper classes. But even though fantasy content varies greatly, the principle as described remains observable throughout this phase. The most changeable aspect of a drive is its object and the most variable component of a fantasy is its manifest content. This variability, which depends on class, region, and historical time should not obscure the role of fantasy in adolescence as a transitory phenomenon interposed between the stages of narcissism and of heterosexual object finding.

Typical for this in-between stage is keeping a diary. Writing a diary is more common for girls in present-day America than it is for boys; perhaps it has always been that way. The emotional self-absorption implicit in keeping a diary easily becomes burdened for the boy with connotations of passivity; his need for extraversive, often defensive, physical assertiveness more often than not turns his attention away from introspection. This has not always been so generally true; it seems that with the arrival of the single standard, new and often more stringent taboos against so-called sex-inappropriate behavior have become established. Be this as it may, the female diarist shares her secrets with her diary as with an intimate confidante. The need to keep a diary is inversely proportionate to the opportunity the adolescent has of sharing freely with the environment his emotional urgencies. Daydreams, events, and emotions which cannot be shared with real people are confessed with relief to the diary. The diary thus assumes an object-like quality. This is obvious from entries addressed to "Dear Diary" or, as in the diary of Anne Frank (1947), to "Dear Kitty." The girl's diary is always a female confidante. The diary stands between daydream and object world, between make-believe and reality, and its content and form change with the times; for material that once was kept as an anxiously guarded secret today is openly expressed.

The older, sophisticated adolescent of today no longer keeps a diary —he writes a "journal." Posterity looks over his shoulder as he writes, however; and what such documents gain in literary quality they usually lose in unselfconsciousness and spontaneity. Diaries today are most frequently kept by adolescents from middle-class families where literary efforts are valued and facility with the written word is not uncommon. Themes which once were dominant in diaries—the instinctual conflicts and their accompanying depressive moods, colloquially known as *Weltschmerz*, a melancholic cosmic grief—have given way to different themes, which may best be summarized as a diffuse anxiousness about life: *Lebensangst* (Abegg, 1954). Also, the political naiveté and provincialism of bygone days have been dramatically replaced by an awareness by most adolescents of world-wide sociopolitical conflicts. This sophistication does not detract from the fact that the diary still serves the same psychological purpose which consists in filling the emotional void felt when the novel instinctual drives of puberty can no longer be articulated on old objects and cannot yet be articulated on new objects, so that fantasy life assumes a most important and essential function. Turning to the diary keeps fantasy life at least partially object-related, and writing down his thoughts keeps the mental activities of the adolescent closer to reality, whether these activities involve either affects or desires, fantasies, aspirations and hopes, or excesses of arrogance or despair. A female diarist reported that as she wrote down her sadomasochistic fantasies, they became more exciting and more real to her. They became more effective by being written down than they were merely as fantasies. Verbalization always brings mental content closer to the quality of realness. Living through experiences and emotions by putting them down in writing closes the door—at least partially and temporarily —to acting out.

Because normally the girl is more ready to turn to heterosexuality, her diary has the function of preventing, through experimentation and role-playing in fantasy, premature heterosexual acting out. Thus the diary fulfills more than one function: it affords role-playing without involving action in reality; according to Bernfeld (1931), the diary stands foremost in the service of identificatory processes; and finally, the diary affords a greater awareness of inner life, a process which in itself renders the ego more effective in its functions of mastery and synthesis.

The use of adolescent diaries for the systematic study of adolescent psychology was first introduced into the psychoanalytic literature by

Bernfeld (1927, 1931), who advanced a methodology for their scientific use. Unfortunately, his studies of adolescent diaries were never followed up; however, some of his remarks are worth recalling: "Diaries of adolescents do not offer source material in the sense of historical data, which is to say, that the credibility of their authors remains irrelevant. One cannot use them to prove facts, or at least only with critical and methodical caution. . . . Diaries are representations distorted by conscious and unconscious tendencies, exactly like dreams, phantasies, and poetic productions of adolescents. They are useful for 1) giving us knowledge of manifest feelings (distorted by various tendencies), of wishes and experiences of adolescence; 2) they are sources for the interpretation of those tendencies and of the psychic material which is distorted by them. This kind of interpretation requires points of reference. This is the reason why a diary as such without further data about the author will remain of limited value as far as the psychological illumination of the author is concerned. Generally, one has to be content with the phenomenological enrichment which can be obtained."

Since Bernfeld conducted his studies, an expanding psychoanalytic experience with adolescents has established certain developmental lines which can be considered as typical for this age. With increasing reliability and indeed with the critical and methodical caution recommended by Bernfeld, we can reinstate the verbal productions of adolescents into a developmental schedule of the adolescent process as a whole. In comparison with direct observation of children, it no longer appears unscientific to recognize in a four-year-old's intolerance to having his toes touched a manifestation of castration anxiety; of course the role this anxiety assumes in the total functioning of the child can hardly be inferred from this observation. The various themes appearing in a diary and running parallel to clinically ascertained developmental lines of psychic functioning offer significant phenomenological data. But beyond this and of greater significance, the diary material can be used to verify typical sequences which permit a more detailed understanding of adolescence. For this reason, the study of adolescent diaries is of great interest, even if we have no other knowledge of the diarist except sex, age, milieu, and historical date. Most of these data usually become apparent from the diary itself.

The first unexpurgated diary of an adolescent published by an analyst was, at the time of publication, considered shocking, and was branded a fraud. Today, in the light of our greater knowledge of adolescent mental life, the authenticity of the *Diary of a Young Girl* (Hug-Hell-muth, 1919) is beyond doubt. Indeed, the same arguments used by Cyril Burt against the diary's verisimilitude could, with equal cogency, be raised against *the Diary of Anne Frank* (1947), and the latter needs no defense on this score. Both these documents, and others (e.g., Golan, 1954) illustrate dramatically the sequence of phases being described in this present book. The diaries also are able to convey the feeling tone accompanying physical changes and emotional shifts in a way that no theoretical discourse can hope to equal.

Closely related to fantasy is the adolescent's propensity to use people in make-believe relationships, namely to endow them with qualities in relation to which the adolescent endeavors to exercise his own needs, both libidinal and aggressive. These relationships lack a genuine qual-ity; they constitute experiences which are created for the purpose of disengagement from early love objects. The complementary self-interest in such relationships between two adolescents, especially boy and girl, is reminiscent of a transient *folie à deux*. The fact that these relation-ships often dissolve painlessly without subsequent grief or identificatory sequelae attests to their character. "The need for reassurance against anxieties concerning the new drives may give all object relationships an ungenuine character; they are mixed with identifications, and per-sons are perceived more as representations of images than as persons. Neurotic characters who remain afraid of their drives throughout life, therefore often given an adolescent impression" (Fenichel, 1945, b).

Anna Freud (1936) has described the role which identification plays in the love life of the adolescent; it is used to preserve a hold on object relations at the time of the retreat to narcissism. "These passionate and evanescent love-fixations are not object relations at all, in the sense in which we use the term in speaking of adults. They are identifications of the most primitive kind, such as we meet with in our study of early infantile development before any object-love exists." The ever-changing attachments and infatuations, the passionate, devoted friendships which are defended by the adolescent against any interference as if life itself depended on them, can be understood as restitution phenomena. They prevent a total libidinal regression to narcissism; by assimilating the ob-ject in terms of the model described by Helene Deutsch as the "as-if" type of relationship, the adolescent enriches his own impoverished ego. All these relationships entail an overevaluation of the friend in order to gratify narcissistic needs, but besides this aspect, we can recognize an experimental role, playing with small quantities of object libido, a state, it is true, which continues to overlap for some time with the essentially narcissistic use of the object. The experimental component is ego-strengthening; it represents that aspect of the total process which could be called adaptive, since it operates in consonance with progressive development.

Before new love objects can take the place of those relinquished, a period exists during which the ego is impoverished because of the withdrawal from the actual parents and the estrangement from the superego; in Anna Freud's (1936) words: "The ego alienates itself from the super-ego." The ego's ally in instinct control has ceased to function in the accustomed dependable way; and in addition, the decathexis of the parental object representations has added to the ego's impoverishment. This state of affairs is not only counteracted by transient identificatory processes but also by the willful creation of ego states of a poignant internal perception of the self. Landauer (1935) refers to this adolescent phenomenon as "heightened ego experience" ("*erhöhtes Ich-Erlebnis*"). This restitution phenomenon can be seen in relation to the body ego, the experiencing ego, and the self-observing ego. In the body sphere it is exertion, pain, and excessive motility; in the experiencing ego it is the overwhelming affective charge and its explosive release; in the self-observing ego it is the keen perception of inner life which characterizes an adolescent condition not wholly relegatable to the mechanisms of defense. In fact, these ego states are important for shaping the specific and ego-syntonic individual variant of adult drive organization.

This matter will occupy us at greater length in our discussion of late adolescence; here I will illustrate it with some excerpts from the analysis of two fourteen-year-old boys:

John entered a new phase in his analysis after he had finally overcome the fixation on the phallic mother. He had to face the submissive weakness of his father while he was not yet able to transfer his libidinal needs to new objects. In this state of isolation and affective impoverishment he suddenly hit on the idea of doing things which were out of the ordinary and which would give him an unknown and unusual sensation of boldness, freedom, and discovery. So he got up at two in the morning, when everybody was asleep, went into the living room, and sat in "father's chair" reading; in school, he specialized in practical jokes, quite to the surprise of his classmates and teachers; he started to wear a funny cap and to observe his own feelings when others watched him. Alan, another boy of the same age, used similar mechanisms. He was always exhausted and excited from hurry, tardiness, and lack of time. He came to realize that the sensations attendant on his rushing around were self-induced states of tension—self-administered stimulants, so to speak, to keep himself feeling alive. He said, "I have discovered that the dither I get myself into when I am attempting to do homework is self-imposed. I really make myself anxious and tense. It's the same thing when I suddenly profess to be terribly interested in baseball, in the World Series; in fact, I don't give a damn." Both these boys recognized only during the course of their analyses that the ego states were self-induced and served partly defensive, partly libidinal and aggressive, partly adaptive and experimental purposes; they were experienced as ego-syntonic. Should adolescent ego states swing toward masochistic gratification, or toward seeking despair, which is expressed in weeping, suffering, self-castigation, then, according to Helene Deutsch (1944), these "narcissistic gratifications through suffering usually yield to moods of depression connected with feelings of inferiority, and may crystallize in a real depression that can lead further to a severe adolescent neurosis."

Into this general category of heightened ego feeling belong those states of self-induced exertion, pain, and exhaustion which are typical of adolescence. Apart from the defensive aspects, the importance of heightened body-ego feeling should not be minimized. Only one illustration need be offered for this well-known phenomenon; this is taken from the biography of Gerard Manley Hopkins (Warren, 1945): "At boarding school, he denied himself salt for a week; another time he went for a week without drinking water or any other liquid, carrying out the bet he had made, though collapsing at the end of it."

Self-induced ego states of affective and sensory intensity allow the ego to experience a feeling of self and thus protect the integrity of its boundaries and its cohesion; furthermore, these states promote the ego's vigilance over instinctual tension. Instinctual tensions are partly relieved in discharge processes to the outside via motor expression; they are partly discharged to the inside and account for the many physiological (functional) disturbances of this period; and they are partly kept under control by defensive mechanisms. In fact, an oscillation between the modes by which ego and instinctual drive achieve a compromise or *modus vivendi* is the rule rather than the exception during this phase of adolescence. Whenever this *modus vivendi* emphasizes moderation, idealism, or instinctual repudiation it receives conspicuous commendation from the environment; should the instinctual drives gain the upper hand, then the adolescent is likely to enter into open conflict with society. Normally, though, he does oscillate between both positions; his turmoil abates with the gradual strengthening of controlling, inhibiting, guiding, and evaluative principles which render desires, actions, thoughts, and values ego-syntonic and reality oriented. This, however, can be achieved only after these principles have become disengaged from the love and hate objects—the images of parents, siblings, and others—which originally brought them into being. As an intermediate step, the ego becomes the recipient of the libido withdrawn from object representations; all ego functions—not only the self—can become cathected in the process. This circumstance gives the individual a false sense of power which in turn impairs his judgment in critical situations, often with catastrophic consequences, a good example being the frequent automobile accidents of teenagers.

The relative weakness of the ego vis-à-vis instinctual demands is ameliorated during this adolescent phase when the ego relents in its acceptance of the drives. This progression parallels the ego's growing resourcefulness in channeling drive discharge along a highly differentiated and organized pattern. However, this step cannot be taken as long as the love objects of early childhood continue to fight for their survival, or as long as the oedipus complex continues to assert itself.

The phase of adolescence proper thus has two dominant themes: the revival of the oedipus complex and the disengagement from primary love objects. This process constitutes a sequence of object-relinquishment and object-finding both of which promote the establishment of the adult drive organization. One may describe this phase of adolescence in terms of two broad affective states: "mourning" and "being in love." The adolescent incurs a real loss in the renunciation of his oedipal parents; and he experiences the inner emptiness, grief, and sadness which is part of all mourning. "The work of mourning . . . is an important psychological task in the period of adolescence" (Root, 1957). The working through of the mourning process is essential to the gradual achievement of liberation from the lost object; it requires time and repetition. Similarly, in adolescence the separation from the oedipal parent is a painful process which can only be achieved gradually.

The aspect of "being in love" is a more familiar component of adolescent life. It signals the advance of the libido to new objects; this state is marked by a sense of completeness, coupled with a singular self-abandonment. Heterosexual object love brings an end to the bisexual position of previous phases, in which the sex-alien tendencies required constant countercathectic charge as they threatened constantly to assert themselves, thus disrupting the unity of the ego (self-image). These tendencies can be fulfilled without restraint in heterosexual love only by conceding to the partner the sex-alien component of the drive. This model was described by Weiss (1950), who called it "resonance phenomenon." It first appears in adolescence and plays an important part in the resolution of bisexual tendencies. One can often and easily observe in adolescence proper how the fact of falling in love or of acquiring a boy or girl friend brings to the fore a remarkable ascendancy in masculine or feminine traits. This shift signifies that sex-alien tendencies have been conceded to the other sex, and thus can be shared in the mutual belonging of the partners to each other. In other words, the sex-inappropriate component has acquired ego-syntonicity by becoming the property of the love object, which in turn is cathected with object libido.

To adolescence proper belongs that unique experience, tender love. Tender love often precedes heterosexual experimentation, which must be distinguished from the roughhousing sex play of earlier stages—although this often extends into adolescence proper in the competitive spirit of boys in their conquest of girls, and the desired form of physical intimacy (which is in great part dictated by the background and group to which the adolescent belongs). The boys' noisy and predatory approaches reach a peak in this phase; but sooner or later these coarse pursuits are suddenly disrupted by an erotic feeling which both enthralls and inhibits the young male. He realizes that a sentiment has entered his life which is new in one respect, namely that his attitude toward the girl involves a sense of tenderness and devotion. Uppermost are a concern for the preservation of the love object, and a desire for the exclusive—if only spiritual—belonging to each other. The partner does not represent merely a source of sexual pleasure (sex play); rather, she signifies a conglomerate of sacred and precious attributes which strike the boy with awe. It must not be overlooked that this new sentiment is first experienced by the boy as the threat of a new dependency, so that the attachment in itself arouses fears of submissiveness and emotional surrender. This reaction appeared clearly in the analysis of a fifteen-year-old boy when tender love made its first appearance. Fear of dependency on the phallic mother had occupied a large part of the analytic work up to this point. The boy described his emotional turmoil as follows: "There is something nutty in my 'sex life' with girls. Several girls are running after me. There is one I like best but at the party last week I hardly paid attention to her. It is crazy the way I behave. I am scared or something to let her know I like her. Only late in the evening I decided to pay attention to her. I felt by that time that I am in control, that I am on top, that I wouldn't risk anything or take chances. The whole thing is silly or abnormal. I am afraid of her knowing of my feelings, of her really loving me and being a pawn in her hand. Then I cannot be on top any more."

The idealization of the love object initiates a refinement and enrichment of feeling life which in the boy derives its intensity and quality from a normal degree of mother fixation. The feeling of tender love in heterosexual relationship can probably be reached only when the narcissistic and bisexual positions are shifted toward a final surrender of the sex-alien component to a member of the opposite sex. The cathexis of the love object with narcissistic libido accounts for its idealization. In cases of extreme infatuation, the cathexis leaves the ego depleted; the result is that essential protection of health, both physical and mental, is often ignored with dangerous heedlessness. At any rate, the emergence of this tender sentiment marks for the boy a turning point: the first signs of heterosexuality are manifest and the adolescent elaboration of masculinity is under way. However, only as he progresses from this early stage of infatuation toward the fusion of tender and sexual love does the genuineness of this early development become apparent. It must not be overlooked that the masculinity of the boy, including that of the passive boy, is powerfully reinforced by pubertal maturation itself. This apparent gain often masks a continuing passivity, which appears once more in force whenever the pubertal upsurge of masculine sexuality has subsided in intensity.

Typically, development follows the schema according to which the male's passive-feminine component is surrendered to the heterosexual partner; a sense of completeness is derived from this polarization. In its early stage the union with the beloved is experienced partly in fantasy; i.e., only a slight stimulus—a memory of a girl known before, or an otherwise unknown girl seen fleetingly or only from a distance—can give rise to strong affective manifestations.

To this latter category belongs the experience of first love which is described by Thomas Mann (1914) in *Tonio Kröger*.

Ingeborg Holm, blond little Inge, the daughter of Dr. Holm, who lived on Market Square opposite the tall old Gothic fountain with its manifold spires—she it was Tonio Kröger loved when he was sixteen years old. Strange how things come about! He had seen her a thousand times; then one evening he saw her again; saw her in a certain light, talking with a friend in a certain saucy way, laughing and tossing her head; saw her lift her arm and smooth her back hair with her schoolgirl hand, that was by no means particularly fine or slender, in such a way that the thin white sleeve slipped down from her elbow; heard her speak a word or two, a quite indifferent phrase, but with a certain intonation, with a warm ring in her voice; and his heart throbbed with ecstasy, far stronger than that he had once felt when he looked at Hans Hansen long ago, when he was still a little, stupid boy.

That evening he carried away her picture in his eye: the thick blond plait, the longish, laughing blue eyes, the saddle of pale freckles across the nose. He could not go to sleep for hearing that ring in her voice; he tried in a whisper to imitate the tone in which she had uttered the commonplace phrase, and felt a shiver run through and through him. He knew by experience that this was love. And he was accurately aware that love would surely bring him much pain, affliction and sadness, that it would certainly destroy his peace, filling his heart to overflowing with melodies which would be no good to him because he would never have the time or tranquility to give them permanent form. Yet he received this love with joy, surrendered himself to it, and cherished it with all the strength of his being; for he knew that love made one vital and rich, and he longed to be vital and rich, far more than he did to work tranquilly on anything to give it permanent form.*

The first choice of a heterosexual love object is commonly determined either by some physical or mental similarity to the parent of the opposite sex, or by some striking dissimilarities. In Tonio's case, the contrast of the blond, plump, prosaic, and teutonic girl to his dark, delicate, poetic, and exotic mother cannot fail to impress the reader. Such first loves are, of course, not mature relationships, but are rudimentary attempts at displacement which will ripen into mature love only with the progressive resolution of the revived oedipus complex.

Tonio's ultimate failure in reaching any stable love relationship may be described here, although it goes beyond the phase now being discussed. In his early manhood he chooses as his love partner a woman

* Reprinted from "Tonio Kröger," in *Stories of Three Decades* by Thomas Mann, by permission of Alfred A. Knopf, Inc. Copyright 1936 by Alfred A. Knopf, Inc.

who is in every way the opposite of young Inge: "Her brown hair, compactly dressed, already a little grey at the sides, was parted in the middle, and waved over the temples, framing a sensitive, sympathetic, dark-skinned face, which was Slavic in its facial cheek bones, and little bright eyes." Apparently the mother who was avoided in the first adolescent love choice had become the central conflict of his later love life. Tonio departs from his father's background and becomes an artist; but he never finds during his young manhood the woman he could marry. Eventually Tonio accidentally meets Hans and Inge, who in the meantime have married each other. Tonio's two early love choices were meant for each other; both were determined by an attempt to please the father. A boy like Hans would have been loved by Tonio's father as a son; and choosing a girl like Inge eliminated Tonio's conflicted desire of possessing the mother or somebody resembling her. Positive and negative feelings toward both parents were thus articulated in the choices which the boy makes with regard to his first homosexual and heterosexual love object.

A fifteen year old boy described his first experience of tender love with these words: "It was the strangest feeling I experienced towards a girl; we were riding together on a train to camp. I loved the girl but was unable to touch her or kiss her. This lasted during most of the summer. I always felt, 'It might be too much for her; if I touch her I will ruin our relationship.' This to happen to me of all people! I who always thought to be fast with any girl, any time; just twenty minutes to the first kiss. This time it was different. About those quick conquests I say to myself, 'Wow! What's a kiss like that?'" This highly egocentric and orally fixated boy became able, through therapy, to overcome his passive dependency by an identification with the active mother; instead of being the object of his mother's nurturing care and protective love, he extended these ministrations to the girl he loved. By so doing he could tolerate increasing tensions of work and abstinence. He achieved a degree of masculinity by conceding the feminine receptive drive modality to the heterosexual partner; in this way he could, by reflection, share in the disowned drive component.

The boy's advance to heterosexuality is greatly aided by the assistance of a deep emotional attachment to a love partner who carries, so to say, half the burden of the polarization process. Whenever the drive organization of early adolescence cannot be abandoned, a rush into premature marriage or into transient sexual relationships may occur as an attempt to sidestep the phase-specific development of adolescence proper. Whenever this occurs in the male, we can discern an insurmountable attachment to the nurturing, i.e., active mother. This fixation during adolescence takes the form of homosexual, passive strivings, which are often held in abeyance by heterosexual acting out.

Homosexual episodes for both boys and girls occur frequently during this phase. There is no way of foretelling their lasting effect on the formation of masculinity or femininity without knowing which specific drive organization is reinforced through these experiences, thus becoming pathologically aligned with pubertal maturation. In the girl, two preconditions favor homosexual object choice. One is penis envy, which is overcompensated by contempt for the male; in these cases the girl herself acts like a boy in relation to other girls. The second precondition is an early fixation on the mother; in these cases the girl acts like a dependent child, slavishly obedient and trusting, overwhelmed by sentiments of bliss and contentment in the presence of the beloved. Eating problems (overeating) often accompany the latter clinical syndrome.

In the boy three preconditions favor the channeling of genital sexuality into a homosexual object choice during puberty. One is a fear of the vagina as a devouring castrating organ; we recognize in this unconscious concept a derivative of projected oral sadism. The second precondition resides in the boy's identification with the mother, a condition which is particularly apt to occur when the mother was inconsistent and frustrating while the father was either maternal or rejecting. A third precondition stems from the oedipus complex which assumes the form of an inhibition or restriction summarily equating all females with mother and declaring introitus to be a father's prerogative. All these stages can be observed, latent or manifest, during adolescence proper, as the resuscitation of early object relations moves ostentatiously into the foreground. Adolescent oedipal manifestations demonstrate the particular vicissitudes which the oedipus complex has undergone during the life of the individual.

The struggle of the instincts which occurs at the close of early childhood is brought to a truce by the attainment of relatively stable object relations within the family, by the establishment of the superego, and by the elaboration (albeit preliminary) of sexual identity. This truce opens the door to the exclusively human experience of the latency period. It is for adolescence proper to achieve similar tasks within a body that has reached physical sexual maturity. Consequently, emotional development must move in the direction of stable object relations to both sexes outside the family and toward an irreversible sexual identity formation. In the wake of these attainments man cannot but fit actively into the social organizations and institutions which are part of his immediate world. Only through alloplastic adaptation will he procure fulfillment of his instinctual needs and in addition give expression to those energies, libidinal and aggressive, which transcend instinctual realization and appear in highly complex, aim-inhibited—that is, sublimated—form. The elaboration of the social and the private role is a process which starts to take shape in adolescence proper, but is not by any means brought to an end during this phase.

Let us return to the oedipal parent. From clinical records pertaining to this phase it is abundantly clear that a decisive detachment from the parent is essential before a nonincestuous object choice can be made. During the prestages of this decisive detachment, spite and revenge attachments are made which are designed to hurt the parent who no longer can satisfy the love needs of the child; these actions signify that childhood status still prevails. We can witness in boys and girls the resurgence of an awareness of the intimate life of the parents; shame and guilt are attached to such curiosity and imagery. The oedipal involvement appears in the critical attitude of the adolescent toward one parent; in the girl it is more often than not the mother who becomes the target of reproach and accusations. Many a girl is convinced that she herself understands her father better than her mother does; she—so runs a typical thought—would not trouble him with the trivialities with which mother greets him at the door after his day of heavy work. The girl is usually only aware of the negative aspect of her feelings toward the mother; the positive side is disguised in fantasies, daydreams, or is experienced in displaced form with a great deal of dramatization and make-believe. One is reminded of the girl who "falls in love" with a boy whose main distinction is that he is misunderstood by others. Depending on the girl's class and caste, this may be a boy of a special race, color, or religion, or simply a "good-for-nothing," an outcast of society. Such an object choice follows the oedipal model of competition and revenge. Ensuing guilt feelings are assuaged by self-punshment, asceticism, and depressed states.

An episode from the psychotherapy of a seventeen-year-old girl illustrates the preceding remarks. Mary had started an affair with a psychotic young man who in her opinion was misunderstood by his family, by his doctor, by the world generally. At home she quarreled with her family about her right to go out with Fred, her boyfriend. This affair bore all the marks of acting out behavior—that is, of discharging conflictual or drive tension in interaction with the outside world instead of experiencing it as an internal, ego-dystonic crisis. Mary clung to this affair, which brought her no apparent happiness but caused her parents great anguish. One day mother and daughter had a violent argument about housekeeping responsibilities, in which the mother found the daughter remiss. Mary felt mistreated, rejected and misunderstood by her mother, and at the height of the argument she left the room in a rage, slamming the door. At this point in Mary's report of the fight, I remarked, "I know what you thought when you walked out on your mother." "What?" "That you will sleep with Fred this weekend." "How did you know?" was the answer.

The startle effect made Mary realize that her turning to Fred for love was prompted by a deep disappointment in her mother. Her relationship to Fred was retaliatory, competitive, and revengeful; it could be paraphrased as "So you won't love me? but somebody else will." From this moment, the girl lost interest in Fred; and material of oedipal content emerged in therapy, material which for the first time was accessible through memories and communicable through words, rather than through action. Acting out, that "special form of remembering in which an old memory is re-enacted" (Fenichel, 1945) bars the memory from awareness and thus renders it unaccessible to transformatory interventions emanating from without or within. In order to do justice to the complexity of Mary's case, it must be added that the girl's defiance of her mother also served another purpose, that of resistance against regression. Anna Freud has referred to the "affective negativism" as a means to resist regression; the problem of negativism as a form of counteracting the regressive pull is of special relevance to adolescence. It appears theoretically convincing and clinically demonstrable that the "wholesale negativism" of the adolescent subsides in direct proportion in which the ego has mastered the regressive pull, either by defensive or adaptive measures but primarily by a forward movement of the libido toward heterosexual, extrafamilial, nonambivalent object relations.

As was pointed out earlier, the paths which the boy and girl follow in the resolution of the oedipal conflict are different. What brings the oedipal phase to a close for the boy, namely, castration anxiety, is instrumental in opening up the oedipal phase for the girl. The resolution of the oedipal phase is never accomplished by the girl with the same rigidity and severity as by the boy. Her turn to heterosexuality in adolescence proper and its defensive use in preadolescence is only in keeping with her loosely repressed oedipal strivings. Because the boy's repression of oedipal strivings is far more severe, their resuscitation is slow and resistant to pubertal stimulation. The resolution of the male oedipus complex is necessarily left incomplete when the child's immaturity necessitates the abandonment of oedipal strivings; the renunciation of them takes the form of repression.

In contradistinction, the girl all through her latency period continues to spin the yarn of the oedipal tapestry. This fact on the one hand sharpens the oedipal conflict, and carries it along into the widening scope of latency experiences; on the other hand, it contributes to the enrichment and deepening of the girl's inner life. The girl, consequently, arrives at adolescence proper with a wide emotional background expressed in fantasy, intuition, and empathy—very well described by Helene Deutsch (1944). These rich sources of inner life enable the girl to tolerate the postponement of genital gratification. It has been pointed out many times that the girl can easily dissociate the sexual urge and its masturbatory gratification from both thought and conscious action, because of the anatomical location of the excitable organ, predominantly the clitoris, more rarely the vagina. The girl's anatomy permits stimulation and excitation by muscular pressure and postural positions, resulting in tension release along a scale extending from orgastic to blunt sensations. In the boy, however, the sexual organ is exterior, visible, and palpable, and any sexual excitation becomes perceptually validated; furthermore, male masturbation is physiologically ejaculatory (orgastic), and its sexual nature cannot escape awareness.

As far as the resolution of the oedipus complex is concerned, once more, we must remember that neither in the boy nor in the girl do we encounter resolutions which live up to the ideal models. In both sexes there remain residues of positive and negative oedipal strivings: that is to say, relics of feminine strivings remain in the boy, and the girl maintains for a long time fantasies of a phallic nature. The analysis of adolescent girls has shown that the resolution of oedipal conflicts prepares her for heterosexual love, and the surrender of the "masculinity complex" releases maternal feelings, for instance, the wish for a child. Helene Deutsch (1944) described this development in the girl. "At any rate," she says, "the girl represses the conscious realization of the direct instinctual claim for a much longer time and in a much more successful manner than the boy. This claim manifests itself indirectly in her intensified love yearnings and the erotic orientation of her phantasies—in brief, in the endowment of her inner life with those emotional qualities that we recognize as specific feminine." The polarity of "masculine" and "feminine" receives its final and irreversible fixity during this phase of adolescence proper. Menarche initiates and emphasizes this polarity. The normal girl's emotional reaction to this event involves two essential psychic processes: the renunciation of maternal dependency on the one hand, and the identification with the mother as the reproductive prototype on the other. Benedek (1959) has pointed out that "the maturation toward the female reproductive goal depends upon the previous developmental identifications with the mother. If these identifications are not charged with hostility, the girl is able to accept her heterosexual desires without anxiety and motherhood as a desired goal. This in turn determines the girl's reaction to menstruation."

The boy, in overcoming the feminine remnants of his negative oedipal position, turns to overcompensatory devices which make him appear belligerently affirmative of his male powers and prerogatives. Furthermore, he turns to male group or gang affiliations ("street" or "school," "low-brow" or "high-brow") which permit aim-inhibited feminine tendencies to find an outlet and at the same time initiate the adolescent into a collective code of maleness.

These solutions can be considered waystations and holding positions on the path of progressive development. In and by themselves they do not indicate any attainment of those internal cathectic and identificatory shifts which may be referred to in their totality as sexual identity. In fact, the unreserved submission to social pressures which force the individual to perform in a given way regardless of his corresponding internal capacity to integrate the experience into the continuity of the ego usually produces a state of inner confusion. As a result, the disruption of ego functions becomes manifest; clinically this presents itself in the typical failures of the adolescent to cope with the normative demands of his life, such as learning, scheduling time, orienting himself to the future, judging the consequence of action, and so on. These states of bewilderment and breakdown indicate an often pathognomic effort to circumvent the internal transformatory processes of adolescence proper by behavior which simulates their achievements. This attempt is universal and usually transient. The tendency to preserve childhood privileges and to simultaneously arrogate the prerogatives of adulthood is almost synonymous with adolescence itself. Every adolescent has to traverse this paradox; those fixated on this way station will have a deviate development.

The decline of the oedipus complex in adolescence is a slow process, and one that reaches into the phase of late adolescence. It is probably accomplished only when in the natural course of events the individual re-establishes himself in a new family; then oedipal fantasies can be dispensed with for good and all. More cautiously—and perhaps more correctly—it may be said that through the formation of a new family the young adult creates an emotional constellation with the help of which he can hope to master any breakthrough of oedipal remnants.

There are two sources of internal danger during adolescence proper which call for measures, both auto- and alloplastic, to avert a state of panic. One is the impoverishment of the ego which leads to the abnormal ego states which have already been described in connection with the psychic efforts toward maintaining contact with reality and continuity in ego feeling. The other source is the instinctual anxiety aroused during the forward movement of libido toward heterosexuality; this anxiety calls into play the defensive mechanisms typical for this phase. All through the years of adolescence, of course, defensive reactions play a significant role; and indeed, some phases have been defined by their employment of specific defenses (e.g., regression is phase-specific for the boy during preadolescence). However, it appears that at adolescence proper defenses are chosen with a more highly idiosyncratic discretion. One might say that the choice of defenses is more in keeping with the progressive emergence of character. Character formation—in its positive and negative aspects, in its ego liberation and ego restriction—under normal circumstances derives quality and structure from ego activities that start more often than not as a defensive measure and gradually assume an adaptive fixity.

Defense mechanisms which appear to be dynamic entities at this phase of adolescence are revealed upon closer inspection to be a composite of divergent component processes. "Closer inspection" here refers to longitudinal observations extending beyond the phase in question in order to study the ultimate fate of the defense—that is, to see how it separates into distinct components which serve different functions, such as, for instance, defensive, adaptive, and restitutive functions. The withdrawal of libido from infantile love objects which is an indispensable condition for phase-adequate progression to nonincestuous object choice is consequently not a defense in the proper sense of this term. It becomes a defense only if the unaltered libido position is repressed and thus withdrawn from forward movement and transformation.

Certain characteristic efforts made by the ego in order to counteract its impoverishment and its weakening hold on reality bear the signs of restitution phenomena. The ego's integrity—its cohesion and continuity —is threatened by the decathexis of infantile love objects; to mend this intrasystemic damage restitutive processes are initiated. The decathexis of infantile objects leads to a rise in narcissism which does not entail a regression to the narcissistic or undifferentiated phase; instead, it can be understood as the consequence of a cathectic shift within the ego in the service of progressive development. Secondarily, we can then isolate, according to Anna Freud (1958), "defenses against the infantile object ties" of which "displacement" and "reversal of affect" are the most prominent. These defenses eventually will open the road to adaptive processes (Hartmann, 1939, a). We know from observation that the transition from restitutive to defensive and adaptive processes is an intricate one, and deserves study. This problem, indeed, goes to the core of the adolescent process itself in terms of differentiation and maturation. The concept of defense is, of course, too narrow to do justice to the complexity of adolescence; too great an emphasis on it has overshadowed other equally significant issues of this period.

The defense mechanisms of adolescence were described by Anna Freud (1936). Asceticism and intellectualization have been particularly well studied. Both appear by and large in a social class in which a protracted state of adolescence is favored by special educational demands. Asceticism prohibits the expression of instinct; it easily plays into masochistic tendencies. "The aim of intellectualization is to link up instinctual processes closely with ideational contents and so to render them accessible to consciousness and amenable to control" (A. Freud, 1936). Intellectualization favors active mastery and allows the discharge of aggression in displaced form. "A negative judgment," according to Spitz (1957), "is the intellectual substitute for repression." Both defenses, asceticism and intellectualization, which are so characteristic for the crisis of adolescence proper, demonstrate well the role of defensive mechanisms in the ego's struggle against the instincts. Furthermore, to some extent they foreshadow the emergence of character and of special preferential interests, talents, and definitive vocational choices. Apparently, intellectualization contains more of a positive potential, while asceticism is essentially ego restrictive; it serves as a holding action and involves little affective effort to communicate with and relate to the outside world.

In *The Portrait of the Artist as a Young Man* (1916) James Joyce minutely and movingly describes his youthful struggle against carnal desire. In the measures which Stephen Dedalus employs in order to control his impulses, following his first sex experience in an encounter with a prostitute, we may recognize two classical defenses, intellectualization and asceticism.

Joyce's description of these defenses indicates the enormity of the struggle which this youth waged. First Stephen attempted to subdue his sexual impulses by simple repression, by a fervent disavowal of his rebelliousness and urges in the hope of finding inner peace. Unconscious oedipal feelings are discernible in the boy's guilty estrangement from his family:

> How foolish his aim had been! He had tried to build a breakwater of order and elegance against the sordid tide of life without him and to dam up, by rules of conduct and active interests and new filial relations, the powerful recurrence of the tide within him. Useless. From without as from within the water had flowed over his barriers: their tides began once more to jostle fiercely above the crumbled mole.
> He saw clearly, too, his own futile isolation. He had not gone one step nearer the lives he had sought to approach nor bridged the restless shame and rancour that had divided him from mother and brother and sister. He felt that he was hardly of the one blood with them but stood to them rather in the mystical kinship of fosterage, foster child and foster brother.*

Stephen's temporary bulwark against his sexual impulses failed. His attempt to establish new filial relations devoid of the pubertal drive component represented the regressive solution of the revived oedipal conflict; it accomplished nothing. He first had to achieve the detachment from his early love and hate objects within the family before he could rid himself of the oedipal guilt, "the mortal sin" of his religious teachings and find that freedom of the soul for which he so fervently yearned. The resolution of oedipal fixations produces crude sexual fantasies and actions which are compulsive and defiant, as well as sublime feelings of tender love.

A dissociation usually exists during the stage of sexual experimentation between physical activity and sensation on the one hand, and ideational content—the re-experiencing of infantile object ties—on the

* Reprinted from James Joyce, *Portrait of the Artist as a Young Man*, by permission of The Viking Press, Inc.

other. The sexual experimentation, if it is not unduly prolonged so that aspects of forepleasure are endowed with permanent satiatory qualities, serves as an introduction to pubertal sexual sensations; the act of dissociation allows them to be less burdened with oedipal guilt. These prestages in the advance to heterosexuality demand their pound of flesh before the stage of consolidation and unification of irreconcilable emotions is attained in postadolescence.

When Stephen Dedalus finally knows who he is and what he wants, he can cry, "Welcome, O Life, I go to encounter for the millionth time the reality of experience and to forge in the smithy of my soul the uncreated conscience of my race." But before he arrives at this milestone of liberation, he has to overcome the conflicts and emotional turmoils of adolescence proper. The following excerpt describes Stephen's masturbatory struggle and the ensuing emotional conflicts which finally lead to his acceptance of an invitation by a prostitute.

He turned to appease the fierce longings of his heart before which everything else was idle and alien. He cared little that he was in mortal sin, that his life had grown to be a tissue of subterfuge and falsehood. Beside the savage desire within him to realise the enormities which he brooded on nothing was sacred. He bore cynically with the shameful details of his secret riots in which he exulted to defile with patience whatever image had attracted his eyes. By day and by night he moved among distorted images of the outer world. A figure that had seemed to him by day demure and innocent came towards him by night through the winding darkness of sleep, her face transfigured by a lecherous cunning, her eyes bright with brutish joy. Only the morning pained him with its dim memory of dark orgiastic riot, its keen and humiliating sense of transgression.

He returned to his wanderings. The veiled autumnal evenings led him from street to street as they had led him years before along the quiet avenues of Blackrock. But no vision of trim front gardens or of kindly lights in the windows poured a tender influence upon him now. Only at times, in the pauses of his desire, when the luxury that was wasting him gave room to a softer languor, the image of Mercedes traversed the background of his memory. He saw again the small white house and the garden of rosebushes on the road that led to the mountains and he remembered the sadly proud gesture of refusal which he was to make there, standing with her in the moonlit garden after years of estrangement and adventure. At those moments the soft speeches of Claude Melnotte rose to his lips and eased his unrest. A tender premonition touched him of the tryst he had then looked forward to and, in spite of the horrible reality which lay between his hope of then and now, of the holy encounter he had then imagined at which weakness and timidity and inexperience were to fall from him.

Such moments passed and the wasting fires of lust sprang up again. The verses passed from his lips and the inarticulate cries and the unspoken brutal words rushed forth from his brain to force a passage. His blood was in revolt. He wandered up and down the dark, slimy streets peering into the gloom of lanes and doorways, listening eagerly for any sound. He moaned to himself like some baffled prowling beast. He wanted to sin with another of his kind, to force another being to sin with him and to exult with her in sin. He felt some dark presence moving irresistibly upon him from the darkness, a presence subtle and murmurous as a flood filling him wholly with itself. Its murmur besieged his ears like the murmur of some multitude in sleep; its subtle streams penetrated his being. His hands clenched convulsively and his teeth set together as he suffered the agony of its penetration. He stretched out his arms in the street to hold fast the frail swooning form that eluded him and incited him: and the cry that he had strangled for so long in his throat issued from his lips. It broke from him like a wail of despair from a hell of sufferers and died in a wail of furious entreaty, a cry for an iniquitous abandonment, a cry which was but the echo of an obscene scrawl which he had read on the oozing wall of a urinal.

He had wandered into a maze of narrow and dirty streets. From the foul laneways he heard bursts of hoarse riot and wrangling and the drawling of drunken singers . . .

He stood still in the middle of the roadway, his heart clamouring against his bosom in a tumult. A young woman dressed in a long pink gown laid her hand on his arm to detain him and gazed into his face.*

The encounter with the prostitute is for young Stephen, as it is for most boys, no solution of the emotional conflict; it is an act of affirmation of male sexuality but it does not by itself sever infantile object ties. The progression to new love objects does not follow sexual experience as a matter of course. Quite the contrary: the internal struggle becomes intensified and the aggressive uprising against male authority (father) figures moves into the foreground. Stephen resorted to defensive measures to prevent the emergence of the aggressive drive into conscious thought; that is, he employed the defense of intellectualization. Toward this end he used—as is always the case—that system of ideas which is rooted in the adolescent's milieu and thus has acquired a prominence of either positive or negative valence. We can clearly recognize the displacement of affect from love and hate objects to ideational controversy and the mastery of psychic conflict by dialectic means. Joyce, the lifelong pupil of a Jesuit school, necessarily articulates the defense mechanism of intellectualization in terms of the ambiguities in religious dogma.

As he sat in his bench gazing calmly at the rector's shrewd harsh face his mind wound itself in and out of the curious questions proposed to it. If a

* *Ibid.*

man had stolen a pound in his youth and had used that pound to amass a huge fortune how much was he obliged to give back, the pound he had stolen only or the pound together with the compound interest accruing upon it or all his huge fortune? If a layman in giving baptism pour the water before saying the words is the child baptised? Is baptism with a mineral water valid? How comes it that while the first beatitude promises the kingdom of heaven to the poor of heart, the second beatitude promises also to the meek that they shall possess the land? Why was the sacrament of the eucharist instituted under the two species of bread and wine if Jesus Christ be present body and blood, soul and divinity, in the bread alone and in the wine alone? Does a tiny particle of the consecrated bread contain all the body and blood of Jesus Christ or a part only of the body and blood? If the wine change into vinegar and the host crumble into corruption after they have been consecrated, is Jesus Christ still present under their species as God and as man?*

A possible breakthrough of the sexual impulse is by no means securely held in check by the defense of intellectualization. The senses, and sensuality in general, must be kept under closest scrutiny. The defense of asceticism, which Joyce describes in the following passage, no doubt operates in closer proximity to the body and its urges; it permits the gratification of component instincts namely sadomasochism. Asceticism as an adolescent defense affords a discharge of libidinal and aggressive drives in relation to the self and the body. This condition favors a fixation on this drive modality whenever a strong masochistic tendency prevails; furthermore, it gives ambivalence in object relations a new vigor through the sadomasochistic reinforcement. Stephen Dedalus's asceticism does not completely obliterate impulse manifestations like anger and irritation, but only removes the sexual impulse, the "temptation to sin mortally." The defense protects him against positive oedipal feelings, but not against his "anger at hearing his mother sneeze." It is the mother as love object against whom the defense operates in Stephen's case; the contact with her can safely be continued only as long as it bears a negative sign. Joyce describes Stephen's elaborate ascetic regime as follows:

But he had been forewarned of the dangers of spiritual exaltation and did not allow himself to desist from even the least or lowliest devotion, striving also by constant mortification to undo the sinful past rather than to achieve a saintlessness fraught with peril. *Each of his senses was brought under a rigorous discipline.* In order to mortify the *sense of sight* he made it his rule to walk in the street with downcast eyes, glancing neither to right nor left and never behind him. His eyes shunned every encounter with the eyes of women. From time to time also he balked them by a sudden effort of the will, as by lifting them suddenly in the middle of an unfinished sentence and clos-

* *Ibid.*

ing the book. To mortify his *hearing* he exerted no control over his voice which was then breaking, neither sang nor whistled and made no attempt to flee from noise which caused him painful nervous irritation such as the sharpening of knives on the knifeboard, the gathering of cinders on the fireshovel and the twigging of the carpet. To mortify his *smell* was more difficult as he found in himself no instinctive repugnance to bad odours, whether they were the odours of the outdoor world such as those of dung or tar or the odours of his own person among which he had made many curious comparisons and experiments. He found in the end that the only odour against which his sense of smell revolted was a certain stale fishy stink like that of longstanding urine: and whenever it was possible he subjected himself to this unpleasant odour. To mortify the *taste* he practised strict habits at table, observed to the letter all the fasts of the church and sought by distraction to divert his mind from the savours of different foods. But it was to the mortification of *touch* that he brought the most assiduous ingenuity of inventiveness. He never consciously changed his position in bed, sat in the most uncomfortable position, suffered patiently every itch and pain, kept away from the fire, remained on his knees all through the mass except at the gospels, left parts of his neck and face undried so that air might sting them and, whenever he was not saying his beads, carried his arms stiffly at his sides like a runner and never in his pockets or clasped behind him.

He had *no temptations to sin mortally.* It surprised him, however, to find that at the end of his course of intricate piety and selfrestraint he was so easily at the mercy of *childish and unworthy imperfections.* His prayers and fasts availed him little for the suppression of *anger* at hearing his mother sneeze or at being disturbed in his devotions. It needed an immense effort of his will to master the impulse which urged him to give outlet to such irritation. [Italics added.]*

What the artist so lucidly describes is only vaguely remembered by the average adult; most often, the emotional vagaries of the youthful mind and body are lost to consciousness. Only the artist keeps open to preconsciousness the full range and depth of the affective and factual experiences of his total existence. Usually, memories of the adolescent period become vague at the close of adolescence, buried under an amnestic veil. Facts are remembered well, but the affective side of the experience cannot be clearly recalled. Repression takes over at the decline of the resuscitated oedipus complex as it once did before at the close of the oedipal phase. However, at the close of the oedipal phase, the memory of facts—the concreteness of the where, when, how, and who—is preferentially obliterated or given a false front, as it were, in the form of screen memories, while the feeling states are more easily available to memory recall. At the close of adolescence, the opposite is true: the recall of af-

* *Ibid.*

fects is obstructed, they fall into an amnestic limbo, while facts remain accessible to consciousness. We shall return to this topic in the discussion of the ego in adolescence.

It appears that the defenses of asceticism and intellectualization are particularly typical for European youth, where they were originally studied. This fact is an example of the way in which culture influences the formation of defenses, especially so during adolescence, when the individual turns away from the family to find his place in society at large. The European educated middle-class, for example, has always put an emphatic premium on intellectual exertions of a philosophical, speculative, analytical, and theoretical nature; the world of peers and adults looks favorably on such endeavors, endows them, so to say, with a preferential value. The same may be said for asceticism. Both these defenses are determined by the child's educational experiences and the suggestive influences of the milieu. Since both these defenses represent a composite of defense mechanisms, it should not surprise us that the particular arrangement of the composite is flexible and susceptible to influences of the environment. The American psychoanalyst does not find an equal prevalence of these defenses in their classical forms in the American adolescent.

From my own experience with American adolescents I have recognized another rather widespread defense which no doubt has its roots in the American family structure—and in particular, the social attitudes favored by American society. I refer to the tendency of the adolescent to resort to accepting a code of behavior in a way which permits him to divorce feeling from action in the ego's struggle against the drives and against infantile object ties. The sexual drive is not denied in this defensive maneuver; to the contrary, it is affirmed, but it is codified through actions which bear the mark of standard peer behavior. Under group pressure toward conformity the gap between genuine emotion and standardized, peer-licensed behavior is widened; the result is that the inner perception of what constitutes manageable stimulation is dulled. Motivation resides in being equal in outward behavior to others, or in living up to a group norm. This goes beyond imitation; its eventual result is an emotional shallowness or sentimentalism due to the overemphasis of the action component in the interplay between self and environment. The drive seems to lose its danger through being shunted into competitive and uniform performance, which in turn favors narcissism due to the inhibited flow of object libido. Group formation is strengthened by the very fact that the greatest source of security lies in the shared code of what constitutes adequate behavior and in the dependency on mutual recognition of sameness.

I call this defense so prevalent in American youth *uniformism*. It is a group phenomenon which protects the individual within the group against anxiety, from any quarter. The boy or girl who does not fit into the particular uniformism which is established by a given group is usually considered a threat; as such, he is avoided, ridiculed, ostracized, or condescendingly tolerated.

Readily recognizable in uniformism are several defense mechanisms, such as identification, denial, and isolation; it also has a counterphobic quality, which appears as a rushing into danger, with the triumphant prediction, "There's nothing to it!" This defense seems responsible for the reaction of young visiting Europeans who gain the impression that the American adolescent is highly regulated in his social forms by obligatory behavior, and follows the adolescent group code for an unusually long time. Uniformism is conditioned by a value order which is modeled along these lines: "The sooner the better, the bigger the better, the faster the better." Individual differences and emotional readinesses are to a large extent ignored in a rush toward self-assertion and equalization which gives a false impression of early maturity. The rush into precocious standardized behavior shortcircuits differentiation and individuality and thus prepares the ground for problems of identity. This condition is adverse to the idealism of youth, to its dedication to knowledge and inquiry, to its revolutionary spirit which desires to improve and reform the world; instead formalism is seen as the safeguard of security. In part this is an answer to a question which Spiegel (1958) asked: ". . . whether there are cultural forces in our country which tend to interfere with the adolescent process, with the establishment of genital primacy, object love and a firm sense of self." (See Chapter VI, Environmental Determinants.)

I shall now illustrate the transformation of a defensive process into an adaptive one during the course of the analysis of a fourteen-year-old boy.

The case abstract shows the simultaneous use of several defense mechanisms loosely or tightly amalgamated but all bent on one purpose, namely to bind anxiety. In this case, broadly speaking, I shall analyze the emergence of an interest, an interest in history, and show how this intellectual pursuit derived its pertinacity from an infantile fixation; furthermore, the interest was related to the pubertal struggle against the instincts and infantile object ties, and last, but not least, was used for the mastery of anxiety and to establish continuity in ego experience. This fragment from an analysis also serves to illustrate how more than one defense mechanism—in this case both denial and regression—intertwine in the total mental effort and become recognizable in the intensity and quality of an intellectual interest, an interest which serves infantile needs and on account of this lasting fixation fails to render any genuine, *i.e.*, ego-syntonic satisfaction.

Tom, a fourteen-year-old boy of unusual intelligence was inhibited, depressive, and plump; he was given to mental rumination and solitary interests. He spent hours in playing alone an intricate game of war with poker chips or pennies in which the weaker one of the contestants, after many threats of annihilation, always finally emerged as the victor. Many versions of this game were worked out; for example, the conquest of an archipelago by a brave hero whose people were driven out by a ruthless warrior chief to a small island from which finally a daring invasion was launched that ended in the destruction of the enemy. This game relieved apprehension and anxiousness by its denial that the weak one will ever be destroyed; there was always still hope. The origin of these games reached back into the phase of preadolescence when it represented the theme of castration anxiety in relation to the preoedipal mother.

The analysis of the interest in history as a defense started when Tom read a book on Greek history in school. He complained angrily about the incompleteness of the information it contained. What he wanted to know was, "what happened *after* the destruction" of a civilization. "Where is it then? What happened to the people? Do they just disappear? Of course not. History never gives a full answer." The effort to penetrate and understand the past proved futile; Tom found that history books always stopped short of telling it all, and reading them became disappointing and irritating. The pastime of doing crossword puzzles did not relieve the boy's tension for long. Suddenly he wanted to "buy something big," but he ended up by playing with his old electric train, which he had not set up for years. This also proved a joyless occupation because the thought forced itself on his mind that he was "wasting his time." At this point he turned against mankind and against teachers in particular. Everybody was declared stupid. Tom hated all people, but especially his friend "who is only good for talking about girls and sex." A depressed mood took possession of him once more, and he returned to his old solitary war games. But these games also no longer suited him. The symmetrical arrangement of the chips, the methodical and neat execution of the battle made him annoyed with himself and he exclaimed in despair, "Oh, I'm so orderly, it's nauseating."

Tom finally returned to the theme of history. "What happened with Athens and Babylon *after* the invasion? I have wondered about this since the fourth grade. I know that Babylon lies between the Euphrates and Tigris, but exactly where? I never found out *exactly*. Why didn't they tell you? By the way, Babylon always made me think of 'Baby.'" Analyst: "A lone baby." "Well, I was five years old when my nurse left me." As a child he had been deeply attached to the nurse, and after the separation he developed a nervous cough which used to wake him from sleep in the middle of the night. He would then go to his parents' bedroom; there his mother would serve him hot cocoa, which stopped the coughing. The child finally went to sleep between his parents. We are reminded of Baby-lon, lying between two protective rivers.

Tom was carried away by a review of his personal history. There were three phases in his life as he saw it, separated by two cataclysmic breaks. He lived presently in his third phase, adolescence. The first break came when he was five years old and his nurse left; this brought early childhood to a traumatic close. The next break came when he moved from Baltimore to New York at the age of eight. "This move," he said, "was the greatest catastrophe; it was the decline and fall of Rome. All my baby things had disappeared." He then enumerated all the lost toys and trinkets, accusing his mother of having pillaged his possessions. His anger was enormous, and with an archeologist's zest he reconstructed the content of his toy chest down to a "small toy soldier or Indian who had lost an arm." He reassembled in his mind the bookshelf of his nursery and recalled the appearance and state of disrepair of each precious item. This stubborn search for the past, *à la recherche du temps perdu,* we recognize as an endeavor to relive the past, to reconstruct his personal history in order to penetrate into the dark stretches of time. The adolescent updrift of the libidinal and aggressive impulses directed toward the oedipal parent were, in Tom's case, mastered by their attachment to thought processes. Infantile inquisitiveness became displaced and diverted toward historical investigations. This intellectual activity, however, could only for short stretches of time avert the recurrence of angry and depressed moods and affects he had experienced in childhood and which now at puberty attached themselves to the defense of intellectualization, rendering it only partially successful.

Tom took a new stab at the historical problem. He now wanted to trace the whole panorama of human migrations, conquests, annihilation of nations, and destruction of empires. What they all had in common was the fact that these violent dislocations had led to a "mixture between conqueror and conquered," culminating in the "birth of a new tribe." Tom embarked on this ambitious project by making a large-scale drawing of the Mediterranean "cradle of civilization." He placed the various peoples on the map, each "tribe" being represented by a piece of cardboard. He then went through historical times, moving populations around. When he became excited and too engrossed in his project he felt guilty and self-accusatory: "I shouldn't be doing this"—that is witnessing the battle of contestants and the birth of new tribes. However, he continued with the project. When he finally reached contemporary history, American soldiers of World War II mixed with "sexy women" in Italy and started new tribes. Sexual associations became more frequent until the gap in history, his personal history, was filled in. This was made possible through reconstruction from the material of primal scene fantasies, sadomasochistic concepts of intercourse, oedipal guilt, ambivalent identifications with both parents, fear of the phallic mother, depression following the separation from the nurse. Finally, history had told the whole story.

The personal historical themes gave world history a decisive persistence and fascination for Tom; they also accounted for the sense of dissatisfaction which accompanied its pursuit. The dysphoria, dissatisfaction, futility, anger, and depression yielded to the analysis of the defensive struggle, but still the interest in history survived; however, its pursuit became rewarding and conflict-free. The historical interest was disengaged from the instinctual fixation and thus was able to advance to the status of an autonomous intellectual activity. It must be remembered that by the time the analysis dealt with Tom's intellectualization, he had already become quite a historian, with a wide knowledge of facts. These facts, to be true, often represented apparently meaningless mental exercises; for instance, the pedantic memorization of the entire lineage of the kings of France. This defensive preoccupation with mere facts gave way to an appreciation and grasp of the larger human issues which the study of history entails. An interest which operated in the service of defense had changed into an adaptive activity, socially and personally meaningful and rewarding, no longer involving the necessary expenditure of countercathectic energy. This transformation promoted in Tom's case a forward movement of the libido. The economy of the ego was affected in terms of a forceful turn to reality, to rational thinking, and to objective observation. An increase in self-esteem followed the ability to master knowledge without guilt.

At the phase of adolescence proper, when the oedipal conflict moves toward its resolution, the withdrawal of libido from the parent "may become attached to the adolescent's body only and give rise there to the hypochondriacal sensations and feelings of body changes that are well known clinically from initial stages of psychotic illness" (A. Freud, 1958, a). Helene Deutsch (1944) emphasizes the role of fantasy in the adolescent process of the girl and describes the conditions in which imagination is experienced as real. If the libidinal attachment to an incestuous object is re-experienced not in relation to a new object but in fantasy only, so that the adolescent remains unconsciously faithful to the early object, then former reality will endow the present love fantasy with the character of reality. "During puberty every reality that might gratify sexual wishes may appear dangerous, and a regression to fantasy and pseudology takes place. Pseudology is used as a defense; the adolescent girl takes her fantasy for reality in order to renounce a reality that she regards as perhaps more dangerous" (Deutsch, 1944).

Children who develop severe superego anxiety during their upbringing are apt to flout all rules at one phase of their adolescence; they are unwilling to make compromises lest weakness and submission once more declare themselves. This is the "uncompromising" adolescent, described by Anna Freud (1958, a). The more moderate adolescent preserves an adherence to a moral code as long as it is of his own choosing and making. Old bottles are filled with new wine. Self-chosen principles of conduct show significant departures from parental discipline, but just the same preserve the modality of discipline in the often revolutionary innovations in morality and ethics.

An example of this step in superego transformation occurred in a fifteen-year-old boy with compulsive-obsessive controls who had reached a more tolerant acceptance of his sexual and especially of his aggressive impulses during analysis. One day he announced that he had developed a new philosophy: "I am a changed boy." His philosophy was made up of "axioms" which were based on the following proposition: "Since I must go on living I might as well enjoy it." Six axioms regulated the conduct of his life: "1) If I am afraid of somebody I say 'to hell with you' and I do as I please. 2) Don't brag so much. 3) Don't eat so much. 4) Don't masturbate so much. Number 2, 3, 4 are of no importance when I have a girl friend. 5) Do unexpected things at unaccustomed times. 6) Endure mother's tirades and don't let her make you lose your control." After the recitation of the axioms, he added, "Please, note that my axioms, at least the important ones, do not say 'do this and not that,' but they say 'don't do this too much, or do this more.' While abstinence is good for me, no axiom says to abstain. Do you realize what difference that makes?" He concluded with a remark of jocular self-irony: "Of course, I don't know how long all this will last. But it makes me feel great."

The various defensive measures employed during adolescence proper are under normal circumstances temporary emergency measures. They are dispensed with as soon as the ego has gained strength from joining forces with the forward movement of the libido toward heterosexuality, as soon as anxiety and guilt have diminished through internal cathectic shifts. From a behavioral or social point of view, this development can be described in terms of adaptive accommodations in consonance or selective correspondency with existing social institutions. In contemporary society this process requires time and is necessarily slow. We know that a chronologically earlier consummation of adult status occurred in the not too distant past; but there are intrinsic difficulties in interpreting these facts, since the societal provisions which allow the adolescent process to evolve by transactional experiences, take different shapes at different historical times (Erikson, 1946). What occurred in tradition-bound, class-structured adolescence a hundred years ago when early marriage was customary and the adolescent process evolved partly within the confines of that institution, we cannot say with certainty. I will explore this point further in a discussion of environmental determinants, in which the different "stopping places," as it were, are viewed in terms of the interrelation between individual development and culture. In today's Western world, there are two dangers of adolescence proper; namely, the rush into heterosexuality at the expense of personality differentiation, and the massive repression of sexual impulses with a consequent character deformation and deviate emotional development.

The decisive progress in emotional development during adolescence proper lies in the progress toward heterosexuality. This stage can only be reached after the pregenital drives have been relegated to an initiatory and subordinate role in favor of genital sexuality or orgastic potency.

Forepleasure is an innovation of puberty; it involves a hierarchical arrangement of genital and pregenital drives. As it did earlier in psychosexual development, the ego again takes its cue from the dominant organization of the drives; and at adolescence proper a parallel hierarchical organization of ego functions appears. A higher order of thinking, recognizable in the development of theories and systems, emerges; consequently, a more discerning order is assigned to percepts. Furthermore, there is a progressive awareness of the relevancy of one's actions to one's present and future role and place in society. The choice of vocation—whether it is engineering or motherhood—requires the relegation of some ego models, ego ideals, possible selves, to subordinate positions. Adolescence proper is the phase during which these stratificatory processes are initiated. During late adolescence they assume a definitive structure. Whenever delay or failure occurs in the hierarchical organization of sexual impulses, there is a delay or failure in corresponding, phase-adequate ego development. Autoplastic alterations such as "splitting of the ego," or "ego deformations" often fail at this early stage to reveal the extent to which the phase-adequate drive organization of adolescence proper has miscarried.

Inhelder and Piaget (1958) studied adolescent thinking in its typical form; their findings bear out this correlative development of "affective life" and "cognitive processes," or drive and ego, to which I am referring. For Inhelder and Piaget it is the "assumption of adult roles" that "involves a total restructuring of the personality in which intellectual transformations are parallel or complementary to the affective transformations." Some of these findings are closely related to my concept of a hierarchical arrangement of ego functions in adolescence. The adolescent "begins to consider himself as the equal of adults and to judge them"; he "begins to think of the future—i.e., of his present or future work in society"; he also "has the idea of changing this sociey." "The adolescent differs from the child above all in that he thinks beyond the present"; he "commits himself to possibilities."

"The adolescent is the individual who begins to build 'systems' or 'theories' in the largest sense of the term. The child does not build systems. . . . The child has no such powers of reflection—i.e., no second-order thoughts which deal critically with his own thinking. No theory can be built without such reflection. In contrast, the adolescent is able to analyze his own thinking and construct theories." This corresponds to the formulation that thinking as trial action becomes, at adolescence, a mode of dealing with the interaction between individual and environment, present and future. Thinking as trial action is in adolescence constantly interfered with by the proclivity to action and acting out. The scope of trial and error becomes enlarged in abstract thought, which eventually becomes formalized in systems and theories. These constructs serve the purpose of furnishing "the cognitive and evaluative bases for the assumption of adult roles. They are vital in the assimilation of the values which delineate societies or social classes as entities in contrast to simple inter-individual relations." Spiegel (1958) has shown that "one type of conceptual thinking, i.e., aesthetic develops at this time."

Inhelder and Piaget (1958) make the point that in the development of thinking the adolescent recapitulates the different stages of the child's development "on the planes of thought and reality new to formal operations." As always, they move from egocentrism toward decentering. The egocentrism which is observed in adolescent thought processes has been described as adolescent narcissism. It precedes the turn to new object relations, corresponding to Piaget's concept of decentering. Decentering promotes "objectivity," decentering is "a continual refocusing of perspective." In the decentering process the adolescent's entrance into the occupational world represents the focal point. "The job leads thinking away from the dangers of formalism back into reality." "Decentering takes place simultaneously in thought processes and in social relationships." What has been referred to as the hierarchical arrangement of ego functions can be described in relation to cognitive functions as the progression from formal structure in adolescent thinking as part of his egocentrism to the objectivity of thought which decentering, namely the analysis of facts, promotes. "Observation shows how laborious and slow this reconciliation of thought and experiences can be." "In conclusion," Inhelder and Piaget state, "the fundamental affective acquisitions of adolescence parallel the intellectual acquisitions. To understand the role of formal structures of thought in the life of the adolescent, we found that in the last analysis we had to place them in his total personality."

The remarkable achievements of the adolescent in the realm of thinking and his equally unusual artistic creativity have been documented and studied over some years (Bernfeld, 1924). The striking decline of this often astonishing creativity at the close of adolescence makes it apparent that it is a function of the adolescent process. The heightened introspection or psychological closeness to internal processes in conjunction with a distance from outer objects allow the adolescent a freedom of experience and an access to his feelings which promote a state of delicate sensitivity and perceptiveness. Adolescent artistic productions are often undisguisedly autobiographical and reach their height during phases of libidinal withdrawal from the object world, or at times of aim-inhibited love, either homosexual and heterosexual. The creative productivity thus represents an effort to accomplish urgent tasks of internal transformations. The cathexis of thought and introspection permits a concentration and dedication to the creative process of thought and imagery that is almost unknown before or after in the life of the average individual. The process of creativity in adolescence enhances infatuation with the self; it is often accompanied by excitement and carries the conviction of being a chosen and special person.

The sublimated creative activity can be described in these essential terms: 1) it is highly self-centered, that is, narcissistic; 2) it is subordinated to the limitations of an artistic medium, and consequently is partially reality oriented; 3) it operates within the modality of "giving life to a new existence," the self; 4) it constitutes a communication with the environment and is, therefore, partially object related. Adolescent creative activity is a complex process, the component parts of which can either work together in relative harmony or else be dominated by one creative component entirely. Thus creativity can gratify narcissistic needs, it can afford a hold on reality, it can replace object love, or it can prepare the channeling of an innate gift into an enduring way of life. Observation has shown that the flourish of creative productivity is by and large restricted to the adolescent of the educated classes; but it must be emphasized that the adolescent who shuns the delay of education and endeavors to reach adulthood via the shortest possible route nevertheless shares in this creative process by borrowing readymade imagery and stereotyped emotions from mass media, like movies and magazines. These stereotypes fulfill his purposes on a very primitive level, to be sure; but they are functionally similar to the creative acts observed in more sophisticated and differentiated adolescents. Spiegel (1958) expressed the opinion that the "creativity of adolescence may be linked indirectly to cathectic oscillations," namely, to the "fluidity of cathectic displacements from self—to object representations. . . . Through artistic creation, what is self may become object and then externalized, and thus may help to establish a balance of narcissistic and object cathexes."

The description of adolescence proper involves a detailed consideration of so many separate aspects that a summary may prove useful at this point. It is apparent that, in terms of drive organization, adolescence proper marks an advance to the heterosexual position; or rather, this organization, while still incomplete, gains in clarity and irreversibility. Toward this end, object libido becomes turned outward again, this time toward nonincestuous objects of the opposite sex; concomitantly, narcissism declines. The turn to new love objects reactivates oedipal fixations, both positive and negative. The disengagement process from the oedipal parent gives this phase of adolescence its special countenance. The sex-adequate task of this phase resides in the elaboration of femininity and masculinity; again, this process is in no way completed, but awaits final consolidation in subsequent phases. However, both the special way in which pregenitality becomes relegated to forepleasure, and the particular way in which oedipal conflicts reach a resolution or compromise portend a drive organization which will operate within highly idiosyncratic confines.

The ego during adolescence proper initiates defensive measures, restitutive processes, and adaptive accommodations. Their choice shows greater individual variation than may be discerned in previous phases, a fact which foreshadows their ultimate selective influence on the formation of character. Furthermore, hierarchical arrangements of ego functions appear, modeled after the emerging drive organization. Cognitive processes become more objective and analytical; the realm of the reality principle increases. The hierarchical innovation in itself brings into prominence distinct interests, capacities, skills, and talents, which are experimentally tested for their usefulness and reliability in the maintenance of self-esteem; thus a vocational choice solidifies or at least makes its voice heard. Late adolescence brings an entirely new quality into this realm of strivings toward possible selves.

In general terms we can say that adolescence proper comes to a close with the delineation of an idiosyncratic conflict and drive constellation which during late adolescence is transformed into a unified and integrated system. Adolescence proper elaborates a core of internal strife which resists adolescent transformations; conflicts and disequilibrating forces move into sharp focus. It is the task of late adolescence to arrive at a final settlement which the young person subjectively feels to be "my way of life." The disquieting question so often posed by adolescents,

"Who am I?" recedes slowly into oblivion. During late adolescence a positive, more self-evident clarity of purpose and awareness of the self emerges which can best be described by the words: "This is me." Such a declaratory statement is rarely if ever spoken aloud; but it is expressed through the particular life the individual leads or takes for granted at the time adolescence comes to a close. We shall now turn to a discussion of this period, which brings about the termination of the adolescent process.

6. Late Adolescence

The closing phase of adolescence has long been taken for granted, and thought of as a natural decline in the turmoil of growing up. The analogy which Freud (1924) used with reference to the passing of the oedipus complex might also be applied to the adolescent process: that it has to come to an end for phylogenetic reasons, that it "must come to an end because the time has come for its dissolution, just as the milk teeth fall out when the permanent ones begin to press forward." However, Freud (1924) also discussed ontogenetic determinants, which are of equal importance. The reasons for and the ways by which adolescence is brought to its termination reveal that the psychological aspects are the only ones in terms of which we may define the closing phase of adolescence. As we have said earlier: pubescence is an act of nature; adolescence is an act of man.

The closing phase of adolescence has attracted more attention during the last decade than the turbulence of the antecedent phases. From experience we know that with the decline of adolescence the individual registers gains in purposeful action, social integration, predictability, constancy of emotions, and stability of self-esteem. In general we are impressed by the greater unification of affective and volitional processes, the amenability to compromise and delay. Another important characteristic of late adolescence is the delineation of those concerns which really matter in life, which do not tolerate compromise nor postponement. These concerns do not always serve an obvious self-interest, since they often result in frustration, struggle, and pain; but regardless of the consequences, the young adult adheres to certain choices which, he feels at the time, are the only avenues to his self-realization. One has the impression that the individual's life, seen in perspective, shows distinct continuities which extend from adolescence into adulthood, as well as discontinuities which in fact mark the upper boundary line of late adolescence. The question, then, is: what processes are at work in the evolution of those novel personality attributes which characterize the advance to adulthood or the decline of adolescence? Another question concerns the conditions that account for the elements of continuity and sameness so familiar to the student of life histories. The clinician will add a third question: what is the particular psychopathology which represents the miscarriage of late adolescence and what is the etiology of these developmental failures? The events that bring a developmental phase to a close seem more difficult to identify than those that bring it into existence. These theoretical problems of the closing phase of adolescence will now be discussed.

Late adolescence is primarily a phase of consolidation. By this I mean the elaboration of: 1) a highly idiosyncratic and stable arrangement of ego functions and interests; 2) an extension of the conflict-free sphere of the ego (secondary autonomy); 3) an irreversible sexual position (identity constancy), summarized as genital primacy; 4) a relatively constant cathexis of object- and self-representations; and 5) the stabilization of mental apparatuses which automatically safeguard the integrity of the psychic organism. This process of consolidation relates to psychic structure and content, the former establishing unification of the ego, and the latter preserving continuity within it; the former shaping character, the latter providing the wherewithals, as it were. Each component influences the other in terms of a feedback system until during postadolescence an equilibrium is reached within certain limits of intrinsic constancy. The threshold of vulnerability shows gross individual differences, since conflict and anxiety tolerance vary enormously. The amount and intensity of stimuli (external and internal) necessary for effective functioning also reveal individual variability, a fact which is not without influence on the emerging ego organization at the time of late adolescence. "There is perhaps an 'optimum' degree of anxiety (varying from individual to individual) which favors development; more or less than this optimum may hinder it" (Brierley, 1951). The same might be said for the maintenance of a stable ego organization; namely, that an optimum of tension is of positive value, giving, as it were, tonus to the personality. I am speaking about general integrative processes: ego-synthesis, patterning, and channeling. In terms of the total psychic organism and its functioning, this refers to character and personality formation.

We might construct a model of late adolescence; but, if we did, it would have to be borne in mind that the transformations described above are attained only partially by any individual. It seems, indeed, that the compromise aspect of late adolescence is an integral part of this phase; the achievement is one of relative maturity. It is well to recall Freud's (1937) words in this connection: "In reality transitional and intermediate stages are far more common than sharply differentiated opposite states. In studying various developments and changes we focus our attention entirely on the result and we readily overlook the fact that such processes are usually more or less incomplete, that is to say, the changes that take place are only partial. . . . There are almost always vestiges of what has been and a partial arrest at a former stage." It seems, then, that the specific "residual phenomena and the partial retardations" account in large measure for the variations in individualization which emerge at the close of adolescence. These aspects, because they are more in evidence in the adult, may be studied better during that stage. What needs emphasis here is the fact that the developmental task of late adolescence resides precisely in the elaboration of a unified ego which fuses in its exercise the "partial retardations" with stable expressions through work, love, and ideology, eliciting social articulation as well as recognition. "Everything a person possesses or achieves, every remnant of the primitive feeling of omnipotence which his experience has confirmed, helps to increase his self-regard" (Freud, 1914).

Late adolescence is a decisive turning point, and consequently is a time of crisis. Here, in fact, resides the final adolescent crisis which so often overtaxes the integrative capacity of the individual and results in adaptive failures, ego deformations, defensive maneuvers, and severe psychopathology. Erikson (1956) has extensively reported on the latter in terms of an "identity crisis." I have described the syndrome of prolonged adolescence (1954) in terms of a reluctance to bring the last phase of childhood, namely adolescence, to a close. Failures in successfully traversing late adolescence have forcefully brought to our attention the tasks of this phase. It has happened many times in the history of psychoanalysis that deviate development has thrown light on normal development; one of these instances has been the study of the failures of late adolescence, which has helped to formulate its phase-specific task.

The phases of adolescence described above fit well into psychoanalytic theory. But with regard to the closing phase of adolescence, concepts such as fixation, defense mechanisms, ego synthesis, sublimation and adaptation, bisexuality, masculinity and femininity—while all involved in the process—are not in themselves either sufficient or adequate to make the phenomenon of personality consolidation at late adolescence comprehensible. Analytical observation has isolated some of the obstacles which stand in the way of progressive consolidation, such as fixations of instincts, discontinuities in ego development, identification problems, and bisexuality; however, the path along which personality consolidation proceeds remains in many respects obscure. Integrative processes are more silent than disintegrative ones.

The phases of adolescence bring into play the drives in their various regressive and progressive constellations or phase-specific organizations. In fact, we might say that all through adolescence the ego is in most intimate involvement—even if defensively—with the drives, and has, along the way, selectively come to terms with their intensity, their objects, and their aims. It was noted above that no progression from one phase of adolescence to the next is ever accomplished without carrying forward "residual phenomena." It must now be added that these residues retain a stubborn buoyancy; only during times of relative calm in adult life do they ever come under complete ego mastery. For instance, the problem of bisexuality is never resolved in terms of its disappearance: it yields to certain accommodations and ego-syntonic dominances. Its continued existence in the unconscious is attested to by the common occurrence of this theme in the dream life of adults.

Shall we assume that repression is the major agent which ushers in adulthood, as previously at the close of the oedipal phase this very defense mechanism and its sequelae initiated the latency period? Obviously this is too simple a solution; it certainly does not offer any explanation for the great variability of individual adaptations or settlements apparent at the close of adolescence. What we must find is an operational principle, a dynamic concept, which governs the consolidation process of late adolescence and renders its various forms comprehensible: first, the psychic apparatus which synthesizes the various phase-specific adolescent processes, renders them stable, irreversible, and gives them an adaptive potential; second, the source of the specific residues from earlier developmental periods which have survived adolescent transformations and which continue to exist in derivative form, contributing their share to character formation; and finally, the source of the energy which pushes certain solutions into the foreground and leaves others in abeyance, thus lending the consolidation process a quality of decisiveness and individuality. These qualities, which often bring about sacrifice and pain, cannot wholly derive from the maturational push; I suspect that other forces combine their efforts within this process.

The concept of trauma must be introduced at this point. The term *trauma* is a relative one; and the effect of any particular trauma depends both on the magnitude and suddenness of the stimulus, and on the vulnerability of the psychic apparatus. Trauma is a universal phenomenon of childhood. Whether trauma is caused by a constitutional or an environmental too-much or too-little has no bearing on the effect of the trauma in individual life. Here I want to emphasize only the fact that the mastery of trauma is an unending task of life, as unending as the prevention of its recurrence. This self-protection is commensurate to the strength of the ego and to the stability of defenses. "Of course, no individual makes use of all the possible mechanisms of defence; each person merely selects certain of them, but these become fixated in his ego, establishing themselves as regular modes of reaction for that particular character, which are repeated throughout life whenever a situation occurs similar to that which originally evoked them" (Freud, 1937).

On the other hand, the aftereffects of a trauma induce life situations which in some way repeat the original one; therefore, the work on the resolution of the trauma, the attempt to master it, will continue. Life experiences springing from this kind of background proceed according to the repetition compulsion. What was originally experienced as a threat from the environment becomes the model of internal danger. In acquiring the status of a model the primal danger had to be replaced by symbolic representations and substitutive equivalents which correspond to the physical and mental development of the growing child. At the close of adolescence the original threat, or rather a component of it, is turned outward again by being activated on the environment; its resolution or quiescence is then sought within a highly specific interaction system. Consequently, the individual experiences his behavior as meaningful, self-evident, urgent, and gratifying.

The progressive mastery of residual traumata determines the prevalent transactional interchange between individual and environment as well as between ego and self. To rid oneself of a noxious influence of the outer world which is precipitated in the trauma and has become part of the inner world remains a psychic task throughout life. A considerable portion of this task is being accomplished during adolescence.

Anna Freud (1952) commented on the possible adolescent "reversal of superego and ego attitudes, though apparently these attitudes had been fully integrated in the ego structure of the latency child." Where new integration is not achieved, persistent ego dystonicity with regard to, for example, certain ego attitudes, bears witness to an only partial adolescent transformation. At any rate, specific unassimilated remnants always reach into adult life; in fact, they exert their claim for continued expression through the personality organization itself.

The extent to which trauma hinders progressive development constitutes the negative factor of the trauma; the extent to which trauma promotes and encourages the mastery of reality is its positive factor. This idea was developed by Freud (1939) in one of his last essays: "The effects of the trauma are two-fold, positive and negative. The former are endeavours to revive the trauma, to remember the forgotten experience, or better still, to make it real—to live through once more a repetition of it; if it was an early affective relationship it is revived in an analogous connection with another person. These endeavours are summed up in the terms 'fixation to the trauma' and 'repetition-compulsion.' The effects can be incorporated into the so-called normal Ego and in the form of constant tendencies lend to it immutable character traits. . . . The negative reactions pursue the opposite aim; here nothing is to be remembered or repeated of the forgotten traumata. They may be grouped together as defensive reactions. They express themselves in avoiding issues, a tendency which may culminate in an inhibition or phobia. These negative reactions also contribute considerably to the formation of character."

Within the problem of character consolidation at the close of adolescence we have to accommodate the problem of trauma as part of the total process. The fixity and irreversibility of character has a favorable effect on psychic economy; like compulsive traits it enlarges the distance between ego and drive. A character trait, then, which forms slowly at the end of adolescence owes its special quality to a fixation on a particular trauma or on a component of a trauma. Through the emotional transformations which adolescence affords, focal traumata, so to say, remain resistive to the adolescent "working over"; they give the consolidating process of late adolescence a selective affinity to certain choices. In addition, they furnish a relentless force which propels the young adult toward a certain way of life which he comes to feel is his very own.

Remnants of traumata fully relate the present to a dynamically active past, and establish that historical continuity in the ego which accounts for a sense of certainty, direction, and harmony between feeling and action. A young patient who had broken down during late adolescence said, when he felt the impact of his rediscovered past on his changing sense of self, "It seems that one can only have a future if one also has a past."

One might ask why a recourse to instinct and ego fixation is not enough to make the specificity of choices and definitive arrangements of ego, superego, and drive claims of late adolescence comprehensible. Fixation aims at the maintenance of a static position; it resists change. However, the positive aspect of trauma lies in the fact that it exerts a relentless push toward coming to terms with its noxious residues through ceaselessly reactivating it on the environment. There is no doubt that drive and ego fixations enter into the consolidation of character and contribute their share to the organization of personality; but among the various components which are unified by integration, a given fixation is merely one of many aspects.

Returning to the questions asked before, it is obvious that the psychic institution where the consolidation of the adolescent process occurs is the ego (ego synthesis). Fixations provide the specificity of choices in terms of libidinal needs, prevalent identifications, and favored fantasies. Residual traumata furnish the force (repetition compulsion) which pushes unintegrated experiences into the mental life for eventual mastery or ego integration. The *direction* this process takes—its preferential emphasis on drive discharge, sublimation, defense, ego deformation, and so on—is to a large extent controlled by superego and ego-ideal influences. The *form* this process takes is influenced by the environment, by social institutions, tradition, mores, and value systems. Obviously, the entire process operates within the confines set by constitutional factors, such as physical and mental endowment.

We come, then, to the conclusion that infantile conflicts are not removed at the close of adolescence, but they are rendered specific, they become ego-syntonic, i.e. they become integrated within the realm of the ego as life tasks. They become centered within the adult self-representations. Every attempt at ego-syntonic mastery of a residual trauma, often experienced as conflict, enhances self-esteem. The stabilization of self-esteem is one of the major achievements of adulthood. "Self-esteem is the emotional expression of self-evaluation and the corresponding libidinous or aggressive cathexis of the self-representations. . . . Self-esteem does not necessarily reflect the tension between superego and ego. Broadly defined, self-esteem expresses the discrepancy between or accordance of the wishful concept of the self and the self-representations" (Jacobson, 1953). It becomes a lifelong effort of the ego to re-establish this accordance and remove discrepancy by judicious interaction with the environment.

This schematic presentation is drawn as a model of the last phase of adolescence; as such, it does not do justice to the many problems which adolescence arouses. In terms of the whole adolescent period, we may say that the adolescent process assumes increasingly individualistic features, which in adolescence proper reach a peak in the revival of the oedipal conflict and the establishment of forepleasure with its effect on ego organization. The resolution of the resuscitated oedipus complex during the adolescent period is at best partial. The part which resisted adolescent resolution becomes the core of a continued effort toward this end; it proceeds within the confines of personal choices, such as work, values, loyalties, love. What we observe at the close of adolescence is a self-limiting process, a staking out of a life space which affords movement only within a restricted psychological area. Those elements of sameness and continuity which embrace childhood, adolescence, and adult life point to the fact that the new mental formation which has now taken shape perpetuates familiar, antecedent trends within the adult personality.

We are reminded here of the oedipal phase at which the residues of previous phases were worked, so to say, into the genital modality. The decline of the oedipus complex leads to compromise formations, but foremost to a decisive structuring of a psychic institution, the superego. During adolescence proper the conflict and dilemma solutions of the oedipus complex, inclusive of pregenital fixations, are again transposed into the genital modality, this time searching for accommodations within the realm of nonincestuous heterosexuality. Failures at this task lead to dissociative processes and result in pathological outcomes. But beyond the reorganization of drives which is characteristic for adolescence proper, there remain oedipal remnants that were not carried along the path of object love. Late adolescence involves the transformation of these oedipal residues into ego modalities. The importance of work for the libido economy was clearly stated by Freud (1930): "Laying stress upon importance of work has a greater effect than any other technique of living in the direction of binding the individual more closely to reality; in his work he is at least securely attached to a part of reality, the human community. Work is no less valuable for the opportunity it and the human relations connected with it provide for a very considerable discharge of libidinal component impulses, narcissistic, aggressive and even erotic, than it is indispensable for subsistence and justifies existence in a society."

Highly idiosyncratic ego interests and preferential cathexes at late adolescence constitute a new attainment in the life of the individual. By the same token, the self-representations assume a stable and dependable fixity. The phase-specific definition of late adolescence could well be formulated in these terms. Freud's statement that the heir of the oedipus complex is the superego might be paraphrased by saying that the heir of adolescence is the self. (For a discussion of the concept of the self, see Chapter V, *The Ego in Adolescence*.)

To demonstrate by clinical example the consolidation process of late adolescence requires recounting a life history. Since this is the best way of illustrating the concepts I have developed, with reference to the closing phase of adolescence, I shall now draw in broad outline the relevant psychological development of an individual. The data are based on memory and reconstruction in the analysis of a thirty-five-year-old man; the analysis of the adolescent period played a prominent role in the treatment of this patient's character neurosis.

John was a younger son; his brother was five years his senior. From birth John was the mother's favorite; she saw in the child the fulfillment of her own artistic dreams. Everything contributed to a fixation on the passive-receptive level. Both mother and nurse indulged him. The boy talked and walked rather late, was given to dreaming and solitary play. As soon as he was able to walk, he ran and became quite independent. He felt keenly the competition with the older brother whose competence he envied. In this struggle John learned to take advantage of his engaging nature, which made him a favorite with women. His reliance on pleasing women and avoiding men (father, brother), in conjunction with the early realization of the advantages of his handsomeness, were his prototypic techniques for avoiding unpleasure; he elaborated upon them through three decades. With these weapons he defeated his strongwilled brother and pushed him out of their mother's affection. This stratagem of dealing with a male rival by bypassing the encounter never ceased to operate in analogous situations.

John's early childhood, then, showed a fixation on the passive-receptive oral modality. Submissive surrender of the body orifices and their
control followed easily. Passivity was dominant in the active-passive balance. A period intervened (age three) during which motility (aggressive
drive discharge) was in the ascendancy, but this attempt to overcome the
early passivity came to naught and was succeeded by an exhibitionistic
period in which looks and charm were used as phallic equivalents.
Within this constellation the boy approached the oedipal phase. The
avoidance of competition with the male gave the oedipus complex a
negative designation. The father was feared as well as admired, and to
be loved by him became a secret but lasting and unacceptable longing.
The relationship to the father reached a negative settlement in terms of
an identification avoidance; in relation to the mother, a submissive, narcissistic, and affectionate attachment persisted far into the latency years.

John sidestepped castration anxiety by passive surrender to the phallic
mother. She became the source of anxiety, but by the same token the
provider of safety as long as John lived—or affected to live—in the
image of a promising and special son. Regardless of whether or not he
possessed the means for living up to these vague and exciting expectations, role and pretense soon became the sole guardians of his security
needs. Rivalry with males, already sidestepped earlier in relation to his
brother, suffered a definitive defeat in the struggle with the oedipal
father. Tentative phallic inclinations were quickly overlaid with a sense
of incompetence (castration anxiety) followed by regressive measures:
the passive-receptive organ mode of the oral phase manifested itself at
the oedipal level in a passive-receptive ego mode. His self-image became
molded by imputed qualities and traits; the reality principle spoke with a
barely audible voice.

John's oedipus complex was resolved by sexual repression, the extent
of which only became apparent at adolescence. Besides the restrictive
and inhibiting influences of the father, the superego contained enough
of the mother's narcissistic seduction to be reminiscent of Alexander's
(1929) "corruptibility of the super-ego" through its secret alliance with
the id. The father remained a threatening figure; anxiety dreams (rob-
bers, giants) accompanied and followed the oedipal phase. John surrendered himself into the hands of women—mother, nurse, and their
substitutes—who became the executors of his ego by doing for him what
he was unable to do for himself. He did not hesitate to take credit for

the accomplishments of his understudies. His conscience always had an alibi: he felt he was a special child, an "adopted prince."

This constellation of drive, ego, and superego augured badly for the latency period. Severe learning disturbances developed; they were covered up all through elementary school by a devoted nurse, who learned to imitate the child's handwriting in order to do his homework. His school work was done, and done well, while he played and daydreamed. In a magical way, then, he was able to enter competition without anxiety, without risk of defeat, and without yielding to the reality principle. His brother was an eager learner with a logical, inquisitive and practical mind; but John felt being privileged was superior to working. An influx of narcissistic libido rescued the ego from feelings of insufficiency and incompetence which in essence were derived from castration anxiety. This narcissistic component added to the boy's charm and gave rise to an imaginative but dreamy mind. John was not dull or stupid except in school.

Puberty brought about complete sexual repression. Neither genital sensations nor masturbation were in evidence. A fixation on the preadolescent drive organization lasted throughout adolescence—that is, fear of castration by the phallic mother. Sexual inhibitions were rationalized as avoidance of venereal diseases; actually they were rooted in concepts such as the cloaca and the vagina dentata. The boy went through the typical homosexual period of idealized friendships; then he turned to girls as a "foothold on heterosexuality." His many girl friends were treated with tender love; and no sexual feelings or urges ever tarnished the purity of these attachments.

The fact that John never gave up the narcissistic position accounted for his prolonged adolescence. He finally became an "intellectual" to please his parents; he was able to fulfill educational demands only to a marginal degree, in spite of excellent intelligence. With advancing adolescence he came to show promising artistic talent.

The consolidation process of late adolescence articulated these various trends into an ego-syntonic configuration. John decided to become a teacher of *young* children, and an educator in a very modern way. By choosing this career he first of all avoided competition with his father and brother, both of whom were learned people with advanced degrees. John prided himself on being a rebel, and spurned family traditions by denouncing his educational past. Being a teacher, he argued, would allow him enough time to pursue his artistic endeavors—which represented the secret bond to his mother. Moreover, John's interest in children was decidedly maternal, and offered a sublimated outlet for his feminine, nurturing needs which were rooted in the identification with the active mother. In advocating educational methods contrary to those by which he was educated, John maintained an oppositional tendency which was successfully sublimated. These trends combined to make John a remarkable and successful educator.

The massive sexual repression at puberty eventually led to conversion symptoms, such as digestive disturbances. These gave way under the influence of genital masturbation at the age of nineteen. John's choice of a heterosexual love object was shaped by an obvious dissimilarity to the oedipal mother. John could only love a girl sexually if she were submissive, passive, simple, nonintellectual, and undemanding. The oedipal mother reappeared in John's life in a constant search for and surrender to women who were powerful, because of social position, intellect, fame, or money. In fact, John's dependency on women like this stifled both his professional development and his marriage. When these aspects of his life were threatened by deterioration, he sought psychoanalytic help.

This case summary indicates that John's synthesis of late adolescence was dominated by narcissistic tendencies, and that the fixation on the passive-receptive modality had influenced his ego and drive development. By his vocational choice he attempted to resolve this ego-dystonic position through an identification with the active mother; his opposition to surrender was maintained by his crusading for modern childrearing methods. The identification with children afforded an institutionalized avenue leading toward repair of the infantile ego fragments in "John the educator." The adolescent oedipal conflict was unsuccessfully resolved by dividing the oedipal mother into a degraded object and an overvalued phallic power. John's proclivity to passive receptivity assumed traumatic proportions during the oedipal phase, when phallic surrender destroyed the capacity for masculine competition with his father through identificatory stabilization. The road toward this outcome had already been paved by his fierce jealousy of and admiration for his older brother. The passive homosexual position in relation to the father was more deeply repressed than any other conflict, and a fixation on this libidinal attachment resulted in a defective masculine identity. The dynamic force behind the drive and ego patterning of late adolescence derived from this trauma, and resulted in relentless and endless efforts to master the propensity to passive surrender, or, simply, to come to terms with the oedipal father.

Some comments of a more general nature may be added here. One striking characteristic of late adolescence is not so much its resolution of instinctual conflicts, but rather the incompleteness of the resolution. Addato (1958) in a clinical paper has suggested that the decision of late adolescent patients to terminate analytic treatment coincides with the resolution of the oedipal conflict and the finding of new love objects. This turning point ushers in a "period of homeostasis," a phase of "ego integration which is normal for this period of development." It follows from his material that a "restorative function of the ego" is typical for late adolescence which somewhat resembles its function during the latency period. What I prefer to emphasize is the fact that the structuring of unresolved drive and ego fixations into an organized totality makes, so to say, the most of a bad situation—although this states the problem somewhat lopsidedly. What was a hindrance and an obstacle toward growing up turns out to be precisely what gives grownupness its special countenance. In John's case, the ease with which he was able to identify with children afforded him the opportunity to overhaul and repair his own infantile ego fixations which had been manifested in his humiliating learning disturbance. Consequently, his role as educator became endowed with both dedicated zeal and imaginative creativity, which in turn earned him social as well as professional recognition. This acquired status, then, broadened the central conflict; to put it more exactly, the status enlarged the conflict-free sphere of the ego and thus instigated a progressive differentiation of adaptive mental processes. We are here reminded of a comment by Anna Freud (1952): "We know from experience that ego interests which originate in narcissistic, exhibitionistic, aggressive, etc., tendencies may persist a lifetime as valuable 'sublimations,' regardless of the fate of the original part instincts which gave rise to them."

The lifelong struggle with unresolved remnants of infantile and adolescent conflicts has been studied in the lives of creative personalities. The focal interest in these bio- or pathographical investigations has usually been directed toward the infantile instinctual life, and only cursory attention—if any at all—has been paid to the contribution of adolescence to structuring of conflicts in relation to regressive as well as progressive drive and ego components. One exception is Erikson's (1958)

study of Martin Luther. Other psychoanalytic studies of creative personalities emphasize the persistent effort to bind conflictual anxiety and to
integrate infantile fixation and trauma into the mature ego organization.
The persistence with which adolescent conflictual remnants extend
their influence into adulthood is described in a letter written by Freud
to Romain Rolland. This letter contains a self-analysis of a memory disturbance on the Acropolis. The mood swing which accompanied the fulfillment of one of Freud's fervent adolescent wishes, namely, to stand
one day on the Acropolis, was caused by the triumphant but ego-dystonic
and depressive feeling, which Freud (1936) summed up in these words:
"It must be that a sense of guilt was attached to the satisfaction in having
got so far: there was something about it that was wrong, that was from
the earliest times forbidden. It was something to do with a child's criticism of his father, with the undervaluation which took the place of the
overvaluation of earlier childhood. It seems as though the essence of
success were to have got further than one's father, and as though to
excel one's father were something forbidden."
    The objection might be raised that experiences such as this belong
only to exceptional personalities, to men of extraordinary talent. But how
do we account for the responsive interest felt by most people to the
artist's creation? Is not this partaking passion proof enough that there are
vital self-interests involved and that corresponding or equivalent desires
and conflicts do indeed exist in most adults to which the artist gives expression in terms of universal essences? The role of the creative artist in
all its various forms both in modern times and in all eras attests to the
residues of unconscious infantile needs which cannot be expressed in
adult life except through institutionalized communal regressions, "in
the service of the ego" (Kris, 1950).
    These formulations are vague; we shall now turn to other data to help
clarify them. At late adolescence recreational, avocational, devotional,
and thematic preferences emerge, the pursuit of which equals in psychic
economy the pursuits of work and love. Instead of Kris's concept of "regression in the service of the ego," these musings of museless man might
more correctly be ascribed to a modality of experience which is derived
from the play of the child. Winnicott (1953), in his study of "transitional objects" in infancy, describes the genetic antecedent of a mental
activity in adult life which was not satisfactorily comprehended before.
He speaks of an intermediate "mental" area of experience in which inner
and outer reality combine, "an area which is not challenged—a resting

place for the individual engaged in the perpetual human task of keeping inner and outer reality separate yet interrelated. . . . It is assumed here that *the task of reality acceptance is never completed* [italics mine], that no human being is free from the strain of relating inner and outer reality and that relief from this strain is provided by an intermediate area of experience which is not challenged (arts, religion, and so on). This intermediate area is in direct continuity with the play area of the small child who is 'lost' in play."

The resolution of the adolescent process in late adolescence is fraught with complications that easily overtax the integrative capacity of the individual, and which may lead to maneuvers of postponement ("prolonged adolescence") or to outright failures ("miscarriage of adolescence"), or to neurotic adaptations ("incomplete adolescence"). The outcome cannot be assured until late adolescence is brought to some kind of settlement. The closing phase of adolescence is the time when adaptive failures take their final shape, when breakdown occurs. Erikson (1956) refers to the consolidation period of late adolescence as the period of "identity crisis"; he has conceptualized late adolescent breakdown in terms of the failure to perform the maturational task of this stage, the establishment of "ego identity."

Whenever early ego deformation with incomplete differentiation between ego and reality underlies the miscarriage of adolescence (defective ego synthesis), the breakdown appears as a borderline or psychotic illness. In the treatment of these cases one has to go back to the pregenital phases: to oral dependency and oral aggression, and to the vicissitudes of "basic trust" (Erikson, 1950). Clinically we recognize the defectiveness of the synthetic function of the ego and the pre-ambivalent aggression directed at object- and self-representations in the persistent defectiveness of object constancy with ensuing affective and cognitive disturbances. The breakdown, to use Brierly's (1951) expression, is related to the distorted internalized objects, and is due to "projected infantile sadism." The consolidation process is further complicated by the necessity at the close of adolescence for assigning aggressive and libidinal cathexes, which originally were fused in object representations, to love and hate objects in the outer world. These ego-syntonic arrangements produce stability of attitudes, feelings, and prejudices. Under normal and benign circumstances they account for people's pet peeves, pet gripes, pet hates, and so on; they are of utmost importance for psychic economy.

The development of neurotic character or symptom formation in late adolescence represents an attempt at "self-healing" after a failure to resolve infantile fixations articulated on the level of the oedipus complex. The love life of the late adolescent demonstrates clinically the various conditions of love which are based on the persistence of the oedipus complex. They were described by Freud (1910): 1) the need for an injured third party; 2) love for the harlot; 3) a long chain of objects; 4) rescuing the beloved; 5) cleavage between tenderness and sensuality. To this list may be added Abraham's "neurotic exogamy."

During late adolescence, sexual identity takes its final form. "By eighteen to twenty," Spiegel (1958) observes, "it seems likely that the *overt* sexual choice is made; at least I have observed that a number of male homosexuals began to view themselves as permanently homosexual at that period." Freud (1920) had made the same observation; he stated that homosexuality in girls takes a final and decisive form during the first years after puberty. He continued, "Perhaps one day this temporal factor may turn out to be of great importance." Indeed, the formation of a stable and irreversible sexual identity is of foremost importance in terms of the phase-specific drive organization of late adolescence.

The consolidation process of late adolescence may be described in terms of workable and abortive compromises or ego-syntheses, of positive and negative adaptations to endopsychic and environmental conditions. The failures to master inner and outer reality can be placed into two categories. On the one hand, the failures are due to 1) a defective apparatus (ego); 2) an impaired capacity for differential learning; or 3) a proclivity to traumatic anxiety (panic of ego loss). These cases, which comprise borderline, schizophrenic, and psychotic conditions, may be called cases of *miscarried adolescence*. On the other hand, if failures are due to 1) intersystemic disturbances; 2) blockages to differential learning (all kinds of inhibitions); or 3) avoidance of conflictual anxiety (symptom formation), we can speak of incomplete adolescence or neurotic disturbance. This division is not presented as an attempt at classification, but rather as a delineation of two essentially different forms of abortive efforts at surmounting the adolescent crisis. They represent the extremes along a continuum of deviate development; clinical observation presents endless mixtures and combinations.

Pseudomodernity in sexual standards is in a large measure responsible for many complications in the development of femininity. The change from the double to the single standard has not given the girl the expansive freedom she hoped to achieve. This social development ignores the fact that the female's sexual drive is far more intimately attached to her ego interests and personality attributes than is the male's. "In the boy as opposed to the girl, at the end of the conflict between the instinct and the defense mechanism, the sexual instinct emerges largely independent of its sublimations" (Deutsch, 1944). The girl reacts to differentiation between the sexes with well-known resentment, which is an expression of the "masculinity complex." In an attempt to formulate the essential qualities of femininity, Helene Deutsch (1944) remarked, "The sequence constituted by 1) greater proneness to identification; 2) stronger phantasy; 3) subjectivity; 4) inner perception; and 5) intuition, leads us back to the common origin of all these traits, feminine passivity." In the effort to assimilate male characteristics rooted in male physiology and anatomy, the girl has acquired a shallowness of feeling and has primitivized her womanliness. Benedek (1956, b) investigated this condition; she says: ". . . the personality organization of the modern woman, through integrating masculine aspirations and value systems, acquires a strict super-ego. Consequently, women might respond with guilt reactions to the biological regression of motherhood. Many women cannot permit themselves to be passive; they repress their dependent needs. . . ." If these dependent needs do not become an integral part of feminine passivity, the dependency need may never become detached from the mother; in that case the girl may transfer to men her defensive hostility toward the mother. This development was apparent in the case of Judy.

During late adolescence, the predisposition to specific types of love relationships becomes consolidated. More often than not these types contain mixtures of and compromises between positive and negative oedipal fixations. I once observed in the analysis of a postadolescent young man that his love for a girl was determined by his identification with the mother, who was rejected by the father as he was himself. In pleading for acceptance and love from his unaffectionate, sexually cold, and egotistic partner, the patient was driven by the relentless oedipal wish for the love of his distant and demanding father. The love relationship—in fact, the marriage—came to the same disastrous end as the oedipal conflict once did, because of its strong negative and extremely weak positive designation: homosexual strivings dominated the relationship. Another form of consolidation was seen in the case of a postadolescent girl who imprinted her first heterosexual relationship with deep yearnings for the protective, preoedipal mother, and for the bliss of oneness with her. This girl said: "I want Don to feel exactly as I do, always; and to be with me whenever I need him. Otherwise I feel frantic and lost, completely lost. No, I don't want to dominate him by dictating to him his feelings, no. What I do want is just curl up in his womb." Of this case we can say that the late adolescent consolidation occurred prematurely due to the fixation on the preadolescent phase. Another girl described the turn from competitive rivalry with boys to what she called "feminine equality." "When I liked a fellow," she said, "I was always in competition with him, not with any other girl, mind you. I wanted masculine equality: just two boys loving each other. Before a date I had my horns and my teeth sharpened. In my love for Bruce it is different: I feel not equal to him, I am not competing with him. I admire him. I never before thought of wanting feminine equality; the whole idea is new to me. Thinking of marriage I always had two alternatives in mind: I either marry a young man and compete with him, or I marry an older man with whom there would be no competition because I expected him to treat me the way a father would." In all three of these cases there appears the consolidation of a compromise without the completion of a satisfactory passage through the adolescent phases. Conditions like these usually augur a deviate development; such deviations influence object choice in adult life and, within certain limits, may be stabilized reciprocally in marriage.

A failure in the resolution of the adolescent process which stems from a different source must be mentioned now: the sexualization of ego functions. In these cases we deal with the seemingly successful integration of vocational choices and ego interests which are secondarily invaded by component instincts—for instance, scoptophilia and exhibitionism. Should their sublimation no longer be maintained, they will burden the ego with sexual excitation and unconscious fantasies which render ego activity highly unstable, and which ultimately will lead to inhibition. This condition has been studied especially with reference to the instability of vocational choices among late adolescents and also in relation to the inhibitions and symptoms of artists. The sexualization of ego functions weakens objectivity, reality testing, and self-criticism; part of the activity based on the related unconscious fantasy becomes ego-dystonic. "An ego-syntonic phantasy will contribute to the pattern of ego-organization and undergo further developmental modification along with the ego, whereas an ego-dystonic phantasy may form the nucleus of a dissociated, and therefore potentially pathogenic, system" (Brierley, 1951).

The case of Tom (page 119) demonstrated that the sexualization of his interest in history "spoiled" the defensive maneuver (intellectualization) and repeatedly aroused feelings of guilt and shame. Sexualization of ego functions renders them intractable, unreliable, and unstable; they become unusable for the maintenance of inner harmony and the patterning of work habits. These sexualized ego functions are poor executors of ego interests; and they behave—to use Freud's simile—like the cook who enters into an affair with the master of the house and then refuses to do her work in the kitchen (Freud, 1926).

The consolidation of personality in late adolescence brings greater stability and evenness into the feeling and action life of the young adult. There is a solidification of character—that is, "a certain constancy prevails in the ways the ego chooses for solving its tasks" (Fenichel, 1945, b). The greater stability of thought and action is attained at the price of the introspective sensitivity so characteristic of the adolescent; the flowering of creative imagination fades during the closing phase of adolescence. Imagination and adventurous and artistic endeavors decline until they gradually disappear altogether. The true artist, of course, is the exception; but his development does not concern us here.

The increasing capacity for abstract thought, for model and system building, the tighter amalgamation of thought with action, give the personality in late adolescence a more unified and consistent quality. The application of intelligence enables man to bring order into the world around him; but it must not be concluded that adult objectivity is in all ways superior to the thinking of the child. In fact, the child, by allowing contradictions in mental operations, is able to make observations and to draw conclusions which are scotomized by the logical adult. "We know that the first step towards the intellectual mastery of the world in which we live is the discovery of general principles, rules and laws which bring order into chaos. By such mental operations we simplify the world of phenomena, but we cannot avoid falsifying it in so doing . . ." (Freud, 1937). The consolidation process of late adolescence is a narrowing down process, a delimitation and channeling. This is well expressed in the autobiography of the English poet, Richard Church (1956), who says of himself at the age of seventeen, "Suddenly I was armed . . . poetry was to be my weapon."

I have emphasized that by the close of adolescence no over-all resolution of infantile conflicts has been accomplished. The residues of fixations and repressions spring to life in the form of derivatives; they challenge the ego and force it into ceaseless efforts to master these disturbing influences; and these efforts give purpose, shape, and color to adult life as it unfolds. The process of consolidation is never one of simple alternatives; therefore, we cannot speak of solutions of disequilibrating tensions, but rather of their becoming organized in terms of patterns or systems. Interferences with their stability are derived, to put it simply, rather from "too little or too much"—that is, from quantitative aspects —than from "this or that"—namely, from qualitative aspects. Freud (1938) expressed this view in reference to the transformations of puberty by saying: "The situation is complicated by the fact that the processes necessary for bringing about a normal outcome are not for the most part either completely present or completely absent; they are as a rule *partially* present, so that the final result remains dependent upon *quantitative* relations. Thus genital organization will be attained, but will be weakened in respect to those portions of the libido which have not proceeded so far but have remained fixated to pregenital objects and aims." By the end of late adolescence, patterns have been formed epitomizing the essential disequilibrating tensions, which have to become an integral part of the ego organization. This idea was discussed in a letter by Freud to Ferenczi: "A man should not strive to eliminate his complexes but to get into accord with them: they are legitimately what directs his conduct in the world" (Jones, 1955).

The late adolescent process of delimitation is achieved through the synthetic function of the ego. It is a final acceptance and settlement of the three antitheses in mental life; namely, subject-object, active-passive, and pleasure-pain. A stable position with reference to these antithetical modalities manifests itself subjectively as a sense of identity. The ego identity of Erikson (1956), as the phase-specific achievement of late adolescence, describes a subjective experience of varying ego states, of libido fluctuations due to conflictual and maturational crises; in short, it is the resultant of heterogeneous psychological processes which accumulatively combine into an ego state best described as a sense of identity, ego identity, or sense of self. The mental representation of the self at the close of adolescence is a qualitatively new formation, and reflects as an organized whole the various transformations which are specific to the phase of late adolescence. (See "The Ego and the Self," page 191.)

After a relative fixity between the three basic antitheses has been established, they will yet vary in combination and emphasis, depending on the various roles the individual assumes in life. The fixity of roles, as well as the specific need-gratification which these roles afford within a circumscribed vector of interaction between individual and environment, is an essential achievement of adaptive mental processes. In the roles of mother and of wife, of wage earner and of lodge brother, not to mention the "unchallenged resting place," the "intermediate area" of Winnicott (1953)—in all these roles the individual pursues different goals, which are not always in harmony with each other, yet are related and unified by a drive toward self-realization.

Many levels of self-realization exist peacefully side by side. In *Orlando*, her epic about becoming a woman, Virginia Woolf (1928) wrote about the various roles the maturing self learns to live with:

Orlando? still the Orlando she needs may not come; these selves of which we are built up one on top of another, as plates are piled on a waiter's hand, have attachments elsewhere, sympathies, little constitutions and rights of their own, call them what you will (and for many of these things there is no name) so that one will only come if it is raining, another in a room with green curtains, another when Mrs. Jones is not there, another if you can promise it a glass of wine—and so on; for everybody can multiply from his own experience the difficult terms which his different selves have made with him—and some are too wildly ridiculous to be mentioned in print at all.

7. Postadolescence

The transition from adolescence to adulthood is marked by an intervening phase, postadolescence, which can be claimed rightfully by both, and can, indeed, be viewed from either of these two stages. There are, however, reasons why postadolescence is discussed here as a continuance of the adolescent process, or, rather, as its waning reflection. These reasons will become clear as we lay bare the essential steps in postadolescent personality formation which represent the precondition for the attainment of psychological maturity. The individual who is described here as postadolescent is usually, and correctly, referred to as a young adult.

Even after the conflicts of bisexuality (early adolescence) and of the disengagement from early object ties (adolescence proper) have found stable settlements, and after selective life tasks have acquired shape, definition, and articulation through the consolidation of social roles and irreversible identifications (late adolescence), even after these phases of development are traversed successfully, the total achievement still lacks harmony. In terms of ego development and drive organization, the psychic structure has acquired by the end of late adolescence a fixity which allows the postadolescent to turn to the problem of harmonizing the component parts of the personality. This integration comes about gradually. It usually occurs either preparatory to or coincidentally with occupational choice—provided that circumstances allow the individual any choice at all. The integration goes hand in hand with the activation of social role, with courtship, marriage, and parenthood. The appearance or the manifest role of the young adult—having a job, preparing for a career, being married, or having a child—easily blurs the incompleteness of personality formation.

From clinical experience with young adults, I am inclined to say that one of their foremost concerns is the elaboration of safeguards which automatically protect the narcissistic balance. This achievement, of course, is made secure only if instinctual needs and ego interests, with their often contradictory nature and unstable stratifications, have achieved a harmonious balance within themselves. This is accomplished if the ego succeeds in its synthetic function. Integrative processes dominate the closing phases of adolescence, and late adolescence is characterized by the consolidation of these essential constituent components of mental life which need to be integrated into a functioning whole. The process could indeed be called the developmental achievement in personality organization which is specific for postadolescence.

We must keep in mind that by late adolescence the drive organization has normally reached a state of permanency and fixity; this fact, however, should not lead us to assume that ego development has caught up with it; quite the contrary is true. What we usually and loosely refer to as adolescence is predominantly restricted to the period of instinctual reorganization. Ego-integrative processes do not cease to be operative after the adolescent storm has passed; in fact, they undergo their most essential and enduring modifications at that time. Greenacre (1958) has given expression to a similar opinion in saying that "no sense of adult functional identity can be completed until after adolescence is well past and assimilated." Experience tells us that, in general, personality development by no means comes to a standstill with the termination of adolescence. Benedek (1959, b) stated, for example, that the psychosexual development of the female is normally brought to completion only through motherhood. She consequently described parenthood as a developmental phase. Motherhood, as Benedek pointed out, facilitates the resolution of residual instinctual, narcissistic, and superego conflicts implicit in female biological functioning—in short, it facilitates resolution of the conflicts which adolescence has not been able to bring to a final settlement. It is obvious that the psychic organization is susceptible to alterations after the adolescent period; however, by extending interest in the adolescent process indefinitely into adulthood, we deprive adolescence as a developmental phase of its meaning. I prefer, therefore, to draw a line of demarcation between adolescence and adulthood; and I will say that adolescence has achieved its task and has therefore been completed when the personality organization can permit parenthood to make its specific contribution to personality growth.

Developmental psychologists and psychoanalysts, for example Pichon (Wolf, 1945), have noted that "emotional development does not stop at puberty. On the contrary, the real achievement of development comes after puberty." It is a common experience that after the cataclysmic struggle of adolescence proper has abated, a period of integrative processes prevails when permanent settlements of intrasystemic conflicts are brought about and disharmonies in the ego are resolved. These processes do not occur independently; the prevailing drive organization throws its reflection on the ego, with far-reaching implications. For example, the polarity of masculine-feminine which is sharpened during adolescence proper and which is subsequently stabilized by the formation of sexual identity, exerts a lasting influence on the ego, evident in the elaboration of ego interests and attitudes consonant with sexual identity. During postadolescence, the process of harmonizing the entire drive and ego organizations, as well as the component parts of each, is at its greatest intensity.

At the close of adolescence, as I have remarked earlier, conflicts are by no means resolved, but they are rendered specific; and certain conflicts become integrated into the realm of the ego as life tasks. This was described as the achievement of late adolescence. It remains the task of postadolescence to create the specific avenues through which these tasks are implemented in the external world. The gratification of disparate instinctual needs and ego interests is characteristic for this period, during which the adolescent articulates his heterogeneous strivings in the form of component pursuits. Many lines of endeavor are followed simultaneously and with equal urgency. This state of affairs represents a typical condition—postadolescent experimentation.

In the realm of the sexual drive, experimentation is evident in the relations with potential love objects which represent all possible combinations of degraded and idealized, of sensual and tender love. Similarly, experimentation with ego interests renders postadolescence a period during which the individual elaborates his very special way of life. Some relevant juxtapositions might be as follows: material gain versus scholarly pursuit; economic uncertainty with independence versus secure employment with the imposition of rules and regulations. Whatever is special about the individual's way of life is always veiled by the commonplace universality of social patterns and roles; however, its idiosyncratic meaning yields easily to investigative inquiry, as every clinician knows. The integrative effort required for the progression from the state of component pursuit to that of unified goal-directedness is often underrated.

We can summarize here and say that the period following the adolescent climax of adolescence proper is characterized by integrative processes. At late adolescence these processes lead to a delimitation of goals definable as life tasks; while at postadolescence, the implementation of these goals in terms of permanent relationships, roles, and milieu choices becomes the foremost concern. The ego, strengthened by the decline of instinctual conflicts, now becomes conspicuously and increasingly absorbed by these endeavors.

The biphasic nature of personality stabilization, which becomes dominant after the chaotic states of early adolescence and adolescence proper are over, requires scarcely any documentation here. Careful observation will readily prove the point. It is of interest in this connection to recall Goethe's developmental novel, *Wilhelm Meister*, which he presented in two parts; the first is entitled *Apprenticeship Years* (*Lehrjahre*), the second is called *Years of Wandering* (*Wanderjahre*). This division is borrowed from the traditional, preindustrial schedule for becoming an artisan and a member of a guild; and reflects a biphasic progression similar to the one made above. In the first part of Goethe's novel Wilhelm leads a life of seemingly wasteful and alarming aimlessness. He starts out as an apprentice in the family business, but this commercial career is soon disrupted by a passionate love for the theater and the idealization of the actor's life. This is followed by a sobering disappointment from which he is rescued by the influence of an older man of intellectual and scholarly wisdom. All these events are interwoven with his romantic love for a half-grown girl and a series of passionate affairs, both sexual and platonic. The second part of the novel, in sharp contrast, is dominated by the two ideas of self-limitation and of work. The theme of renunciation implies the dedication to a limited goal. Wilhelm becomes a surgeon. He ceases to be attracted to the many temptations of life and reduces his many inclinations to those which matter in his now dedicated existence. He has changed from an impulse-driven individual and an idealistic seeker and follower to a citizen of the world. He has become aware of his social obligations and of the sense of dignity derived from being useful to his fellowmen.

Metaphorically, Wilhelm's second period describes the ego activity of postadolescence, which prepares the young adult for the ultimate step of settling down. This final step is taken at the time when the various life tasks—in terms of instinctual needs and ego interests—have reached a satisfying and relatively harmonious organization which can be maintained within certain limits by a patterned interaction with the environment and the self.

During the postadolescent period emerges the moral personality with its emphasis on personal dignity and self-esteem rather than on superego dependency and instinctual gratification. The ego ideal has in many ways taken over the regulatory function of the superego, and has become heir to the idealized parent of childhood. The reliance once vested in the parent now becomes attached to the self, and sacrifices of all kinds are made in order to sustain the sense of dignity and self-esteem. The moral tenor of the postadolescent period is well conveyed by Joseph Conrad's (1900) *Lord Jim:*

It was solemn, and a little ridiculous too, as they always are, those struggles of an individual trying to save from the fire his idea of what his moral identity should be, this precious notion of a convention, only one of the rules of the game, nothing more, but all the same so terribly effective by its assumption of unlimited power over natural instincts, by the awful penalties of its failure.

After the completion of puberty, after physical maturity has been reached, one psychological task remains, the fulfillment of which often requires a good many years. Erikson (1956) described this period (postadolescence) while discussing Bernard Shaw, who "granted himself a prolongation of the interval between youth and adulthood." This interval Erikson calls a "psychosocial moratorium." Shaw, during these intervening years, molded himself into a writer. By determined self-discipline he made himself adept in the metier through which he could best come to terms with the residual trauma, with conflictual residues, thus giving shape to his life tasks. After these life tasks had become organized, Shaw turned to articulating them on the environment. As he said, "If you cannot get rid of the family skeleton, you may as well make it dance." Erikson's psychosocial moratorium is defined by him as a period "during which the individual through free role experimentation may find a niche in some section of his society, a niche which is firmly defined and yet seems to be uniquely made for him. In finding it the young adult gains an assured sense of inner continuity and social sameness which will bridge what he *was* as a child and what he is *about to become,* and will reconcile his *conception of himself* and his *community's recognition* of him."

In a study of the postadolescent period in the male, Braatöy (1934) emphasized its high psychic mortality; it is the time when mental illness often reaches a manifest state. He concluded that this period, which he called an "interregnum," i.e., lying between puberty and adulthood, makes integrative demands on the ego which overtaxes its resourcefulness for many a young adult, and the result is failure to achieve the postadolescent personality organization.

As always in the progression of developmental stages, failure at any one of them is due either to an insufficiently completed prerequisite development or to an insurmountable obstacle which precludes the fulfillment of the stage-specific task. With this in mind, one can say that failure in completing the adolescent process will occur whenever the organization of a stable self is not attained, or whenever the ego fails to render any conflict ego-syntonic; both these constellations lead to a deviate completion of the postadolescent task. Failure might take the form of foreclosing the integration of diverse and contradictory strivings in an effort to keep, so to say, the doors open permanently to many possible lives. This developmental impasse will be discussed in the syndrome of prolonged adolescence. What has been said here must be supplemented by stating that partial task fulfillment at each phase and consequent compromise formation are the rule rather that the exception.

One typical roadblock encountered in traversing postadolescence is what I shall refer to as the "rescue fantasy." Rather than living in order to master life tasks, the adolescent hopes that life circumstances will master the task of living. In other words, he expects that the solution of conflict can be alleviated or side-stepped altogether by the arrangement of a beneficent environment. In this case it seems that the original dependence on the environment, namely the mother as the extinguisher of tension and the regulator of self-esteem, has never been abandoned. The overvaluation of the parent has been transferred to the environment, which, so goes the fantasy, could bestow if it only wanted to its favor and fortune on the chosen child.

Obviously, the rescue fantasy is closely related to the family romance and to the typical daydreams of adolescence, which in postadolescence often reach a particular urgency, persistence, and elaboration in content. "If these daydreams are carefully examined, they are found to serve as the fulfillment of wishes and as a correction of actual life. They have two principal aims, an erotic and an ambitious one—though an erotic aim is usually concealed behind the latter too" (Freud, 1909, b). Such fantasies are guarded, more or less dissociated, intimate thoughts which often give rise to neurotic disturbances. Hysterical fantasies have, according to Freud (1908), "a common source and normal prototype . . . to be found in what are called the day-dreams of youth." Of course, these fantasies spring into existence as early as adolescence proper, but abandonment of them can become a major effort of postadolescence.

The formulation of the adolescent rescue fantasy should not be confused with that concerning several conditions of love described by Freud (1910) which is expressed by "the impulse to rescue the beloved." The difference lies in the fact that the latter fantasy is marked by the desire to rescue someone, while the adolescent rescue fantasy which I describe is concerned with the wish, or rather, the expectation, of being rescued by a person, by circumstances, by privilege, by good fortune or luck. The forms of the adolescent rescue fantasy are, of course, legion. What is readily voiced represents only the communicable aspect of the fantasy; the major portion of it remains submerged. What we hear are simplified versions of a complex thought process, which may take the following forms: "If I only had a different job"; "If only I were married"; "If only I could live in Europe, the west, the east, the country, the city"; "If only I had a different name"; "If only I were two inches taller or shorter"; and so on. What all these wishes have in common is a global quality, a reduction of intricate problems to a single condition on which everything seems to hinge.

Forerunners of this powerful fantasy can be observed during late adolescence. If they persist, they will short-circuit postadolescence by premature settlements which allow the rescue fantasy to survive for good. Even if this developmental failure does not lead to manifest emotional illness, it is responsible for many ego restrictions and inhibitions. The fact that the clinical picture of these cases shows a high degree of similarity does not imply that the rescue fantasy presents homogeneous content. In terms of previous formulations, this fantasy can be considered as the failure to make a specific residual trauma an integral part of the ego organization. The failure does not lie in the lack of an impelling life task, but in the expectation that its fulfillment will come from the beneficent influence of circumstances. The internalization of the trauma has been undone, and its mastery is expected, as if it were a reparation payment, from the outside world. The specific fate of this constellation depends on its amalgamation with drive components; for instance, masochistic needs will produce the well-known "injury collector" (Bergler), who searches for a gratification rightly due him but unjustly withheld by a hostile world. The insurmountable impasse of postadolescence which is described as the rescue fantasy here is abstracted from clinical material similar to that which Erikson (1956) has described in terms of "identity diffusion" and "negative ego-identity." The rescue fantasy is a useful formulation because it promises to throw light on the integrative process of postadolescence. From the analysis of young adults, I have gained the impression that the detachment from the parent of early childhood, or better, from parental object representations, is not complete until postadolescence has passed. That is to say, the loosening of infantile object ties is the task of adolescence proper, but coming to terms with parental ego interests and attitudes is most effectively and most deliberately done during postadolescence. Only then does a lasting settlement of these concerns take shape. The competition with the father which the boy experienced in the resuscitation of the oedipus complex during adolescence proper normally recedes gradually into relative oblivion. In the years that follow, the postadolescent undergoes a revision of his rejected, provisional, and accepted identifications. "The character of the ego" Freud (1923, a), "is a precipitate of abandoned object-cathexes." However, it must not be overlooked "that there are varying degrees of capacity for resistance, as shown by the extent to which the character of any particular person accepts or resists the influence of the erotic object choices through which he has lived." The final step in this process, namely, of acceptance and resistance to identifications, is not taken until postadolescence.

We often observe that young adults, after having found a love object to whom they can relate with a minimum of ambivalence, become selectively—that is, positively or negatively, by identification or by counter-identification, but at any rate definitively—oriented toward parental images. The desexualized object libido invested in these identifications can now be transformed into ego libido or narcissistic libido without conflict; it can be bound in stable sublimations. At such a time, for instance, a young woman who had been opposed to any orderly domestic tasks, resisting identification with the "good mother," might say, to her own surprise, "I am really quite a good housekeeper; I learned it from my mother; I am proud of it." One often sees attitudes, traits, and tendencies of the parental egos become, although, to be sure, in selective variations, lasting personality attributes of their adult children. Often the ego at this period brings to life abandoned object choices on the level of ego attitudes in fantastic combinations and inventiveness and in a surprising reversal of preceding patterns. This is to say that identification and counteridentification with the object proceed in relation to object aspects or object qualities, and not in relation to object-subject totalities. A remark by Grinker (1957) actually describing earlier stages of identification, is relevant here: "The overt personality or character of the object is viewed by the subject as an assemblage of qualities, some parts of which are needful, useful, or dangerous and with which identification may result or is avoided by a counteridentification."

One special aspect of postadolescence deserving attention is the ceaseless effort to come to terms with parental ego interests and attitudes. This effort constitutes a decisive step in character formation after the sexual drive has become increasingly stabilized by its disengagement from infantile love and hate objects. During early adolescence and adolescence proper the ego is predominantly engaged in the mastery of conflictual anxiety. In contrast, during the succeeding period, the adaptive and integrative function of the ego is in ascendancy.

James Joyce (1916), whose novel, *Portrait of the Artist as a Young Man*, was quoted in the section on adolescence proper, may once again serve as an illustration. This novel opens and closes with the same theme: the father. The opening sentence is spoken by the father who is telling a story to the little boy. The last sentence of the book is an invocation of the father figure: "Old father, old artificer, stand me now and ever in good stead." Nothing can be accomplished without one's having come to terms with the father, or rather, with his image or object representation. To accomplish this particular task was Joyce's lifetime occupation. When he invoked the blessings of the old artificer, he was twenty-two years old, he had met his future wife, and he knew he was destined to become a writer. He could only accomplish this goal by determinedly exiling himself, distantly reliving and re-creating his family. Joyce never ceased to write about one subject: his city and its people; and in the end he succeeded in making Dublin an eternal city of literature. To put it another way, an ego-syntonic residual trauma never ceased to exert its positive influence on the ego, which took, in this case of genius, the form of creation.

From therapeutic work with older adolescents, one learns that the struggle to integrate ego interests and attitudes of the parent of the same sex proves to be a formidable task. In order to reach maturity the young man has to make peace with his father image and the young woman with her mother image. Failure at this juncture of development will result in regressive solutions, ego deformations, or a break with reality. Erikson's study of Martin Luther (1958) demonstrates clearly, especially in its pathographic material, how Luther's postadolescent failure to detach homosexual libido from the father image raised conflictual anxiety to the point of a psychotic break.

The incomplete solution of this phase-specific task can often be endured for a while until it flares up again during parenthood in relation to a child of the same sex. The paper by Jones (1913) on the fantasy of the reversal of generations contains ideas which are relevant in the present context. "It is no exaggeration to say that, to a greater or lesser extent, there always takes place some transference from a person's parent to the child of the corresponding sex. . . . The child's own personality is thus molded, or distorted, not only by the effort to imitate its parents, but by the effort to imitate its parent's ideals, which are mostly taken from the grandparents of the corresponding sex." By unconscious substitution, failures at the postadolescent task are stabilized, often pathologically, in the family life of the next generation.

The typically rebellious adolescent of adolescence proper not only turns against his early love objects in his attempts to detach himself from them; he simultaneously turns against the view of reality and morality which was imparted to him by them. The infantile sexual tie has to be irrevocably severed before a reasonable *rapprochement* between the self and parental ego interests and attitudes can be effected. Hand in hand with this process goes an acceptance, or rather an affirmation, of social institutions and cultural traditions in which component aspects of parental influences become, so to speak, immortalized. The negative aspect—that is, the resistance against or the rejection of certain parental influences—appears in the repudiation of and the antagonism toward certain institutions and traditions, following the same externalizing process of rendering impersonal what was once a part of object relations. Conservatism and reformism may receive moral and emotional impetus from these sources. In similar fashion, many superego components become reprojected into the outside world where they first originated. By this process, the postadolescent becomes more firmly anchored in the society of which he is an integral part. At this period, then, instinctual conflicts recede into the background and ego integrative processes become prominent. As a transitional stage, postadolescence has a bridging function; the integration described in the foregoing paragraphs brings the adolescent process to its completion. Conversely, adulthood has an initial and firm toe hold in this terminal stage.

Throughout the discussion of the adolescent process, it has been apparent that progressive development ceaselessly effects higher orders of differentiation in psychic structure and personality organization. By processes of integration a state of stabilization and irreversibility is finally reached. The plasticity and fluidity of development typical of adolescence diminishes with time; it is, indeed, restricted to a limited time span. The psychology of adolescence may thus be viewed in terms of an energic system which tends to reach higher levels of differentiation until it eventually stabilizes itself in patterning. This general concept of energic systems underlies all processes in nature, animate and inanimate, as modern science has come to view them.

IV

Masturbation

ALL THROUGH OUR DISCUSSION of the phases of adolescent development, repeated reference was made to masturbation. The significant role of masturbation during adolescence as a whole has, however, not been spelled out in detail. The importance of this typical form of adolescent sexual activity requires a comprehensive inquiry about its phase-specific modality, its emotional vicissitudes, and its phenomenology or clinical picture.

Adolescent masturbation—or, to be exact, genital, autoerotic gratification—becomes the regulator of tension and the bearer of fantasies which accompany, in their shifting content and pattern, the various phases of adolescent development. Adolescent masturbation is built on a long history of autoerotic sensations and experiences which reach into the dim past of infancy. Masturbation comprises a wide range of sensations; it extends from the soothing and lulling to the "orgastic kind, in

159

which there is a gradual, usually steplike, rise of mounting excitement and strain" (Greenacre, 1954).

Masturbation as a complex psycho-physical act is associated in the course of development with the erogenous zones, and leads to more or less fixated drive proclivities. Furthermore, masturbation gradually moves away from being a simple pleasurable activity to being closely linked to the child's primary love objects in terms of specific instinctual wishes. Fantasy, including the mental image of the object, thus becomes the vehicle which connects instinctual wishes with memory traces and their elaborations and distortions; until fantasy of and by itself comes to suffice for the attainment of instinctual gratification. The nature of these unconscious fantasies is well known. Whenever this form of masturbatory gratification without physical—or, more precisely, without consciously acknowledged erotic—sensation takes place, we speak of mental masturbation.

The complex history of masturbation implies that it must always be considered in its various and often heterogeneous aspects. I need hardly mention that masturbation performs a phase-adequate function insofar as it facilitates the forward movement of the instinctual drive. On the other hand, it easily asserts a conservative tendency by perpetuating infantile sexual positions, often in a partial mode or in a disguised form. This conservative tendency constitutes a detriment to progressive development.

In this connection we might recall Freud's (1909, a) comment that, "the problem of masturbation becomes insoluble if we attempt to treat it as a clinical unit, and forget that it can represent the discharge of every variety of sexual component and of every sort of phantasy to which such components can give rise."

Genital masturbation during adolescence is the phase-specific sexual activity which divests pregenital drives of their independent aims and progressively subjugates them to genitality. This is to say that these drives become relegated to an initiatory rather than a satiatory role, the latter being focused in the genital aim. Any function of masturbation which furthers this development represents its positive aspect. The ultimate achievement of adolescent masturbation lies in the elaboration of forepleasure.

Masturbation, by its very nature, tends to work against this goal; nevertheless, it is an indispensable transitory sexual activity which normally brings infantile autoerotic experiences into contact with objects through mental imagery that is fantasy. This closer linkage facilitates object relatedness, the *conditio sine qua non* of genitality. Schilder (1935) referred to the social connotation of genital masturbation which he considered "an act by which we attempt to draw the body images of others, especially in their genital region, nearer to us." In this connection a comment by Freud (1909, a) is relevant. He also emphasized the effort typical of adolescent masturbation which aims increasingly at object directedness: "We must above all bear in mind that people's 'childhood memories' are only consolidated at a later period, usually at the age of puberty. . . . It at once becomes evident that in his phantasies about his infancy the individual as he grows up *endeavors to efface the recollection of his autoerotic activities;* and this he does by exalting their memory-traces to the level of object-love, just as a real historian will view the past in the light of the present."

Masturbation normally promotes new shifts, linkages, and delineations of mental images and their cathexes; it consequently stabilizes object- and self-representations, thus facilitating the approach to genitality. Total absence of masturbation during adolescence indicates an incapacity to deal with the pubertal sexual drives. Furthermore, it indicates that infantile masturbation has been repressed to such a degree that the necessary alignment of pregenital drives with genital sexuality cannot be accomplished. Consequently, cases of total abstinence represent an arrest in psychosexual development which in itself is pathognomic. But whenever masturbation serves a solely regressive function, or whenever it renders alloplastic adaptation, as part of object finding, dispensable, then masturbation has miscarried its phase-adequate function.

Along the path of adolescent development, both the mental content and the functional character of masturbation undergo typical changes. Masturbation can be viewed in two ways: either as being consonant with the organization of instinctual drives and ego development, or as obstructing these processes. The latter is in evidence whenever masturbation becomes an indispensable habitual tension regulator, or whenever masturbation is prematurely patterned and stabilized by personality formation; such an autoplastic integration usually results in a more or less pronounced compulsive or narcissistic character. It follows from this that there exists an injurious aspect to adolescent masturbation.

In genital masturbation we usually distinguish the physical act from the attending fantasy. It is the fantasy that exerts a harmful influence on personality formation. Here again one has to differentiate between the damaging effects stemming from two sources: either they are due to severe superego anxiety and guilt feelings or they derive from the amalgamation of genital masturbation with infantile sexual aims. The latter condition will result in the arrest of psychosexual development. These comments have to be viewed within the wider scope which Freud (1909, a) has given this problem when he said: "The injurious effects of masturbation are only in a very small degree autonomous— that is to say, determined by its own nature. They are in substance merely part and parcel of the pathogenic significance of the subject's sexual life as a whole."

Adolescent masturbation can only be fully understood in its relation to the total psychosexual development. Masturbation assumes pathological features whenever it consolidates regressively infantile fixations. One such pathological outcome would be the masturbation fantasies of a fifteen-year-old boy who fantasies self-fellatio in a defensive struggle against homosexuality. Another example would be an older adolescent who combines masturbation with defecation, thus diverting the anal stimulation to the genital. However, only when such practices acquire a compulsive character do they become harmful to progressive development. An astounding tolerance of the most bizarre and perverse fantasies exists and is attached to genital masturbation at adolescence. Such transient conditions either promote disengagement from infantile modes of gratification, or effect an ever closer amalgamation of pregenital drive components with genital drive discharge. The outcome will depend on two factors: first, the strength of fixation points; and second, the degree of the ego's surrender, acquiescence, or weakness vis-à-vis the regressive pull. Genital masturbation, especially in the boy, serves as an anchorage on the genital level and normally counteracts regression (Reich, 1951).

It is generally agreed that the physical act of masturbation is not harmful in itself, but that the fantasy attached to it becomes the bearer of injurious influences. Beyond this, however, the dependence on masturbation per se can prevent object libido from flowing outward, in which case the genital acquires an object-like quality. A concentration of narcissistic libido on one's own genital is accompanied by voyeuristic and exhibitionistic tendencies. Low tension tolerance or a weak ego invites masturbation; and conversely, masturbation keeps tension tolerance at a low level. Tausk (1912) in the famous discussion on masturbation already mentioned the "damage to object choice" and stated that when masturbation "provides full satisfaction it perpetuates and fixates infantilism. The individual has no reason to compete with others for a sexual object since he finds all sources of pleasure easily within himself. *Omnis sua secum portat.*"

When both the fantasy outlet of instinctual tension and the transformation into symptom are blocked, a special condition arises which Anna Freud (1949) has described, in which the masturbation fantasy is displaced from sexual life to ego activity, from fantasy to outer world. In this way masturbation fantasies are acted out on the external world. It has been my experience that the social maladjustment which follows is always built on a fluid and easy substitution of inner and outer experiences, on a lack in essential object constancy, and, *pari passu*, on impaired reality testing. Glover (1956), in his paper on delinquency, refers to social maladjustment of this kind as a "symptom equivalent."

When physical masturbation and fantasy outlet are both blocked, transient symptom formation in adolescence often appears. Reich (1951) speaks of compulsions and phobias, Tausk (1912) of obsessional symptoms. To these should be added the psychosomatic disturbances of adolescence. Lampl-de Groot (1950) discusses the harmful effects of masturbation in terms of emotional symptoms, such as depression, nosophobia, inferiority, and guilt feelings, and also in terms of neurasthenic symptoms, such as headaches, gastrointestinal disturbances, and fatigue. The adolescent's need for physical activity and social interaction; his inability to be alone without becoming restless and anxious; and his habit of combining his solitary study with listening to music—all these forms of behavior at least partially represent typical maneuvers in the battle against masturbation.

Masturbatory activity may appear in displaced form without genital manipulation or sexual fantasy; these cases remind us of the host of masturbation equivalents involving other body parts or compulsive hand-object manipulation. Scratching, nose picking, cuticle tearing, nail biting, hair twisting, pencil chewing, endless play with rubber bands or other objects, all these activities can be considered masturbatory equivalents. Whenever displaced masturbation undergoes a symbolic elaboration of orgastic discharge, it brings about a state of high excitement the sexual nature of which is not recognized by the subject. Such activities are, however, followed by self-accusations, guilt, and inferiority feelings typical of the aftereffects of masturbation itself. Activity of this nature is represented, for example, in gambling (Freud, 1928) or reckless driving (Reich, 1951); furthermore it can be recognized in some forms of procrastination, where the usually conscious postponement of action produces small doses of anxiety which arouse a constant trickle of excitation with slowly mounting crescendo. A passive, masochistically-tinged drive organization is a prerequisite for the employment of procrastination as a masturbatory equivalent. A catastrophe which is invited by these various activities can be understood as "a mixture of punishment and disguised orgasm" (Reich, 1951).

One often meets adolescents who experience no conscious conflict about masturbation, who practice it freely without feelings of guilt; these adolescents were never intimidated as children in matters of genital play. Nevertheless they show in dreams and actions that their equanimity and unconcern is illusory. Children from so-called modern or laissez-faire families have been reassured that masturbation can do no harm and that the practice of it is normal and universal. For these children, the physical aspect of masturbation has become totally divorced from the fantasy accompanying it, and consequently, each has undergone separately its specific elaboration (Arlow, 1953). This development often leads to symptom formation, which reveals the conflictual nature of masturbation that, especially in the form of genital manipulation, is not experienced as ego-dystonic. In dealing with these cases, the task of therapy is to link guilt feelings and parapraxes to the masturbatory act. The unconscious fantasies which analysis uncovers tend to be of oral and sadomasochistic nature. This was apparent in a fifteen year old boy, a compulsive eater, who masturbated without conscious guilt feelings. He revealed the oral sadistic component of his masturbation by saying, "It feels good to go to sleep and not masticate—I mean masturbate." Another boy of the same age endowed masturbation with bisexual fantasies in which the genital assumed the role of an object: a penis and a nipple. The masturbation fantasy revealed in a dream ran as follows: "There are two milk bottles and they look alike; however, one contains milk and the other contains semen; I argue with somebody how I could tell the difference in case I wanted to drink one." An older adolescent girl reported her vividly remembered sadistic masturbation fantasies which dated from the time she was thirteen years old. In these fantasies, a male slave or prisoner was elaborately tortured by injuring his genitals. All through her adolescence this girl never realized that her fantasies and her masturbation were related to sex; she never experienced guilt feelings. Nevertheless, she developed the compulsion to urinate after each masturbatory act in order to reassure herself that no damage had been done to the genital.

Masturabation guilt appears often in disguised form as accident proneness. A fifteen year old boy recalled that his masturbation at the age of twelve and thirteen was followed by the expectation that an accident would befall him. "You know," he said, "such things do happen." He described how he would suddenly jump when crossing a street, expecting that a car was about to hit him; to his astonishment he would realize that there was no car near him. But one time when he was darting out into the street, he actually was hit by a car. The need for punishment and the wish for castration are usually both at the source of such self-induced accidents. It was interesting to observe in this case that the turn to heterosexual object finding reduced the need for masturbation and for bodily injury (accident proneness).

Adolescent masturbation of boy and girl follow different lines which can be understood as the consequence of the difference in the male and female castration complex. The fact that sexual excitement in the boy results in an erection, and later in ejaculation, makes the connection between stimulus and genital reaction an undeniable and obvious fact. It forces the boy's attention early in life directly on the penis as a pleasure-giving organ which can be manipulated at will. Guilt feelings, lowering of self-esteem, and castration anxiety interfere, in one way or another, with the uninhibited masturbation of the boy.

The girl, in contrast, masturbates without any observable and conspicuous body change. The manipulation of the clitoris which is practised during childhood is often given up at some point following menarche. At this time, according to Horney (1935), a profound personality change occurs in the female. An antagonism to the mother develops and guilt reactions to masturbation increase. If masturbation is physically suppressed, it survives in crude sadistic fantasies, of which the rape fantasies are typical representatives. Fear of body damage leads to hypochondriacal fears; the sense of being unworthy of love and being ugly represent concomitant subjective feelings. Resistance against masturbation is more common in the girl than in the boy, a fact which is consonant with the development of femininity, namely, with the gradual repudiation of clitoral, i.e., phallic sexuality. Masturbation may, however, continue to be practised by the girl in a masked form by positions which stimulate the clitoris, e.g., by sitting on the arm of a chair, by horseback riding, or similar activities. One adolescent girl reported the practice of sleeping with a pillow between her legs; the pressure on the pillow led to orgasm with the vague accompanying notion of possessing a penis. The change in body ego feeling did not progress to the awareness of a phantom organ (illusory penis), but rather stimulated the girl's imagination and found an outlet on that level. Vivid fantasies involving boyish or manly activities, heroic and cruel feats of phallic-sadistic nature constituted the repertoire of her masturbatory ritual. The use of thigh pressure often results in a vaginal sensation or an approximation to it. Clitoral masturbation is, in most instances, not totally given up until the finding of a heterosexual love object. The state of being in love facilitates the conceding of the sex-alien drive to the idealized partner who then becomes the source of narcissistic as well as of object-libidinal gratification. This move toward femininity occurs only slowly and partially until it reaches a state of completion in late or postadolescence.

A revival of the girl's narcissistic disappointment of castratedness is avoided by giving up clitoral and manual masturbation, and also by the cathexis of her whole body with narcissistic libido. "With the onset of puberty the maturing of the female sexual organs, which up till then have been in a condition of latency, seems to bring about an intensification of the original narcissism . . ." (Freud, 1914). Freud continues by saying that this narcissism affects unfavorably "the development of a true object choice with its accompanying sexual overevaluation." The narcissistic self-love, the adornment of the body, the socially-sanctioned emphasis on the display of body parts such as the breasts, of physical charm and beauty generally—these forms of narcissistic and exhibitionistic gratification facilitate a postponement of a surrender to sexual love until a time when a permanent relationship, so essential for the rearing of a child, is likely to present itself. Harnik (1924) in a cogent paper, states: "In men the genital continues to be the centre of their narcissism, whilst in women there is a secondary narcissism which becomes attached to the body as a whole." The erotic sensitivity to touch of the female body surface as it develops at puberty shows the novel distribution in cathexis which occurs at this period. Harnik calls attention to the "genital qualities developed by the female breast and especially the nipples." Infantile sexual fixations encourage adolescent masturbation, which then continues to persist side by side with the narcissistic use of the whole body as an object to be admired and looked at.

In contrast to the girl, any boy who attempts to call attention to his beauty or who parades it with exhibitionistic pleasure is always considered effeminate. It is the prerogative of the female to display her physical charm—indeed, to emphasize and enhance it through the use of cosmetics, adornments, and dress. Her need is to be loved. The boy is permitted only to display what he can do; he therefore focuses his pride on prowess and accomplishment. His attainments may lie in athletic, intellectual, academic, sexual, occupational, or creative endeavors. Daring, perserverance, speed, and power are the attributes considered masculine, which can be displayed publicly by the male. His masculine tenderness, gentleness, and sensitiveness can only unfold when his sexual polarization becomes stabilized at late adolescence, when dependency needs have become fused with genital sexuality, with assertive, protective, and intimate love.

Masturbation is often linked to an unconscious fear of injury to the genital, and, by displacement, to specific ego functions as well. This becomes apparent in the frequent association of insignificant physical manifestations or common performance vacillations with the masturbatory act. There seems to exist a basic enmity between masturbation, on the one hand, and ego and superego interests on the other. The tolerance for this enmity differs widely among individuals. It certainly must be considered responsible for the tendency for masturbation to assume a compulsive character; that is, the fear of possible damage caused by masturbation is assuaged only by repeating the masturbatory act. The vicious circle which ensues is reinforced by additional factors which render masturbation a progressive deterrent to the turning outward of libido to new objects.

Certain adolescents in whom the homosexual drive is overwhelmingly strong, completely sidestep masturbation and enter into a heterosexual relationship at an early age. The compulsive urgency with which heterosexuality is pursued, in conjunction with a persistent lack of object relatedness, reveal the defensive nature of the sexual act. Masturbation in these cases can often only be practiced as an adjunct to the heterosexual acting out.

The general defensive nature of masturbation should be stressed. Masturbation for the boy serves to reassure him of his masculinity, and it subsides markedly with the resolution of the homosexual conflict and with heterosexual object finding. What Kinsey (1948) refers to as the sexually most active, i.e., virile, period of the male, namely adolescence, coincides rather with a period of intense conflict during which the frequency of masturbation, Kinsey's "outlets," is determined by its defensive function and compulsive nature. Kinsey equated frequency of sexual outlet, such as masturbation, with virility; but this idea is contradicted by the clinical observation that the most compulsive or frequent masturbation occurs in boys with strong passive homosexual trends.

Masturbation, by its very nature, tends to act against progressive development and to affirm regressive and fixating influences. It needs to be emphasized that masturbation is objectless and involves no forepleasures. The object of masturbatory activity resides in fantasy. The masturbator experiences a fluctuating self- and object-representation, since he is simultaneously subject and object, male and female, active and passive. Prolonged adherence to masturbation, therefore, counteracts sexual polarization. It establishes a state of bisexual fixation which results, on the one hand, in the improverishment of object directed interests, and on the other, in the proliferation of an over-cathected fantasy life.

Spiegel (1959) referred to the fact that a dichotomy of the self exists in masturbation: the object-directed masturbation represents the genital part of the self, while the narcissistic component of masturbation takes the genital as an object. The strain put on the ego by this vacillating cathexis of self- and object-representations can be considered in and by itself as pathogenic. This threat to the self gives the progression to genitality in adolescence an additional sense of urgency. "There is a connection between disturbance of self-feeling (loss of personal identity) and the striving to reach the genital level of the libido" (Spiegel, 1959). It should be added that masturbation in which the genital is taken as an object has nevertheless its phase-adequate place during pre-adolescence. Looking and being looked at draw the object closer. However, masturbation in which the opposite sex is taken as object in fantasy is established only gradually during subsequent phases; it reaches its full bloom during adolescence proper.

When the bisexual position becomes intolerable to the ego, it often happens that the ego-dystonic, sex-inadequate drive component will be counteracted or neutralized by genital masturbation. This attempt to transcend the bisexual position will fail; the result will be either a suppression of masturbation altogether, or a precocious and defensive turn to a heterosexual object. The consequence of both these drive accommodations on ego development and on personality formation generally has been referred to in other chapters; similarly, the vicissitudes of object finding have occupied us elsewhere and need no repetition here.

Because masturbation by its very nature is devoid of forepleasure, it works against or prevents the hierarchical arrangement of drive components; this adverse development delays or blocks an advance to psychosexual maturity. It seems that abandoning masturbation altogether before the heterosexual stage of adolescence proper is established results in some form of psychosexual immaturity. Adolescent masturbation, then, initates and promotes the forward movement of the libido by experimental quasi-action in fantasy. This interlude eventually leads to heterosexual experimentation and concomitant modifications which find their clearest reflection in the definitive consolidation of the self. The regressive or infantilizing nature of masturbation must constantly be counteracted by the articulation of the newly-won adolescent drive organization on the object world.

V

The Ego
in Adolescence

THE TOPIC of the ego in adolescence has been singled out for special consideration because its study will permit a more detailed view of the adolescent process in terms of psychic restructuring as manifested in transient ego activities and permanent ego alterations. Taking the ego as the focus of study will enable us to weave many strands of observation and theory into a coherent texture. The clinical examples which were given above in the description of the developmental phases are sources of reference; consequently in this discussion I shall concentrate on theory. In brief, then, an attempt will be made here to render a systematic treatment of ego aspects which were in previous chapters treated as segments of the entire problem of adolescence.

1. Introductory Remarks

The ego—its nature, operation, and function—can best be studied during periods of maturational dislocations when the balance between drive and ego is upset. Under these conditions the mental apparatus is confronted with the task of accommodating new instinctual drives—new in quantity and quality and also involving new demands from the outer world. The ego is, by definition, the sum total of those mental processes which aim at safeguarding mental functioning; toward this end the ego mediates between drive and outer world. We recognize in the sense of reality the fruits of this mediation process. To these pressures—id and outer world—should be added a third which is, however, a derivative of the environment, namely, the superego.

The methods by which the ego mediates as well as its pattern of operation can be observed during adolescence. Considering the origin of the ego, we have to keep in mind that it is the result of differentiating processes and constitutes a corollary to the young human organism's prolonged dependency on the external world. Throughout its lifetime, the ego preserves the earmarks of this origin; in fact, it continues to be stimulated toward progressive differentiation by the two-fold impact of the instinctual drives and the external world. This fact has been previously alluded to by saying that ego development takes its cue from the phase-specific drive organization.

The ego in its operational definition is a relative concept, determined by the degree of pressures exerted on it. Consequently, an ego which has maintained adequate mental functioning during times of relative calm can be overwhelmed by increasing pressures evidenced during puberty; the character of its resources will then prove itself as either sufficient or insufficient for the acute task. This latter condition is precipitated during adolescence by the increased pressures from the three sources mentioned. Anna Freud (1936) referred to the adolescent ego by saying that "a relatively strong id comfronts a relatively weak ego." Furthermore, the support which the ego obtained in childhood from education ceases to operate in the accustomed fashion, due to the adolescent's massive rejection of external controls as mere excrescences of infantile dependency.

The patterned reaction to inner dangers is modeled along early experiences of threats emanating from the environment. "Frightening instinctual situations can in the last resort be traced to external situations of danger" (Freud, 1933). In other words, all defensive processes once had an adaptive function in the face of external exigencies.

In both instances—those of internal and external danger—the problem of overexcitation has to be considered: in the infant an inborn apparatus provides a stimulus barrier against the outer world, but the stimulus barrier against instincts has to be developed (Hartmann, 1939, a). In this sense, any psychic mechanism which protects the mental organism against overstimulation serves a positive function; this is equally true for early childhood and for adolescence. The developing psychic apparatus must, so to say, constantly catch up with maturational conditions, which in turn give impetus and direction to ego differentiation and integration. This process reflects the mutual influences of ego and id on their respective development. When this process is not kept fluid, but produces instead a premature crystallization of character or neurotic symptom, the function of the ego has miscarried. What should normally operate as an adaptive or defensive mechanism has taken on a different quality: instead of initiating progression and differentiation, the development of certain ego functions has either miscarried or been arrested.

In any crisis the ego resorts to emergency measures aimed primarily at the protection of its basic function—the maintenance of psychic cohesion and reality contact. For instance, quite apart from its defensive aspects rooted in conflictual anxiety and in the fear of drive intensity the withdrawal of cathexis from the outer world during adolescence operates to preserve and protect basic ego functions. This is to say that both quantitative and qualitative factors have to be considered as separate variables in evaluating ego activities directed at self-protection. Here, as in so many psychic phenomena, the principle of multiple function (Waelder, 1936) has to be kept in mind in order to appreciate the individual variability and combination by which the demands from several sources are effected with least effort. The adolescent situation no doubt calls for extreme measures to avert trauma or disintegration. The huge amount of psychic energy absorbed in this task reduces, if only temporarily and intermittently, adaptive processes to a minimum. When psychic energy is bound in defensive operations or in countercathexis, a depletion of movable energy within the ego will result.

The conflictual aspect of adolescence has dominated the discussion of adolescence for a long time; but it is proper to call attention to the fact that not every balance disturbance in the psychic apparatus is *ipso facto* a conflictual manifestation (Hartmann, 1939, a). This consideration has special importance for adolescence, a time when disturbances in balance, with ensuing regulatory mechanisms often extreme in nature, are the rule rather than the exception.

2. The Ego at the Onset of Adolescence

The phase-adequate adolescent ego can only develop appropriately if the preparatory phase of the latency period has been traversed more or less successfully. Otherwise, as in the case of an abortive latency period, a prelatency ego must cope with pubertal drives. The result is a mere reintensification of infantile sexuality; nothing new or specifically adolescent makes its appearance. Pseudoadolescent manifestations are simulated attempts at being an adolescent: the ego resorts to the use of tension regulators in direct continuation of early childhood. The ego, in order to be able to cope with puberty and adolescence, requires the achievements of the latency period; only then can it deal with the approaching maturational tasks in terms of new differentiating and integrative processes.

The onset of puberty brings with it a quantitative increase of instinctual drive energy. A recathexis of pregenital instinctual positions occurs which in many ways resembles drive diffusion. Component instincts come blatantly to the fore, the attempt to control them is evidenced in typical adolescent reactions: scoptophilia leads to shyness, embarrassment or blushing; exhibitionism to modesty and self-consciousness; sadomasochistic trends to impassivity and indifference; and smelling and tasting are drawn into the sexual realm of conflictual body sensations. Of course, the direct and uncontrolled expression of these instinctual trends during adolescence is well known to every observer of this age.

It is well to remember that "all pregenital impulses, in their aims of incorporation, seem to possess a certain destructive component. Unknown constitutional factors, and above all, experiences of frustration, greatly increase the destructive element" (Fenichel, 1945, b). In the total picture of adolescent instinct control we may have underestimated the ego's effort to tame the aggressive drive by directing our attention almost exclusively to the libidinal conflicts and the attempts to master them.

It might be helpful to define the preconditions which the ego must possess at the onset of adolescence to an appreciable degree in order to develop those qualities and functions that are specifically adolescent and that will bring about those ego transformations which result in the ego of adulthood. The essential ego achievements of the latency period are the following: 1) an increase in cathexis of inner objects (object- and self-representations) with resultant automatization of certain ego functions; 2) an increasing resistivity of ego functions to regression (secondary autonomy) with a consequent expansion of the nonconflictual sphere of the ego; 3) the formation of a self-critical ego which increasingly complements the functions of the superego, so that the regulation of self-esteem has reached a degree of independence from the environment; 4) reduction of the expressive use of the whole body and increase in the capacity for verbal expression in isolation from motor activity (Kris, 1939); 5) mastery of the environment through the learning of skills and the use of secondary process thinking as a means to reduce tension. The reality principle stabilizes the use of postponement and anticipation in the pursuit of pleasure.

Often, what at the onset of adolescence looks like a regressive phenomenon turns out, on closer inspection, to be the result of retarded ego development, or, indeed, of an abortive latency period. Schematically one might say that the psychic achievement of early childhood lies in the mastery of the body, that of the latency period in the mastery of the environment, and that of adolescence in the mastery of the emotions. The completion of one of these tasks and its stabilization can, by and large, be defined in terms of an orderly sequence of ego functions which have to parallel the maturation of the body in order to safeguard normal development.

3. Hierarchy of Ego Interests and Functions

The history of the ego reveals that it models itself progressively on each prevalent phase of drive organization. A mutual influence of ego and id never ceases to be in evidence. For example, projection and introjection are ego mechanisms which derive from the oral modality. The "existence and importance of primal, congenital ego-variations" (Freud, 1937) in their interplay with constitutional drive factors account in part for preferential drive and ego modalities. However, in the pursuit of our particular study, the question to be asked at this point is the following: What is the instinctual modality specific for adolescence alongside of which the ego develops its own corollary characteristics? The novelty lies in the subordination—only gradually, and most often only partially, achieved—of the erogenous zones to genital primacy. To put it differently: The new modality of adolescent sexuality lies in the elaboration of forepleasure (Freud, 1905, b). Pregenitality, consequently, becomes relegated to an initiatory rather than a satiatory role; this different emphasis in sexual economy makes pregenitality qualitatively different from its early childhod state.

We are reminded here of Freud's (1914) remark: "It is possible that for every change in the erotogenicity of the organs there is a parallel change in the libidinal cathexis in the ego." Possibly, then, there is an ego feeling or self-experience which is essentially as new in the realm of the adolescent ego as forepleasure is in the realm of the instinctual organization. Federn (1929) speaks of the quality of the experience of "healthy ego feeling" as an "agreeable fore-pleasure."

In an analogous way, ego interests and functions become stratified into a definite hierarchy. Selective ego components are elevated to a dominant position; others are subordinated to them. This irreversible fixity in the ego's relations to the outer world, to the id and the superego, based on a hierarchical order of ego interests and attitudes, is referred to as character. Character does not acquire its final countenance until the close of adolescence. In the emotional sphere of adolescence, we speak of the destruction of infantile ego institutions. Both these destructions lead to a rearrangement of the remnants which is in accordance respectively with the new sexual aim and with the newly-created ego ideal. "Ego institutions which have resisted the onslaught of puberty without yielding generally remain throughout life inflexible, unassailable and unsusceptible to the rectifications which a changing reality demands" (A. Freud, 1936).

The serious damage which ego fixations can inflict on progressive development is often underrated; these fixations are easily eclipsed for the observer of adolescence by sexual manifestations—which, taken in and by themselves, are the most unreliable indicators of progressive development. There exists what might be called an "optimal reciprocity" between ego and id which is tested during adolescence to its limits.

The experimental period of adolescence—at its height during adolescence proper—is the last fling before the final limitation of possibilities left open to the self is reluctantly accepted, before ego interests become narrowed down to specific and essential ones, before identity formation assumes its definitive outline. The most outstanding aspect of the hierarchical arrangement of ego interests occurs in the area of the vocational commitment during late adolescence. This commitment process operates with equal decisiveness in male and female; it requires in both the refinement of some and the stratification of other ego interests. Whenever the ego functions which are employed in this process become sexualized—i.e., become a source of exhibitionistic, voyeuristic, sadomasochistic excitement—their reliability, usefulness, and stability will be severely curtailed. Many ego disturbances, for example, learning disturbances, are caused by the inundation of ego functions by sexual and aggressive drives. The sexualization of hitherto autonomous ego functions such as perception, for instance, as an aftermath of the radical suppression of masturbation was described in detail by Joyce (1916), and was quoted above, page 116. Usually only a segment of an autonomous ego function, e.g., in perception, motility, judgment, or memory, becomes subject to conflictual involvement. This selective disturbance is due to the specific associative links which are stimulated by particular reality situations. Under such circumstances ego functions can serve as masturbatory equivalents; they are then resorted to as satiatory regulators of instinctual tension, or they are warded off and inhibited altogether. In either case, these ego functions are ineffectual in terms of their intended purpose and aim. Autonomous and defensive ego functions are often difficult to distinguish. Instinctual drives and ego functions maintain a constant mutual influence, the scope of which normally narrows down and acquires by late adolescence a fixed, harmonious, and patterned interplay.

Attitudes and behavior patterns of secondary autonomy, such as punctuality and orderliness, can also become reinvolved in emotional conflict. What gave rise originally to a reaction formation is re-experienced as a controlling imposition, a submissive surrender to the will of others; anal stubbornness reappears on the scene. The same reinvolvement in conflict occurs with certain attitudes which originated in the various libidinal phases and had apparently been absorbed in nonconflictual traits. These adolescent reactions thus reveal the existence of fixation points. This course of development is part of normal adolescence; and it illustrates the fact that personality attributes already well-established before adolescence may still undergo momentous alterations. Anna Freud (1952) has remarked: "Even as late as adolescence, revolt against the parents is followed by the rejection of identification with them and can lead to reversals of superego and ego attitudes, though apparently these attitudes had been fully integrated in the ego structure of the latency child."

The adolescent ego that yields to the dangers of a radical reorganization will evidence signs of temporarily maladaptive behavior and mentation. Nevertheless, such an ego often proves to be a strong one in the sense that trust and confidence in the cohesiveness of its existence, in fact, in its indestructibility, is never shaken. The source of this confidence is, of course, the positive quality of early object relations.

For the clinical observer, a clear line of demarcation between revolutionary reorganization and regressive disintegration is often difficult to establish. Disregarding obvious pathology, any prognosis during adolescence must be made with scepticism and uncertainty. The eventual outcome may not be known until late or postadolescence, since the ego's synthetic capacity becomes apparent with clarity only during these phases. The closing period of adolescence presents fascinating problems and has been studied in the last decade more exhaustively than in any other. It has spelled out for many observers the ultimate aim of adolescence as a whole, namely, to endow the individual with a stable arrangement of ego interests and with sexual differentiation and polarization as the core of the sense of identity. Both these achievements have to be exercised and refined in interaction with the outer world.

The closing phase of adolescence is characterized by integrative and adaptive, rather than defensive, ego activity. Several authors have recognized the momentous ego alterations of a definitive nature as the outstanding psychological achievement of this phase. Erikson (1956) speaks of the formation of "ego-identity"; I emphasize the total process of consolidation and the definitive formation of the self as the paramount ego alteration characteristic of late and post-adolescence; Gitelson (1948) in a more general way has summarized the same observations as "character synthesis." Hartmann's (1950, a) reference to a "rank order" of ego functions should also be mentioned here. "We have seen, for instance," he says, "that fitting together, the synthetic function, must be supra-ordinate to the regulation by the external world." The same applies to a host of ego functions which will not acquire the stability and fixity of a hierarchical structure until the close of adolescence. In fact, the end phase of adolescence is marked by this very achievement.

4. Stabilizing Mechanisms

The ego is prepared by the achievements of the latency period to cope with increasingly complex conditions, both inner and outer, in differentiated and more economical ways; it is not prepared, however, for the magnitude of the task with which puberty confronts it. The pressures to which the ego is exposed in adolescence change both quantitatively and qualitatively, as was outlined above in my description of the developmental phases. Not capable of mastering the critical situations with which it is presented, the ego resorts to various stabilizing mechanisms as temporary devices for safeguarding its integrity. Almost exclusive attention has been paid to the defenses against the instincts; and indeed, they do play a major role in the adolescent effort to ward off anxiety which cannot be mastered by integrative processes. However, the anxiety is not necessarily conflictual anxiety; neither is it always due to a repudiation of the sexual drive. Partly, it is the consequence of dammed-up drive energy or of the imperfection of phase-adequate discharge channels. Spiegel (1958), who agrees with some of Bernfeld's (1935) ideas on this subject, comments: "Indeed, some of the symptomatology of adolescence can be viewed as direct sequelae, as actual neurotic symptoms, of the instinctual influx which the still imperfect psychic apparatus is not able to handle at the beginning of adolescence."

Another source of tension is to be found in the parents' retaliatory restrictions meant to deal with the sexual maturation of their offspring. We often witness an exaggerated prohibiting and punitive attitude of parents toward their child as he reaches sexual maturity, gains in physical stature, and acquires a more independent turn of mind. Jones (1913) and Pearson (1958) have shown that the arrival of puberty in the child arouses in the parent fearful and retaliatory reminiscences which hark back to the times when their own smallness foiled their attempts at interfering with the envied and exaggerated privileges of their own parents. The greater sexual permissiveness of the modern parent creates a situation in which the parent accepts the sexual strivings of the adolescent and offers himself as an equal, as a comrade or pal to his pubertal child. This parental attitude aggravates the oedipal involvement through the contrived actuality of an earlier parent-child relationship.

It is obvious that diverse tensions confront the ego of the adolescent and a variety of processes are employed to keep these tensions within manageable limits. What needs emphasis is the fact that the stabilizing mechanisms are not limited to the defenses, in the strict meaning of that term. Hartmann (1939, b) speaks of the two sides of a defense, the unsuccessful pathological one and the adaptive one; Fenichel (1945, b) differentiates between pathogenic and successful defenses, i.e., sublimation; Lampl-de Groot (1957) introduces the distinction between adaptive processes as part of normal development and their distortions, called neurotic defenses; Anna Freud (1936) discusses the normal aspects of defensive reactions as "preliminary stages of defence,"—all these authors stress the fact that we are dealing here with a multifunctional concept. To differentiate between the heterogeneous aspects of this concept seems relevant in a discussion of the adolescent ego.

One further distinction must be mentioned which was introduced by Hartmann (1956), who speaks of "defensive maneuvers" and "defense mechanisms." The latter are located in the unconscious; defensive maneuvers operate in the preconscious and are kept from consciousness by censorship. What appears in adolescence as easy access to unconscious determinants in terms of insight is, in fact, more often than not preconscious content. Consequently, the fear that in the treatment of adolescents the weakening of defenses will always mobilize primary processes is in many cases without foundation. The stabilizing mechanisms characteristic for adolescence include defensive, adaptive, restitutive, and compensatory mechanisms. Ego deformation which occurs, for example, in the splitting process takes its place alongside these stabilizing mechanisms; it was described by the author (1954) in a clinical study of prolonged adolescence. Dissociative processes shown in this adolescent syndrome are more often employed to avoid conflict formation than to control conflictual anxiety.

The delineation between the various mechanisms enumerated above is obviously tenuous. This fact, however, should not deter us from an attempt to systematize clinical observations. Several or all of the stabilizing mechanisms can be employed simultaneously; we deal with intertwined psychic mechanisms. In order to single out their specific natures, it is necessary first to establish dynamic characteristics which will permit, by definition, the tracing of discrete unitary processes.

Implicit in the definition of the mechanism of defense is the fact that it is maintained by countercathexis; consequently it results in a permanent deficit in available, i.e., movable, psychic energy.* The depletion of available energy due to its being bound in the maintenance of a defense may become critical in adolescence. It must be kept in mind

---

* The question about the source and nature of the energy employed in countercathexis (defense), namely, whether the energy is the same as the one of the warded-off drives, or whether neutralized aggressive energy is to be postulated, cannot be taken up here. Hartmann (1950, a) has discussed this question extensively.

that the employment of each one of the stabilizing mechanisms may reach a point where a pathological state begins to set in. The etiology of specific stabilizing mechanisms takes into account the individual's history, his endowment, and, furthermore, the encouraging or discouraging influence of social institutions such as family, class, caste, school, and church which favor or disfavor certain types of control or mastery.

The stabilizing mechanisms, as stated, should not be thought of as sharply delineated from each other. In fact, one may gradually blend into the other in terms of a slow shift in emphasis until the process has acquired a distinctly new character. This, for example, occurs in the various forms of identification. Besides defensive identification, we also speak of primitive, transient, and adaptive identification. Primitive identification, for example, has annihilated by regression the distinction between object and self; it is, more or less, a merger with the object. In this connection, Geleerd (Solnit, 1959) speaks of a "partial regression to the undifferentiated phase of object relationship"; she claims this is a normal occurrence during adolescence. I am of the opinion it is always of pathognomic significance. Defensive identification and counteridentification leave permanent marks on the character of the ego, while transient identification remains close to experimental psychic maneuvers ranging from fantasy to ego ideal formation and sublimation. Finally, an adaptive identification is to be thought of as a function of the autonomous ego. Transitions and combinations of these various forms of identification are typical of adolescent development. The case of Tom offered a clinical illustration which shows the transition from a defensive (intellectualization) to an adaptive (scholarship) ego function.

Intellectualization was described by Anna Freud (1936) as a typical defense mechanism of adolescence. It represents an attempt to master instinctual dangers by displacement; beyond that, it also has an adaptive aspect which becomes apparent whenever the displacement has acquired the status of an ego interest, i.e., whenever the intellectual activity has become disengaged from instinctual involvement. Hartmann (1939) commented on this by saying that a defense mechanism such as intellectualization has "another reality oriented aspect also, showing that this mechanism of defense against instinctual drives may at the same time be regarded as an adaptive process." In this connection Hartmann makes the point that denial and avoidance as defenses have also an adaptive side—considering the avoidance of the too dangerous and the seeking of the at least possible. Another remark by this same author

(1950, b) illuminates the problem further: "Every reactive character formation, originating in defense against the drives, will gradually take over a wealth of other functions in the framework of the ego. Because we know that the results of this development may be rather stable, or even irreversible in most conditions, we may call such functions autonomous, though in a secondary way."

Creativity, especially artistic creation, must be mentioned in this context. Spiegel (1958) has alluded to its special function in ego differentiation and to its stabilizing faculty. "Through artistic creation," he says, "what is self may become object and then externalized, and thus may help to establish a balance of narcissistic and object cathexes." Bernfeld (1924) speaks of the creative products of adolescents as "also-objects." In addition to this function, creativity serves the internal mastery of emotional conflicts. Wolfenstein (1956) has shown the intricacies of this process by her analysis of a poem written by A. E. Housman when he was fifteen years old. The decline in creative activity at the close of adolescence coincides with the emergence of a stable ego organization and the establishment of firm boundaries between self- and object-representations. In the ego organization of the artist this delineation is probably never drawn as sharply as it is in other people.

Adaptive ego functions operate in the nonconflictual sphere of the ego. Consequently "adaptation" is not a value-determined concept, but is defined in terms of an intrasystemic organization. Behavior can be adaptive yet still be in conflict with the environment. The point at issue is whether the behavior is the externalization of an infantile wish, or whether it originates in the nonconflictual sphere of the ego and contains no secondary gain of a sexual nature. In this connection, a mechanism which is akin to the repetition compulsion should be mentioned. Simply by repeating an action, thought, emotion, or affect the adolescent can establish a familiarity with and a tolerance of them. This method is especially effective if the dosage of the quantitatively and qualitatively new drive discharge is regulated and kept within tolerable limits. This repetition, then, is another stabilizing mechanism used by the ego in its effort to master instinctual tension.

The restitutive stabilizing mechanism can be observed, for example, in the transient identifications of adolescence proper. As explained earlier, these transient identifications prevent object libido from being totally drained through deflection on the self. The adolescent's need for group belongingness as an expression of social hunger has characteristics of a restitutive process. By gaining access to a full and exciting outer life, the adolescent counteracts his unbearable feelings of emptiness, isolation, and loneliness. Anna Freud (1958, b) has presented a dramatic example of the restitutive mechanism from the study of orphaned children. The children under study "were deprived of the relationship to a stable mother figure in their first years. This lack of a mother fixation, far from making adolescence easier, constitutes a real danger to the whole inner coherence of the personality during that period. In these cases adolescence is preceded frequently by a frantic search for a mother image; the internal possession and cathexis of such an image seems to be essential for the ensuing normal process of detaching libido from it for transfer to new objects, i.e., to sexual partners."

Compensatory mechanisms are a means to maintain the narcissistic balance. Mental or physical shortcomings which are experienced as a narcissistic slight stimulate the—often forced—proliferation of special endowments and thus offset the threatening decline of self-esteem. Observation shows us that the re-establishment of object relations renders the narcissistic balance less precarious and reduces compensatory mechanisms in scope and intensity. The uneven rate of pubertal development which results in the striking maturational differences to be found in the same age group is often modified individually by overplaying or underplaying the respective maturational level. Here again the narcissistic problem lies at the root of the compensatory ego activity. This device for stabilizing the narcissistic balance often initiates an "experimental accident" which brings to the fore latent abilities which may then flourish under the positive acknowledgement of others and self. The transition to an adaptive ego function under such auspices is most favorably promoted.

The vicissitudes of the instinctual drives, in conjunction with the environmental influences on adolescence (such as greater freedom of movement and enforced social responsibilities), both stimulate certain ego functions toward accelerated development, while they stunt and retard other ego functions. In this connection, Hartmann (1950, b) comments: "Influences acting on the ego's development do not always exert a parallel effect on all of its functions in the sense of developing or retarding them. We know that in some cases not only single ego functions but whole sectors of the ego may be retarded." This distinction is particularly relevant for adolescence, when ego development progresses unevenly, at one time advancing the defensive functions, at another the experimental (acting out, imitating, and learning by repetition), at another the adaptive—in brief, giving priority at different times to distinctly disparate ego mechanisms. As Hartmann remarked "the intellectual or the defensive functions of the ego have prematurely developed, while, for instance, the tolerance for unpleasure is retarded."

Not only is conflictual anxiety responsible for "lopsided" ego development in adolescence, it also underlies the intolerance of tension, and this immaturity of the ego often leads to pathological ego formations. This last consideration is especially pertinent to an understanding of "modern youth," for whom sexual promptings and activities cause little conflictual anxiety. However, taking prolonged refuge in sexual relief through masturbation without advancing to meaningful object relations only perpetuates the state of low tension tolerance characteristic for the immature ego. Sexuality, which in previous generations constituted a source of anxiety based on the more or less conscious, ego-dystonic sexual strivings described as the typical conflictual distress of adolescence, has in recent times become overshadowed—at least for an appreciable section of so-called sophisticated adolescents—by a typical ego-syntonic condition of retarded maturation of certain ego functions. The result is an intrasystemic structural imbalance in the ego. This conflict within the ego leads usually to transitory splitting processes as a means of forestalling a state of disorganization or ego regression.

A typical adolescent trait, the adolescent's proclivity to action, must be mentioned here because it touches on a fundamental antithesis of this period—that between passivity and activity. The fear of passivity in terms of infantile receptivity and submission is equally strong in both sexes. The merger of passivity with aspects of femininity, of course, makes it an anathema to the boy, in whom action and self-assertion often serve as negations of passivity. By projection one experiences an inner threat as if it existed in the outside world; hence the adolescent predilection for "acting out." Closely related to this phenomenon is Anna Freud's (1951) adolescent "negativism" as a defense against emotional surrender and the loss of the sense of identity.

I shall close this discussion of stabilizing mechanisms with a quotation from Freud (1938, b) in which he views this problem in dualistic terms, and precludes any comforts of a simple alternative. "Whatever defensive efforts the ego makes in warding off dangers, whether it is repudiating a position of the external world or whether it seeks to reject an instinctual demand from the internal world, its success is never complete or unqualified; there results always two opposing attitudes, of which the defeated, weaker one, no less than the other, leads to psychological complications."

5. The Ego Ideal

The concept of the ego ideal has played of late a rather insignificant role in the psychology of adolescence. I shall use this concept here because it permits the delineation of an ego modification typical for the adolescent period. The ego ideal is a differentiated part of the ego, cathected with narcissistic and homosexual libido; it assumes a guiding role similar to that of the superego; but it differs from the superego in being more personal and in lacking uncompromising tyranny and primitive cruelty.

Both superego and ego ideal can be differentiated by considering their respective origins. The superego can be traced from early infancy through its many precursory stages until it assumes the definitive structure of a psychic institution at the decline of the oedipal phase. Its origin, or better, its formation, is due to the settlement or the Pyrrhic victory which brings the oedipal struggle to a close. Similarly, the ego ideal attains its definitive organization only belatedly at the decline of the homosexual stage of early adolescence. Precursors of the ego ideal are in evidence all through childhood. The psychic institution of the ego ideal continues to integrate during adolescence an ever variable content; its structure, however, remains constant and permanent. The origin of the ego ideal is to be found in the irreversible surrender of the negative (homosexual) oedipal position during early adolescence. The ego ideal, consequently, promotes the formation of sexual identity and serves to stabilize it. Both institutions are goal-directing and choice-determining. Infractions against superego demands result in feelings of guilt, fears of retaliation, and abandonment, and a need for atonement; the neglect of ego ideal expectations, in contrast, results in a shock to the narcissistic balance and a contamination of the ego with social anxiety. The ego ideal embodies, as Freud (1914) indicated, not only an individual but also a social component.

The ego ideal, at least in its typical and predominant form, has its roots in the identification with the parent of the same sex. It receives a decisive formative push during the passing of the oedipus complex when the child stops clamoring to be equal to the parent and devotes his efforts to being and becoming like him. Primitive identification, which disregards the distinction between subject and object, is replaced by identification with abstracted part-objects, such as traits, values, attitudes. These identifications gradually gain ascendancy over their precursors of body or body-part emulation and global idealization of the parent. Greenacre (1958) refers to this period by saying, "It is, then, the period of the beginning of ideal formation, both through partial identifications, deferments, anticipation, and an increase in opportunity for outer-reality experience and testing." Analytic observation of late or postadolescent cases reveals the negative oedipal attachment, namely, the homosexual component, which has not been transformed into ego ideal formation, with the result that the adolescent process breaks down under the impact of an infantile sexual fixation. We shall return later to the role of the ego ideal in adolescence and its significance for the resolution of the infantile homosexual tie.

The ego ideal gradually takes over some superego functions. This change takes place in its most dramatic form during adolescence when the ego-superego relationship is under radical revision, that is, during the phases when the loosening of early object ties or the decisive detachment from the oedipal parent occurs. Certainly as late as adolescence, as Anna Freud (1952) has remarked, superego and ego attitudes are susceptible to alterations. Elements of the superego become thus either positively or negatively modified and integrated into the ego ideal. Identifications of the adolescent period play a major part in giving the ego ideal additional content and specific direction. Normally, they lack in the irrationality characteristic of the superego and are, by definition, ego-syntonic.

The libidinal model of "I love what I would like to be" establishes narcissistic completeness; this was described above in terms of the homosexual phase of early adolescence. The heir of this phase is the ego ideal in its final organization. Thus, the ego ideal advances to the status of an ego institution by the transformation of homosexual object libido into ego libido, and in the concomitant state of sexual completeness to be found in heterosexual polarity. This crucial modification on the one hand closes the door to bisexual self-sufficiency (megalomanic self-aggrandizement of adolescence proper), and on the other hand to narcissistic, that is, homosexual, object choice. About this Freud (1914) said, "In this way large amounts of an essentially homosexual kind of libido are drawn into the formation of the narcissistic ego-ideal and find outlet and satisfaction in maintaining it." It seems that the development of the ego ideal in adolescence has received insufficient attention in terms of the influence it exerts on the stabilization of masculinity and femininity and *pari passu* on the character of the ego. Benedek (1956, b) mentioned a conflict typical of the modern girl who attempts to integrate opposing goals in her personality: a masculine (active) ego ideal which is rigidly opposed to regression as an essential step in the development of motherliness. Benedek (1956, b) continues, "Through integrating masculine aspirations, modern woman has acquired a strict superego."

Any discrepancy between ego ideal and self-representation is felt as a lowering of self-esteem; this state can assume intolerable proportions. In the adolescent we often observe a self-image formation with "paranoid" reactions caused by a hostile identification with a degraded parent image. This state is followed by a narcissistic restitution of the depreciated self; and only in this way are certain adolescents able to counteract the self-criticism and negative environmental reactions which incessantly pound at him. Helene Deutsch (1954) has discussed this problem in relation to the psychology of the imposter.

6. Cathectic Shifts

The withdrawal of object cathexis and its deflection on the self has been described by several authors as typical for adolescence: (Bernfeld, 1923); (Landauer, 1935); (A. Freud, 1936); (Hartmann, 1950, b). In this case, the ego takes the self as object. There exists, as Freud (1914) stated "a certain reciprocity between ego-libido and object-libido. The more that is absorbed by the one, the more impoverished does the other become." The libidinal shift in the direction of the self leads to an increase in secondary narcissism with impaired function of reality testing.

The efforts of the ego to counteract the withdrawal of object libido necessitated by emotional conflict are unrelenting. The phenomenology of these efforts was described above in the discussion of the developmental phases; they all are directed at forestalling a break with reality.

Estrangement from the outer world, with resultant narcissistic inflation, may precipitate mental states with psychotic-like qualities; this condition was mentioned first by Bernfeld (1923). These normally transient states diminish when object libido is again turned outward and becomes invested in new objects in the outer world. Changes in this condition parallel the gradual cessation of autoeroticism (masturbation) and the turn to heterosexuality.

The typical adolescent query, "Who am I?" represents the subjective experience of this cathectic shift. The loss of the sense of identity which adolescents often describe as feelings of depersonalization—"This is not me"; "I feel nothing"—follows the withdrawal of object cathexis. This state becomes aggravated when the emotional disengagement from the parent represents the abandonment of a strongly narcissistic relationship on which the sense of identity almost exclusively depended for regulation and maintenance. The rupture of such an object tie necessarily involves, more or less seriously, a fragmentation or loss of the sense of identity. Federn (1929) in his investigations of the phenomena of estrangement adds to these considerations by emphasizing that object loss induces a concomitant narcissistic distress, and that the mood swings following such a loss are a healthy sign of the struggle between narcissistic self-sufficiency (denial of the external world) and object-directed libido. Clinically we can observe that the proverbial mood swings of adolescents decline when object libido is again directed outward after a period of increased narcissism.

The object loss which the adolescent experiences in relation to the parent of his childhood, that is, in relation to the parent image, contains features of mourning. This adolescent loss is more final and irrevocable than the one which occurs at the end of the oedipal phase. Root (1957) has shown that "the work of mourning is an important psychological task in the period of adolescence." This work of mourning involves the ego in well-known reactions. It accounts in part for the depressive states of adolescents, as well as for their grief reaction as a postponement of affect. To complete the work of mourning requires repetition and time. The appearance of states of narcissistic regression in the service of the work of mourning would then constitute a positive reaction, and presage the development of a strong ego.

Hartmann (1950, b) formulated a significant distinction between the various forms of the withdrawal of libido from reality. It must be considered he marks, "whether the part of the resulting self-cathexes localized in the ego is still close to sexuality or has undergone a thorough process of neutralization. An increase in the ego's neutralized cathexes is not likely to cause pathological phenomena; but its being swamped by insufficiently neutralized instinctual energy may have this effect (under certain conditions)." This distinction may account for the different possible outcomes of withdrawal of libido from the outer world— that is, for relatively benign or pathological consequences of this cathectic shift.

Ego activities typical for this phase of libido withdrawal have the purpose of providing by self-stimulation that ego feeling which is essential for the maintenance of ego boundaries and the preservation of ego continuity. This stimulation is ordinarily provided by the outer world. With reference to adolescence Landauer (1935) speaks of "heightened ego-feeling," by which he means the arousal of affective states which furnish a sense of intensive ego experience. These "heightened ego-feelings" are aimed at counteracting the impoverishment of the ego, which is caused by the "decathexis of the outer world" (A. Freud, 1936), or, rather, by the decathexis of the object representations in the ego. This state of ego impoverishment seems to be subject to fluctuations (mood swings) which reflect successes or failures in loosening infantile object ties.

The rapid shift and instability of these ego states is characteristic for the phenomenology of adolescence: at this period of development, shiftlessness and instability do not indicate a weak or fragmented ego, but rather represent the ego's alert attempts to safeguard its continuity, cohesiveness, and reality contact. Adolescent development is characterized throughout by oscillating progressions, regressions, and standstills; I have referred previously to these standstills as "holding actions" which consolidate or organize inner changes and gains before they become articulated on the environment. The positive aspect of the withdrawal of libido from the outer world lies in the "internal mastery" through thinking, experimental feeling states, self-observation, and cathectic shifts in the ego with reference to self- and object representations; these are all preparatory stages to a decisive turn to the object world, which occur before "outer mastery" is initiated. The preparatory and anticipatory stages of internal change assure a more likely success in the adaptation to a new reality.

7. The Stage of Consolidation

The decisive test of the ego, at least as far as its integrative and synthetic capacity is concerned, comes with late adolescence, the phase of personality consolidation in terms of preferential, fixed ego interests as well as highly personalized love needs. These integrative efforts of the ego are carried over into postadolescence, with the specific aim at activating the inner gains on the environment. Several observers of adolescence have been struck by the fact that the period of emotional reorganization is followed by a period during which ego integrative and adaptive processes absorb a major part of psychic energy. Wittels (1948) spoke of a "second latency"; Braatöy (1934) of an "interregnum"; Erikson (1956), who emphasized the time span required by ego-integrative processes and their activation on the environment, has called this period the adolescent "moratorium."

It was stated earlier that conflicts are only partially resolved at the close of adolescence; but nonetheless, a synthesis is achieved which proves to be highly individualistic and stable. One might say that certain conflictual complexes attain the rank of a leitmotiv by being rendered ego-syntonic. At any rate, it is my contention that this definitive ego synthesis at the close of adolescence incorporates unresolved (traumatic) remnants of early childhood, and that these dynamically active remnants in turn furnish an urgent and determined driving force (repetition compulsion) which becomes apparent in the conduct of life. These ego processes are subjectively felt as an awareness of a purposeful and meaningful existence. The intrasystemic organization of the ego is affected by differentiative and stratificatory processes; that is to say, ego interests become more narrowly defined with the result that a halt is called to the unlimited scope of "possible lives." This organization marks the end of a childhood state which is typical up to and inclusive of adolescence proper.

The consolidation at the close of adolescence is accompanied by repressions, producing a state of amnesia reminiscent of the beginnings of the latency period. However, there is an essential difference between the two: at the end of early childhood, memories are closer to the emotions experienced, and the facts are deeply repressed. In contrast, at the end of adolescence, memories contain precise factual details, but the emotions experienced are repressed. This was illustrated by a male patient of twenty-one who said, "I remember that wonderful feeling from the time I was five or six—I can feel it now—that I could fly up and down the staircase." The factual details of this period were not remembered. He continued, with reference to his memories of adolescence, "I remember clearly my friend and I masturbating and trying to observe the spermatozoa under the microscope. But the only feeling I can remember is the embarrassment at having made a spot on the rug when I ejaculated." It has often been pointed out that the reconstruction of adolescent emotional life deserves greater attention than is usually accorded to it in the analysis of adults.

The above-mentioned ego alterations, which are essential for the attainment of adulthood, considerably tax the synthetic and integrative capacity of the ego; therefore the major psychic mortality of adolescence falls in this phase. Descriptive psychiatry of the past denoted dementia praecox as the psychotic condition which typically has its onset in adolescence. Braatöy (1934) in a study of men between the ages of fifteen and twenty-five commented on the frequency of psychosis (schizophrenia) in males occurring "exactly in those years when the individual should make a start of putting into practice what up till then had been training, dream and school work."

Whenever the ego is victorious in the struggle of this phase, a legitimate narcissistic gratification—pride, self-reliance and self-regard—lends durability and stability to the achievement. The study of the ego at the close of adolescence has increasingly supported the opinion that rectifications and reparative changes can be instituted spontaneously at a developmental phase as advanced as late adolescence. Studies (Beres and Obers, 1950) of children who suffered extreme deprivation in infancy have indicated that the "distortion of psychic structure" which they had experienced was "not immutably fixed." As late as adolescence reparative processes counteracted, at least partially, early deficits, and considerable growth in ego functions took place. We still are in a quandary as to the factors that enable children who were severely damaged emotionally in early childhood to effect, nonetheless, significant reparative changes in their adolescence.

The ego at adolescence has the task of counteracting the disruptive influence of infantile trauma by pathological solutions; this is achieved by the employment of stabilizing mechanisms, and finally by processes of differentiation, stratification, and integration which are the psychological hallmarks of a cohesive personality. Individuality is determined by the specific set of conflictual themes (traumata) which have become permanent, integrated aspects of the ego. Their resolution is destined to remain the task of a lifetime.

8. The Ego and the Self

With the concept of the self we touch on a distinctly new phenomenon in the development of the maturing ego. Of course, I do not imply that the self takes shape at adolescence; however, at this period the self does acquire a quality it heretofore did not possess.

Clinical observers of adolescence have often alluded to a qualitatively novel formation in the mental life of late adolescence which cannot be explained solely by the fact that psychosexual development has progressed to genital primacy. A new level of homeostasis in the mental apparatus is in evidence. This circumstance suggests that the stability is not based merely on the decline of conflict or on the ego syntonicity of specific tensions—as described above—but that the innovations reflect an organizing principle of a new order, here designated as *the self*. "We need a term," Grinker (1957) remarked, "to apply to a supra-ordinate process which functions in integrating the sub-systems, including the many identifications that constitute the ego, ego-ideal, and superego, and in organizing behaviour into available social roles. The most suitable available term is the self." Paraphrasing an axiom of gestalt psychology, which states that the whole is more than the sum of its parts, it may be said that the ego at the close of adolescence is more than the sum of its abandoned object cathexes or the sum of its identifications; in brief, a new formation, or better, a new organizing principle has arisen which can be defined in terms of the self.

For a definition of the self, I will turn to Jacobson (1954): "By a realistic concept of the self we mean one that mirrors correctly the state and the characteristics, the potentialities and abilities, the assets and the limits of our bodily and mental ego: on the one hand, of our appearance, our anatomy and our physiology; on the other hand, of our conscious and preconscious feelings and thoughts, wishes, impulses and attitudes, of our physical and mental activities." It needs to be emphasized that the self has a long individual history and does not emerge as a psychic formation at adolescence. What is new at the entrance into adulthood is the quality of the self, its relative stability and the effect it exerts on both reality testing and realistic self-evaluation as the basis for thinking and action. Subjectively, the young adult feels he is a different person after the adolescent turbulence is over. He feels "himself," he senses a unity of inner and outer experiences instead of the fragmented excesses of his adolescence. This all amounts to a subjective self-experience which Erikson (1956) has described as "ego-identity." Spiegel (1958) comments on the fact that by this time—the closing stage of adolescence—"the *overt* sexual choice is made."

The final, late adolescent stage in the organization of the self can be compared to an individuation process similar to the one which occurs when the infant of about eight months experiences the separateness from the environment in terms of "I" and "non-I" which does not take the object into account (Spitz, 1957); this step in ego differentiation precedes by several months the distinction between self and object. Both individuation processes have in common the progressive resistance to the disorganizing effect of inner and outer stimuli (stimulus barrier), and consequently an increasing independence from the mother through the distinction between mental image and percept.

The self is equally centrifugal and centripetal in its perceptive and cognitive aspects. "All self-awareness combines the ego's awareness of one's own person, tinged with the consciousness of the 'other's' reaction to it" (Spitz, 1957). While for the infant the physical limitations establish the physical self as the core of self-awareness, for the adolescent the formation of the self is dependent on the recognition of his emotional, intellectual, social, and sexual self. In other words, the self as an effectively organized entity depends on the relinquishment of infantile megalomania and magic powers. This process may also be viewed in terms of progressive objectivation.

The difficulty of relinquishing the inflated self-image of childhood is usually underestimated. It can only be assessed correctly if the comfort and pleasure derived from the accompanying ego state is taken into account. The merging of self and object represents a primitive identification which permits one to disregard the painful and undesirable aspects of reality and self. Thus it becomes possible to partake of the attributes and qualities of the object; this, however, is only achieved at the price of falsifying internal and external reality.

It follows, then, that firm boundaries between the cathexis directed to the self and that directed to the object are essential for a constancy of reality perception. A fluidity in cathectic flow from self- to object-representations or the reverse will preclude the stability of the self: either the self-representation becomes invested with the properties of the object, or the properties of the self are imparted to the object world. In both instances, the faculty of reality testing (sense of reality) is disturbed; mood swings will constantly alter the sense of self, and concomitantly determine the ego's attitude toward and perception of the outer world (Jacobson, 1954). The influence of adults serves children as a regulator which keeps cathectic fluidity in relative check; this is another source of the child's dependency on adults' normative authority.

The mental life of many adolescents—and this is particularly true in cases of prolonged adolescence—is reminiscent of early object relations and their attendant fantasies of "being one with the other," by imitating gesture and affect of the love object without relating them to their functional aspects: *i.e.*, the adolescent is unconcerned about the distinction between outer reality and self. Recourse to this rescue maneuver is taken in instances when the adolescent is threatened with a narcissistic defeat at the hands of an inflated ego ideal. This archaic method of coping with frustration aims to acquire, through primitive identification (transient merger), that modicum of self-esteem which allows the disregard of disagreeable aspects of reality. Whatever the adolescent has achieved through these means affords him but a false sense of security. Instead of the formation of a stable self based on firm boundaries between self and object, he has resorted to primitive identifications based on a weakening of these boundaries, and he lives in a state which subjectively is felt as a loss of the sense of identity. Transient states like these are normal adolescent phenomena. The omnipotent elation which the child experienced when self- and object-representations merged in a state of ideal grandeur, as well as the disillusionment in the parent and the formation of the degraded parent image resulting in self-debasement and a sense of worthlessness—both these typical childhood vicissitudes of the self have macrocosmic counterparts at adolescence when the world at large is made to partake in similar reflections of cathectic shifts which occur in the self. These cathectic shifts within the ego contribute their share to the changing ego feeling and to the mood swings of the adolescent (Jacobson, 1957). In the event that the aggressive, destructive component of object cathexis in conjunction with the degraded object-representation becomes lastingly deflected on the self, then the adolescent's conduct of life will assume a self-destructive, self-abasing, and ruinous course. Erikson (1956) has referred to this phenomenon as "negative ego-identity."

The dangers of the passage through adolescence seem to lie in the fact that the detachment from infantile object ties involves reverting to early object relations during the effort of disengagement. In the course of this reorganization, the boundaries between self- and object-representations necessarily become blurred. Cathectic shifts produce affect and identity disturbances which only subside when these boundaries are again firmly established. The defectiveness or incompleteness of a sharp distinction between self- and object-representations in the ego precludes any successful personality consolidation. Viewing the same adolescent dilemma from another angle, one can say that the difficulty is one of overcoming a basic ambivalence deriving from projective-introjective processes of the oral modality. It hardly needs repeating that preoedipal object relations are highly ambivalent; this condition is reflected in the typical emotional instability of adolescence.

Self- and object-representations do not acquire firm boundaries, i.e., do not become resistive to cathectic shifts, or, in other words, constancy of self-esteem and inner regulatory controls (superego, ego ideal) for its maintenance are not fully effective, until adolescence comes to a close. In fact, the close of adolescence is defined by the fact that this very process is completed. The completion is evidenced in a decline of adolescent mood swings and a change from the extreme attitudes of idealism and cynicism to one which automatically takes reality into account. The inflated expectations and the fatal disappointments in the self gradually are replaced by the setting of reasonable goals and by an acceptance of achievements and gratifications which lie within the reach of a correctly perceived self. Thus an operational area within the scope of self-realization is staked out, the boundaries of which are determined by such factors as endowment, circumstances, and time.

The ego at this stage of maturation "accomplishes at least a partial victory of the reality principle, not only over the pleasure principle, but also over exaggerated 'idealism' and thus over the super-ego" (Jacobson, 1945). As was said earlier, the ego ideal takes over some of the superego functions, serves as guide, and gives direction to the ego; at the same time it binds homosexual libido and offers a flow of narcissistic supply in terms of abstract values, ideational constructs, and concrete goals. The realization of these goals, or rather their approximation and relentless affirmation and pursuit, are impressed on the ego with less exacting intolerance than superego domination ever afforded.

Firm boundaries between self- and object-representations (often described as ego boundaries) separate the individual from the external world. The formation of the self at the close of adolescence permits the individual an independent pursuit of ego interests and an assurance of object-directed tension discharge. By the same token, it brings him face to face with his realistic limitations and the realization of the human condition. Conrad Aiken (1952) speaks of this fateful moment in his autobiography: "To be able to separate oneself from one's background, one's environment—wasn't this the most thrilling discovery of which consciousness was capable! And no doubt for the very reason that it is a discovery of one's limits, it is therefore by implication the first and sharpest taste of death." The two Greek goddesses, Tyche and Ananke, the philosophical principles of Fortune and Necessity, replace the parental figures and become the forces to which man bows. The sense of the tragic does not develop until late adolescence. The child only experiences a sense for the happy or sad, the fair or the unjust, the enchanting or the horrible, the good or the bad. Even a child genius like Mozart could not express in his music the dimension of the tragic until his adolescence was completed.

One aspect of the self-representation needs special consideration at adolescence, namely, the body image. The young child is always cognizant of his body as far as size, skills, sex differences, and tabooed and approved areas and sensations are concerned; these various components, including their cathexes, are unified in the body image. With the maturation of the genitals and the appearance of secondary sex characteristics at puberty, the body awareness is revolutionized and the body image radically revised. This change is often accompanied by transient feelings of depersonalization. Anna Freud (1958) referred to the fact that libido cathecting the mental representations of body parts gives rise to hypochondriacal sensations and feelings. Precocious, delayed, or asymmetrical maturation may introduce severe disturbances in the body image, leading to ego dysfunctions—often seen in school failures. The direct effect of body image defect or distortion on the breakdown of ego functions—with a minimum of intervening conflictual anxiety—has been studied by the author on preadolescent cases of cryptorchism (Blos, 1960). The case material demonstrated how the genital defect of cryptorchism, if aggravated by the environment, results in a distorted, vague and incomplete body image which in turn exerts a pathogenic influence on ego development. A bisexual sense of identity in these cases reflected the physical reality of anatomical incompleteness. A perseverance of the female body image and the defense of castratedness (body-part surrender) was directly related to a body reality rather than to a psychologically integrated drive and ego organization. This became evident when the body image confusion proved to be reversible after operative intervention.

A direct and corrective influence on the body image—a component of the self-representation—and an indirect influence on ego function is no doubt possible at adolescence. What often appears as an endopsychic conflict is in fact the result of a body reality confusion, aggravated by reality fear, such as abnormality. Consequently, maturational thrusts in sex-appropriate body changes at puberty have a directly beneficial effect on ego functions, such as learning, thinking, and reality testing. Sex-appropriate body changes in puberty can rectify—at least partly—a distorted self-image with the result that the defenses bound up in it become dispensable. It goes without saying that such crises in delayed or inappropriate pubertal maturation reinforce infantile body-intactness anxiety which constitute lasting points of vulnerability.

The psychology of the self was enriched by a study which Spiegel (1959) undertook in relation to perceptual problems. The novelty of his approach lies in the application of perceptual, that is, Gestalt psychology to the inner perception of one's person (self-representations), a process which may be subject to analogous vicissitudes. The concept of "framework" is employed by Gestalt psychology in order to study the stability or instability—in essence the relativity—of perceptual evaluations. It appears that subjective evaluation is governed by a framework which can be scaled from a zero point of reference. With varying framework, the perceptions of the same object are judged differently. Constancy of perception depends on the constancy of ratio between percept and frame of reference.

In applying these findings to the field of inner perception, Spiegel refers to the self as framework. He concludes that "the operational significance of the concept 'self' is its function as framework. This constant frame of reference (the self) thus acts as a steadying flywheel to overcome the disturbing discontinuity of intermittent self-representations." The interrelatedness of self-feeling and the constancy of inner perception are significant for an understanding of adolescent oscillations in self-feeling and the final stabilization of self-feeling at the close of adolescence. As long as single self-representations cathected with new quantitics of narcissistic or aggressive energy are not "pooled by the ego to become part of the self," no stable frame of reference exists on which the stability of self-feeling can depend. When finally a new cathectic level of the self is fixed, a "steady ratio between single self-representation and self is re-established. This occurs especially toward the end of adolescence when a relatively steady self-feeling begins to emerge." The relatedness of Spiegel's hypothesis to Jacobson's concept of cathectic shifts between the constituent elements of the self is apparent.

The nature and function of the self have been presented here because it appears that the concept of the self is becoming an investigative and conceptual tool of increasing moment for the study of adolescence. The extensive exploration of defenses during the adolescent period seems to be giving way to an investigation of the self in its genetic and pathologic aspects, and the study of psychic organization and psychic restructuring is complementing the concentration on instinctual conflict as the paramount feature of the adolescent process.

VI

Environmental
Determinants

IT HAS ALWAYS BEEN a basic proposition of psychoanalytic theory that psychic structure takes its origin from the child's awareness of a separateness between the "I" and "non-I," between self and object, between ego and external reality. "The rudiments of the ego, as they emerge gradually in the first half of the first year of life, take their pattern from the environmental conditions which have left their imprint on the infant's mind by way of his early pleasure-pain experiences, the conditions themselves becoming internalized in the ego structure" (A. Freud, 1954).

The child's dependency on the mother's care, on the alimentary inflow, and on the stimulation of the sensorium for its normal maturation, all these conditions render the object world an intrinsic aspect of infantile existence. It follows that a social situation is the condition for psychological development. The psychosexual development of the child which, it is true, follows a schedule of physical maturation, can only undergo those transformations which insure the child's emotional growth if the environment provides concomitant opportunities for the psychic elaborations of instinctual drives. To speak of "instinctual man," is as misleading as to speak of "social man," unless one bears in mind that both are but reciprocal and partial abstractions of "total man."

The child's environment always and everywhere is represented by the specific practices and attitudes with which significant persons meet his physical and emotional needs. The outer world is initially modelled in congruence with the body schema, the mental representation of which constitutes the body ego. This basic spatial and sensory orientation is permanently fixed in the unconscious analogy of body schema and outer world, and never loses its archaic associative similitude. Peto's (1959) remarks are relevant to this point: "Symbolism in dreams and folklore indicates that finding and evaluating external reality is to a great extent determined by refinding one's own body in the environment. Thus the body image is of decisive importance in grasping the world around us. Peculiarities of one's body image may then cause to be conceived as a world which is different from that visualized by the average human being."

Reality resides in the mental representations of the outer world—the environment—which contains meaningful objects, values, and ideas with which the child becomes familiar. These mental representations, due to their varied cathexes, become the basis for judgment, motivation, and conflict. In describing psychic processes in man, a social reference is always implicit because without it no psychic life can exist. The fact that psychic life springs from an interaction between biological givens, including instinctual endowment, and the impingement of the outer world leaves no doubt as to their complementary function. There are degrees of complexity, but no alternatives as to priority. The internalization of the external world, the growing independence from the environment, the unfolding dependency on mental institutions, on complex mental functions such as fantasizing, symbol formation (speech), and thinking— these processes in their genetic, dynamic, and structural vicissitudes have always been the special concern of psychoanalytic investigation.

The first reactions of the infant to the environment are reflexive only. With the development of memory traces alongside the maturation of the sensory system, a distinction between the inner and outer world, between "I" and "non-I" becomes established. Maturational processes, such as increasing muscular co-ordination in, for example, walking, stimulate recognition of the outer world and selective awareness of it. Outer reality is always different as far as its signal specificity or meaningfulness for different individuals is concerned, and this distinction persists throughout life despite the fact that individuals partake in consensual similarities of behavior and attitudes which constitute an empathic bond between members of the same culture. The primitive similarities by which individuals view the environment are based on the twofold fact that, on the one hand, they share a similar body structure and functioning, and on the other, they exercise the same instinctual drives in relation to their basic environment. This genetic link becomes increasingly blurred as mental institutions achieve a state of progressive autonomy, but the link remains traceable in dreams, speech (metaphor, simile), and fantasy. Psychic processes, as well as psychic structures, are more or less the same for all individuals of a given society; however, the associated emotions and psychic content diverge enormously, and their variations and manifestations are, indeed, boundless.

At this point I would like to mention the "fitting in" of the human organism into his social environment, a process which Hartmann (1950, a) called the "average expectable environment" to which the organism is preadapted, an environment which is a precondition for survival. The average expectable environment is consonant with the physical and mental equipment of the child. Indeed, the interaction between both, supported and directed by maturation and development, effects differentiating processes of increasing complexity. Hartmann (1950, a) refers to this phenomenon as "social compliance." At any rate, the interpretation of the environment in terms of selective awareness and obligatory rememberings constitutes the rudiment of learning, and is tendered by the significant persons in the child's world. These significant figures provide ego content and effect its structure; they account for the selection of percepts which become cathected, and for the mental representations of the outer world of which the child takes special cognizance and to which it cannot fail to react. The reality principle receives an added dimension after the establishment of the rudimentary self on the basis of the shared and identical, that is, learned, evaluation of events, objects, and feelings. Identification with parental figures establishes an increasing experience of the constancy of the external world, a process which is aided and stabilized by symbol formation, namely, the use of language. Only after the relinquishment of primitive ambivalence is the child able to take the feelings and motives of others into account. Only then do we see what Fenichel (1945, a) called the "rational component of social fear." He continues by saying "that an objective judgment of the probable reactions of the environment must, in normal persons, supplant the rigid and automatized superego reactions of the latency period and adolescence. The full development of the reality principle includes a certain reasonable reprojection of parts of the superego into the external world."

Every child knows the behavior which is expected of it by the environment, and uses this knowledge to achieve maximum gratification. Postponement, i.e., tension tolerance, and the ability to anticipate the future also play an essential part in this process. Unacceptable stimuli from inner or outer sources are blocked from direct discharge, and effect inner changes—for example, reaction formations. On the other hand, they also contribute their share to the private world of thought, fantasy, and feeling which lends an individual quality to every experience. Modifications of ego and superego attitudes by social conditions have been amply demonstrated by clinical as well as by anthropological studies.

We can now say that component aspects of the environment are differently experienced by different individuals, and conclude that environment is what is perceived, while reality is what is cathected. We may add that in the first instance the sense organ is cathected, and in the second instance the percept. It follows that reality in the psychological sense is only a fragment of the environment; the latter, being supraordinate, is theoretically limitless. The dichotomy between inner and outer perception, however, remains unalterable. The capacity of reality testing as well as the sense of reality are both rooted in the fixity of this separateness. Each culture possesses its idiosyncratic, patterned, outer world image which it transmits to the child. The relativity of reality in terms of description, evaluation, cognition, and emotional aspects has been demonstrated by psychoanalysis, psychology, anthropology, and sociology. The consensual congruence of reality remains a statistical matter. What often seems rational and identical social behavior—such as conforming with the law—has quite varied motivations when viewed in relation to the total personality. The uniform usage of logic and causality establishes objective reality in its scientific and definitive sense.

Psychoanalysis has studied the ways in which the psychic organism develops in order that it may fit into a given social environment and maintain itself in it. The theoretical explanation which relates average individual behavior to social institutions and which describes the effects they have on each other is the contribution of sociology. Parsons (1950) clearly expresses this idea: "What is meant by social structure is a system of patterned expectations of the behavior of individuals who occupy particular statuses in the social system. Such a system of patterned legitimate expectations is called by sociologists a system of roles. Insofar as a cluster of such roles is of strategic significance to the social system, the complex of patterns which define expected behavior in them may be referred to as an institution." Parson emphasizes the fact that no direct correspondence exists between personality structure and social structure; however, there is no doubt that "the behavior of individuals is motivated to conform with institutional expectations, even though personal structure as such does not give an adequately effective background for it." Any elaboration of a theory which explains such postulated mechanisms of social behavior lies in the domain of sociology. One is led to believe that constantly changing social conditions exert a decisive influence on psychic organization, as is exemplified by the changing picture of the prevalent neuroses of a given time. However, psychic processes seem to remain the same.

Biological needs are gratified or frustrated by the environment represented consecutively by persons, objects, and social institutions. The response of the environment to the child's needs is specifically patterned in the interest of the preservation of social institutions such as kinship system (family, monogamy), dietary customs, types of clothing, economic system, and so on. Cultural patterning is anchored in emotional reactions, consistent attitudes, and value codes of the environment. These learned specificities are the result of the particular practices employed by society to transform infantile instinctual drives into social conventions and customs. What has begun in the molding of the instinctual drive through pleasure-pain experiences is soon extended to the system of ego and superego. In these respects we may speak of the progression from a somatic to a symbolic acculturation level.

Erikson (1950) has paid particular attention to the specific methods of child rearing which utilize the plasticity of the infantile organism in the interest of society. He demonstrated this process with clinical and anthropological material, by describing the "psycho-social development" of the child in terms of an intrinsic mutuality between child and society. Society uses biological givens to develop attitudes, sensitivities, interests —both positive and negative—which serve its conservation by the establishment of ego congruity among its members and ego continuity within each of them.

Just as the time-honored dichotomy of body and soul fell into oblivion under the influence of psychoanalytic investigation, for the same reason it now seems unwise to contemplate as antithetical the biological and social determinants in the behavior of man. Biological needs and social conditions must be viewed as complementary: the former remain static and conservative; the latter appear changeable and fluid. Theoretically, there is no limit to the social variations by which the instinctual needs of man can be expressed. Grinker (1955) has voiced similar ideas: "Although physical growth is self-limited, we have as yet observed no limits to psychological growth except that set by the ageing of somatic organs, and no limit to social and cultural change. Human individuals and their collective societies seek new experiences, new challenges, and new concepts. They seem as much involved with growth, development, and change independent of self-preservation, although new devices of internal regulation and homeostasis closely follow each other." These remarks are well-illustrated by the social phenomenon of adolescence in Western culture.

It has often been remarked that Western democratic, capitalistic society provides hardly any uniform processes or techniques to define the adolescent role, nor does this society recognize ritually the adolescent status change. In many primitive societies, and also in political systems of nationalistic or totalitarian structure, the adolescent is recognized and inducted into the privileges and responsibilities pertaining to his rank or status in the culture or system. Ritualistic procedures often symbolize the stage of coming of age. Anthropology has provided ample descriptions of the *rites de passage*. "Changes of dwelling, entrance into youth societies, ordeals, tests of personal skill and endurance, acquisition of a guardian spirit, the importance conceded to adolescent dreams and visions, separation from the family group, disappearance from home into forest or desert, initiation into sexual life, freedom from childhood restraints, use of decorations, mutilations, serve as symbols of the enlarged status" (Van Waters, 1930).

We can view the social institutions of Western culture and the way in which they impinge on adolescence under a teleological aspect similar to the methods employed in childrearing. The particular way in which society takes cognizance of the pubescent child is significantly relevant in terms of the character structure which a given society, in this case Western culture, requires for its intrinsic preservation. It is no mere accident when educational principles undergo changes, nor is the direction these changes take a matter of chance. During adolescence, in sharp contrast to early childhood, the lack of institutionalized patterning is striking. Society, so to speak, abandons youth and lets it fend for itself.

Social institutions in their effect on the individual aim at the elaboration of attitudes and character traits, at the selective responsiveness to social stimuli and value systems which restrict reactions to a circumscribed scope. Social anxiety is the signal which warns the individual that he is overstepping the limits and is treading on dangerous ground. It seems of intrinsic significance that modern democratic capitalistic society does not offer youth any status confirmation, no initiation rites nor consecration. Adolescents left to their own devices will spontaneously form competitive organizations within their own ranks. Gangs, cliques, groups for all kinds of purposes, and unified by all kinds of principles set themselves against each other: their emphasis is on aggressive dominance, competitive superiority, and hostile exclusiveness. In the structure of these adolescent groups a dual-value principle operates, according to which the attitudes (ethics) applied to the ingroup but not to the out-group are not experienced as moral contradictions.

The vacuum of uninstitutionalized adolescence in Western society thus allows, on the one hand, a high degree of personality differentiation and individualization, since there are no obligatory models, but on the other hand, the discontinuities in social patterning and the burden of self-determination facilitate deviate and pathological development. What on the surface often appears to be rational and adaptive behavior, proves, on closer inspection, to serve an individual's instinctual gratification in such areas as competition, acquisitiveness, and vindictiveness —gratification which society condones or even encourages. Each society favors certain rationalizations, reaction formations, and sexualization of behavior; and the hypocrisy of society inherent in its organization is exposed, caricatured, and challenged by the asocial and antisocial behavior of youth. The aggressive competitive behavior of adolescent social organizations merely reflects the social pattern of the culture of which they are a part. The reciprocity between the need of the individual and the social conditions can be viewed as the social determinism of human behavior. This social compliance allows, on the one hand, patterned drive satisfaction, and on the other hand, parallels the defensive functions of the ego by binding or controlling anxiety.

What arouses interest in this connection is the critical limit of social institutions beyond which the biological needs of man cannot any longer find adequate, i.e., adaptive expression; at this critical point physical and emotional health shows signs of breaking down. These considerations are of special significance in relation to those periods in human development, such as adolescence, when the transformation of drives becomes solidified into permanent reaction patterns—in short, when the formation of character is taking place. The environment represented by social institutions and role designation can be viewed as supplying both beneficial or noxious stimuli. Its noxious influences are overexcitation of the organism, both somatic and psychic, resulting normally in protective reactions, adaptive and pathological. An optimal stimulus and discharge level exists for the individual relative to all areas of functioning. Each developmental phase requires a specific experience in kind and in range; furthermore, each developmental phase requires protectiveness in relation to specific points of vulnerability which, in some way or other, are perpetuated throughout life. We have followed this resurgence in adolescence proper and its integration into the personality at late adolescence. Normally, then, a stimulus barrier protects the child against noxious influences from the environment. In an analogous way, the adolescent ego protects its integrity against disorganizing, noxious influences emanating from the id, the superego, and the outer world by psychic processes which were described above. Beneficial stimuli or experiences have to be consonant with phase-specific needs; some such experiences in adolescence might be found in peer affiliation, extrafamilial identification, opportunities for experimentation, and reasonable equality with adults—for instance, in employment. One is tempted to define the average expectable environment of adolescence, but the problem soon grows into a state of staggering complexity, and besides, it lies outside the scope of this discussion. However, to arrive at an operational definition of this concept would represent a decisive methodological step toward a positive mental health program for adolescence. Hartmann (1947) summarized the underlying problem in abstract terms: "We shall not forget that social institutions and a psychological climate develop, or are created, in such a way that when action takes place in agreement with the changed attitudes toward the instinctual drives and the superego, it will tend to gratify interests of the ego (for social status, influence, wealth and so forth) at the same time."

To record the phenomenology of adolescence would require a most extensive inventory which would only have to be amended as each day passes. Let us consider just one behavioral item of adolescence, the wearing apparel which characterizes and distinguishes certain groups, cliques, coteries, and gangs of more or less definable cohesion. Many styles have paraded as teenage garb. These self-chosen clothing styles give expression to the adolescent's changing body- and self-image besides serving the social purpose of establishing a group identity in our society. Of course, adolescent attire is only one item, selected at random, which calls attention to the infinite variability found in any one aspect of adolescent behavior. Other areas of equal interest are adolescent slang, dance styles, ritualistic behavior, party etiquette, coded male and female prerogatives, and obligations in heterosexual conduct.

Typical adolescent behavior could be described indefinitely, since there are not only constant shifts and innovations, but also neighborhood nuances, class and caste modifications, and, indeed, geographical mutation—influenced, no doubt, by climate, local history (e.g. the West, Texas), by glamorous or dominant occupations (e.g. movies, cowboys), and by the prevailing ethos of a respective country or region. One could well envisage an ecology of adolescent behavior; its systematic study would add valuable data to the behavioral sciences. We are accustomed to see in the patterned behavior of childhood the prevailing ethos of a society and its institutions; it is of equal interest to investigate the influence of this same ethos on adolescent fads, costumes, rituals, and mores. American youth, for example, clearly reflects the dominant features of its society: extroversion, chumminess, popularity hunger, being "on the go," being a "good mixer," and "minding one's own business."

Sociologists have studied regions and communities where the influence of the milieu on the prevailing forms of adolescent behavior is well documented. However, the phenomenology of adolescence is not the purpose of this investigation, and we must instead concentrate on unifying the variations of manifest behavior by subordinating them to developmental principles, *i.e.*, by recognizing in them a pervasive adaptive process which has been initiated by puberty and which takes innumerable forms. As universal as puberty itself are the inherent tasks which must be met in order to grow up in Western culture. The adolescent process has many facets because it is affected by the sum total of conditions—social, economic, political, religious, historical, educational—which constitute the matrix of individual and collective life. The adolescent must elaborate his maturational tasks in terms of their articulation with a given environment. Consequently adolescent characteristics vary widely, but we can assume that the underlying processes reflect teleological similarities.

Bernfeld was the first to study this problem extensively, and to investigate the influences of social conditions on the adolescent process. He described the similarities and dissimilarities of development typical for different social milieus such as those denoted by caste or class within the same social system, and concluded that psychological development is not fully intelligible without reference to the social environment as an independent variable. Bernfeld (1929) states: "The vicissitudes of the instinctual drives at a given epoch receive—apart from the correctness of all Freudian mechanisms and dynamisms—their unique imprint from the milieu in which they occur. . . . We suggest that the question as to the historical aspect and to the impact of the milieu on a given psychic process be delineated and summarized as the aspect of the 'social locus' [sozialer Ort in the sense of 'social environment']."

Bernfeld concluded that both a historical and a milieu aspect can be delineated in all normal and pathological processes, and applied this concept to the description of the "simple male puberty" (1935) which is milieu-bound in that it follows the shortest possible distance to adult sexual organization. This development typical for abbreviated adolescence always results in a certain primitivization of the personality. As I pointed out above, adolescence requires an optimal, indeed culture-bound, time span, for only under such conditions will the various phase-specific drive organizations elicit corresponding ego interests and attitudes, or, generally, lend the personality a complex countenance. The influence of the environment is thus recognizable in the relative complexity or primitivization of the personality due to goal and time allotted by the social milieu for the completion of the adolescent process.

Returning to the fact that manifestations of the adolescent process permit endless variations, we shall view these here as epiphenomena. On the other hand, the adolescent process as the psychological reaction to puberty, produces intra-psychic changes which we shall view as core phenomena. In order to describe any segment of the adolescent process, it becomes necessary to abstract a given epiphenomenon to the level of the corresponding core phenomenon; only then shall we be able to recognize the dynamic and structural references within the psychic organization. These correlations are essential aids in the psychological description and the diagnosis of adolescent behavior.

An illustration may clarify the above remarks. Two adolescent boys whose behavior and attitude are antithetical have in common the fact that they struggle with the identical psychological problem, namely, the disengagement from early object ties. One of them accepts the value system and the class standards of his family; he concentrates his "rebelliousness" on usurping as quickly as possible the pleasure privileges of adults. In contrast is the boy who focuses his "rebelliousness" on the value system of his parents and of the milieu to which he belongs. He does not desire their privileges; he only wants to be different from them. Everything which is alien to his milieu becomes desirable and worth doing, thinking, and feeling. This kind of adolescent may grow into an artist, a reformer, a delinquent, a social rebel, or a crackpot mender of all ills; he has a tendency to marry out of his class, religion, and ethnic group.

What is the situation when society or, better, the state, turns the rebelliousness of youth to its own advantage? When this happens, the channels for rebellion with which we are familiar in a democratic, capitalistic society necessarily dry up and an entirely different picture of adolescence presents itself. A report on the status of the adolescent in a totalitarian state illustrates this:

Communist youths are to be made responsible in the East German republic for seeing that their elders behave themselves in trade and commerce . . . members of the Communist Federation of German Youth were to be installed as controllers of trade and business transactions. Youth control posts will be installed in all state stores and cooperatives. They are to check on weaknesses and oversights in commercial undertakings. They are to be "ruthless in dealing with waste, bureaucracy and deficit operation." . . . Youth brigades are at work in industry checking to see that the norms of the first five-year plan now in its final year are being carried out. . .members of the Communist Youth Federation check up on the teaching given in the schools. Any variation from the plan laid down by the regime is immediately reported to the authorities. Teachers who are not themselves Communists of standing are reported to treat with deference and respect students in their classes who hold some rank in the youth organization. . . . Youth is apparently becoming rapidly a ruling caste with a vested interest in the regime, which is regarded by the adult generation as an alien imposition. The conflict came to the fore again last week between the church and the Communist regime over the ceremony of "youth consecration," by which young people solemnly assume their obligations with the Communist society.*

It can be expected that youth which is thus aggrandized and given caste status by the leaders of government will be prevented from turning its rebelliousness against the existing social and political order. These heirs of the regime will grow up to become conservative and live in rigid identification with the past order. But should however the powers which "consecrated" this youth ever be defeated, then a narcissistic disappointment and a loss of identity (devaluation of narcissistic identification) will mobilize restitutive measures. Several Italian writers have dealt with this problem and the tragic condition of youth after the collapse of fascism: Berto (1948), Pratolini (1951) and others have shown in their novels how disillusioned youth, the aggrandised *giovinezza* (youth organization) of Mussolini, turned either to new, mostly radical, political ideologies, to self-deception (denial), to self-degradation, or to cynicism, delinquency and criminality.

Social realities in which the individual adolescent finds himself afford avenues for gratification and modification of drives within a limited array of behavior patterns and discharge channels. In order to be adaptive the pursuit of these open channels has to be paralleled by appropriate ego positions. The interrelatedness among drive, ego, and environment is neither static nor linear, but can best be described as a circular response. Let us consider the following: before a conflicted wish is executed in the outer world, it goes through several preparatory stages, such as preconscious mentation, trial action in thought and fantasy, experimentation (not yet ego-syntonic) and eventually becomes ego-syntonic action without conflict or anxiety. Each step toward the expression of a conflicted, but phase-specific, drive becomes less anxiety-producing because of the realization derived from experience that the feared danger is exaggerated and imaginary. This process of reality testing enhances the ego's mastery of the environment, an achievement which the individual experiences as an increase in self-esteem and in self-assurance, and as a firmer sense of identity.

One reason for the adolescent's propensity to social experimentation lies in the opportunity such experiences afford him to separate fact from

---

* Report by Albion Ross from Berlin, *New York Times*, February 21, 1955.

fancy, that is, to extend the sovereignty of the reality principle. A small child often imputes to certain of his actions grossly distorted and exaggerated consequences; severity is due to the child's projected aggression. This factor plays a decisive role in the formation of the superego and is partly responsible for the intensity of guilt feelings. The severity of the superego is thus partially independent of reality. Observation has indicated that many adolescents brought up by benign and permissive parents exhibit the most severe superego problems; these are, in fact, problems of unresolved ambivalence. Adolescent aggression which is not turned against the parent or the superego, or against the self, is projected on parental images in the social environment—police, teachers, bosses.

"During puberty the oedipus complex is revived and declines by nonincestuous authority figures taking the place of parents . . . postambivalent series become established in which objects of love and hate are represented by different persons and, consequently, love and hate occur relatively independent of each other" (Landauer, 1935). Society provides objects for shared hate (aggression), a condition which sustains the cohesiveness of the group. The objects of shared love reside more firmly in values and ideas which are often represented by "a central person" (Redl, 1942). This dichotomy is slowly achieved. The adolescent wages a battle against authority figures with the collaborative support of the group, the influence of which mitigates superego as well as social anxiety. Through transient identification with the central person of the group, or with the egos of its members, the individual is aided in separating out the projective component from objective fact. This process can extend over years; it shows how important adolescent group life is and demonstrates the conventionalizing influence which the group exerts on the individual: the environment is viewed in identical terms by all members of the group. The transformation through group psychological processes often involves so-called delinquent behavior of the type which Glover (1956) designated as "functional delinquency"; this behavior is the expression of an acute growth problem rather than the consequence of an infantile pathogenic fixation.

The contributions of Redl (1942) to the problem of group formative processes in adolescence should be mentioned here. He studied the types of group formation which correspond to the respective developmental levels of the child. The latency child accepts a "patriarchal or matriarchal sovereign-type of group pattern," but the preadolescent is "intensively attracted by the gang type of group relationship. . . . Even very egotistic and spoiled persons may go through a phase of intense loyalty to a gang. It brings prestige. . . . A considerable degree of security is derived from this type of group relationship. They [preadolescents] are desperately in need of expressing suppressed drives and urges. Many of them need drive protection more than drive sublimation. . . . The adolescent exhibits a growing preference for a more sublimated group formation. The needs of youth seek outlets in the group which also protects them from guilt feelings and anxieties, and leads into more mature patterns of life. . . . The delinquent youngster, however, retains his need for preadolescent drive protection against the educative process. This is why so-called 'criminal' gangs are obviously fixed at the preadolescent level of gang formation."

Which experiences or which mental content in the life of an adolescent assumes imaginary and distorted qualities are questions that can hardly be answered in general terms; but the way in which reality distortion is corrected follows typical lines. From the therapy of adolescents it is known that the individual's selective awareness of the environment changes with, for example, the resolution of a conflict or a fixation and also with a shift in defenses. The same processes which have been explored in the analysis of adolescents are generally at work in this age group. However, what interests us here is the active use of his environment which the adolescent makes or fails to make. His experiences are the subjective aspect of this process, and they vary in accordance with his ability to use environmental resources and stimuli to support his progressive development. In many cases I have had occasion to observe, for example, that boarding school placement of an adolescent can forestall deviate development caused by continued noxious overstimulation by one or both of the parents.

Redl (1942) referred to a scantily explored problem by saying "that many children, who have trouble in making their group adjustment, need a change in their personal drive patterns before they can adapt effectively, although it is equally true that many children are only assisted in effecting personality developments under certain group psychological conditions." Normally, the adolescent creates for himself an environment which is conducive to his phase of development. The stabilizing mechanisms which he employs were described above; here we shall add the identification with a family-alien milieu. By making this move, the adolescent displaces needs and libidinous dependency ties which can no longer find gratification in the original family. This attempt to solve an inner conflict by social action, which can be either conforming or rebellious, often represents acting out rather than adaptive behavior. This is especially true for adolescents whose permanent social oppositionalism is determined by an ambivalence conflict with the family. However, flight into family-alien, subcultural milieus may also serve progressive development. Transient identification with an adolescent group of a specific peer culture, or with adult groups of a specific ideological or social bent permits the young person to try himself out in various roles, and thus test their desirability. Such flights are often used as holding actions. The removal from noxious parental stimulation and the exposure to an environment with a positive identification potential often mobilizes progressive development after it has almost come to a standstill. The usefulness of the environment as a stimulus factor depends on the adolescent's selective receptivity; this receptivity depends greatly on his self-image, and no doubt is widened and modified by the social sanctions which prevail in his group as well as by available models for identification and counteridentification.

Redl (1942) studied the particular effect of the group on individual conflict situations; he referred to it as the "guilt-and-fear assuaging effect of the initiatory act." He elaborates: "I have noticed that children are obviously helped in their decisions, either in favor of the drives or of the superego demands, by association with other children who definitely represent the one or the other solution. . . . I found, as a condition for this effect, [that] the first person must be on the verge of having to make either the one or the other decision. Moreover, the influential person must have definitely resolved his own conflict." This is what is meant when we speak colloquially of good or bad company and its influence on young people.

To the two adaptive principles of alloplastic and autoplastic behavior, Hartmann (1956) added a third, "in which neither the outside world nor the individual is really changed; instead their relationship is changed: I am thinking of the search for and finding of a more appropriate environment." How many individuals in their late adolescence have successfully changed their environment, not being content with the kind and scope of opportunity for self-realization which the original environment offered! Temporary flights from conflicted family relationships will often aid in a loosening of infantile object ties and permit a less conflicted return to life with the family.

The pathognomic aspect of the shift from one social milieu to another was described by Bernfeld (1929). "This change of social locus deserves our attention as a special kind of displacement of instinctual gratification. We know this process well . . . it is not infrequent among adolescents from a middle class milieu who show various symptoms of delinquency. One finds among these adolescents successful or not so successful attempts to change the social locus with the aim of avoiding the efforts of repression or sublimation. Most adolescents, however, cannot accomplish this shift realistically. The libidinous or social tie to their original milieu remains too powerful."

A case to illustrate this particular problem is that of Frank, who at the age of nineteen had failed in college and had fallen into a state of indecision and lethargy. He was the adopted son of highly intellectual parents. In the course of psychotherapy, Frank decided to become a laborer and started to work in a factory. He felt happy and at ease with his fellow workers and soon decided to move in with one of their families. He deeply enjoyed the simple pleasures and interests of his new milieu. In making this change in his milieu, Frank followed the relentless pull of the infantile object tie to his foster parents. He had lived in a family of uneducated people before he was adopted when he was three years old. As Frank became able to recall the memories of his childhood as well as the love he had felt for his foster parents, a gradual disengagement process occurred. The acting out as a special form of remembering was translated into the concrete memories of his past. When the reliving of this past became dispensable, Frank returned to his adoptive family. Freed from the regressive pull to his original milieu, the abrupt separation from which had been traumatic, Frank returned to college, successfully studied for a doctorate, and became equal in intellectual pre-eminence to his parents.

Fenichel (1945, a) remarked: "Certainly not only frustrations and reactions to frustrations are socially determined: what a human being desires is also determined by his cultural environment." The prevalence and type of mental disturbances are both profoundly influenced by social conditions. The classical hysteria of the turn of the century has become rare now that the atmosphere of the nursery has given way to less prohibitive and rigid attitudes in child rearing. The prerequisite for the development of hysteria—severe sexual repression due to strict prohibitions—has largely disappeared. No doubt the enlightened approach was sparked by the discoveries of psychoanalysis; but it should not be over-

looked that these ideas played simultaneously into man's wish for omnipotence. The ambitious hopes of parents for their children seemed sci-
entifically realizable once the shackling limitations of an outmoded
heredity were disposed of for good. It is no surprise that the prevailing
disturbances of the present time reflect in their structure the prevailing
tenor of enlightened educational principles and their less conspicuous
but nonetheless irrational motives. "The inconsistency of the modern
neurotic personality corresponds to the inconsistency of present-day
education. The change in neurosis reflects the change in morality. Different societies, stressing different values and applying different educational measures, create different anomalies" (Fenichel, 1945, b).

Analysis of adolescent girls and older women, has made it apparent
that the shift from the double to the single standard has not affected the
fantasy life of the girl (Deutsch, 1944). Women have acquired equal
place to man in society, but the double standard has really never been
relinquished; certainly not by men. Modern man's fear of passivity or
of the active woman proves to be as eternal as modern woman's struggle
to come to terms with her femininity. The conservatism of infantile
fantasies remains stronger than the influence of enlightened education.
Helene Deutsch (1944) notes that "it is unbelievable how many even
modern girls still imagine during adolescence that the apertures of their
bodies serve only 'dirty' purposes and have nothing to do with love."
The cloaca conception continues to persist in the unconscious. Sexual
conflict continues to persist in spite of greater tolerance of instinct expression and sexual enlightenment, and the new situation thus created
has brought about an increase in neurotic character formation.

The keen mind of the child is quick to discover the discrepancy between parental permissiveness and institutional sanctions. This dilemma
of the modern child in a progressive home is illustrated by the following
anecdote. An enlightened mother who found that her eight-year-old son
and his playmate had secretly undressed decided to treat the incident
lightly. In a matter of fact way she explained that a penis is really nothing so special; after all, "it's just another part of your body like your
arm or your nose or your foot." The boy turned to his mother, and said,
"There is a difference, mom. The teacher told us how to spell arm and
nose and foot; she never told us how to spell penis."

The assessment of adolescent behavior is always complicated by the
fact that the "principle of multiple function" (Waelder, 1936) operates
in all behavior. A multitude of trends operate in each psychic event; the

synthetic function of the ego permits purposeful action to emerge. Adolescent behavior is always complex and overdetermined: it does not speak for itself, but requires interpretation. The confluent determinants of behavior originating both inside and outside of the organism acquire a psychological unity insofar as the ego is able to integrate them in the service of progressive development. Whenever the cohesiveness of the ego is weakened, and whenever isolated motivations become rampant, as they do in emotional disturbances, the clinical observer gains insight into the course of adaptive processes by this very failure. It is an accepted fact that we learn about the normal progression of development through developmental disturbances and their disruptive influence on the homeostatic controls of the personality.

In this discussion of social determinants, I have singled out relevant areas which may be viewed under the aspect of a unifying principle. The concept which gave rise to the psychosocial determinism of human behavior originated in the confluence of three tributaries, namely, the constitutional equipment, the sequence of drive and ego organization, and the environment. None of the three possesses priority in determining men's behavior: each exerts an influence on the other. Constitutional equipment cannot be changed by environmental influences; we are accustomed to define congenital variations in terms of activity types (Fries), temperament, intelligence, or barrier against stimuli (Escalona). Freud (1937) was convinced that the id and the ego possess a constitutional *Anlage* which influences individual propensities to specific body zone needs, to degrees of bisexuality and, generally to preferential modes of stabilization effected by the ego. This constitutional factor makes individual adaptation in a given culture either more difficult or less difficult, dependent on the dominant trend of its institutions, its preference for and commendation of certain personality characteristics. For example, American society favors the child who is active, outgoing, bouncy and a "go-getter."

The fact that puberty first of all is a biological event has been stressed often in order not to lose sight of its basic significance. By following the model of psychosexual and ego development of early childhood, we may conclude that the sexual maturation of puberty also implies a similar adaptive task to social conditions, the continuation of a process, which has been active since life began. The adaptation to the social reality during adolescence acquires a fixity and stability which childhood never possessed. A certain degree of continuity, constancy, and sameness in the environment has a functional significance for the stability of psychic structure and function. The creation of an idiosyncratic environment is the task of the closing phase of adolescence; in the extent to which this endeavor succeeds one can gauge the individual's alloplastic potential. The critical point of disequilibrization as well as the rate of environmental changes which can be tolerated and integrated varies from individual to individual.

The adaptive tasks of adolescence will always be accomplished in terms of the inner reality which has been shaped by antecedent experiences of having been a child in a given family, at a given place, during a given epoch in history, with a given *Anlage*. The particular articulation on the environment of adolescent needs proceeds within these fixed conditions, and determines the manifest course which each individual passage through adolescence will take.

VII

Two Illustrations
of Deviate
Adolescent Development

In THE COURSE of delineating the phases of adolescence, I made repeated reference to phase-specific psychological tasks. These steps in progressive development were defined in terms of drive and ego organization; they were thought of as critical points in the epigenesis of adolescent development, because failure at the attainment of essential transformations within a given crucial period necessarily leads to deviate personality formation.

It goes without saying that deviations from normal development never occur without antecedent events exerting their significant influence. What we observe clinically is simply a definitive break in progressive development. We refer to these failures as fixations on one of the various

217

phases of either early childhood or adolescence. This failure can occur at any of the critical developmental junctures of adolescence, which were defined above. In fact, it often becomes apparent only at the adolescent level, when progressive development has become arrested, just how persistent an early childhood fixation remains, and to what an undiminished degree it asserts itself. While it may have been possible for the child to go forward until adolescence, it often becomes evident at this period whether transformatory changes effect compromise solutions in the form of "adaptive repairs" (see the case of John, page 136), or whether progressive development will come to a standstill. Pathological development is usually masked by the fact that ego and drive partially progress despite their continued subordination to early fixations. In considering a development which suffered defeat in the preadolescent phase, we should not be misled by the fact that a degree of social adaptation and heterosexual orientation have manifested themselves. We may recognize in derivatives of preadolescent phase-specific drive and ego modalities, in poorly organized hierarchical arrangement of drive components and ego interests, and especially in the—often wildly overcompensated—fear of the phallic, castrating woman the indisputable signs of a fixation on the preadolescent phase. An analysis of the clinical picture reveals that primitive, i.e., phase-alien, ego and drive modalities assert themselves on a somatic and mental level which has been brought forward by the function of growth. Pubertal growth, after all, proceeds independently of emotional growth, although under normal circumstances, to be sure, there exists an optimal correspondence between both. The concept of adolescent fixation is illustrated in the clinical material which follows.

It seems opportune at this point to repeat the fact that no natural course of adolescence can be mapped out with the precision and predictability which pubertal growth can claim. All we can say is that adolescence allows infinite elaborations of its progressive psychic transformations within the confines of a sequential pattern and within certain limits of individual tolerance.

There are several specific courses the adolescent process can take. The schematic outline which follows is offered as an attempt at classifying observations along typical lines of clinical variances. 1) *Typical Adolescence*: progressive modification of the personality in consonance with pubertal growth and changing social role; 2) *Protracted Adolescence*: a culturally determined prolongation of the adolescent status; 3)

Abbreviated Adolescence: pursuit of the shortest possible route to adult functioning at the expense of personality differentiation; 4) *Simulated Adolescence:* an abortive latency period makes puberty manifest itself in a simple intensification of one of the prelatency drive organizations; 5) *Traumatic Adolescence:* regressive acting out, an example of which is to be found in female delinquency; 6) *Prolonged Adolescence:* perseveration in the adolescent process caused by the libidinization of adolescent ego states; 7) *Abortive Adolescence:* psychotic surrender with loss of reality contact and breakdown of differential learning. The first three of these categories are in the range of normal adolescence; the last four represent deviate developments. It is hoped that the formulation of phases will be useful in that it offers insight into the dynamics and etiology of developmental failures.

The two examples of deviate development presented below illustrate the theory of adolescent development in terms of specific breakdowns of the adolescent process. The significance of certain processes as defined in phase-specific ego and drive alterations can be confirmed and refined through the study of deviate adolescence. Deviate development, in turn, will indicate the latitude which phase-specific development can tolerate and spell out the pathogenic consequences of a departure from essential developmental requirements. This clinical material, then, will primarily illuminate normal development—the chartering and description of which has been my major purpose throughout this book. The two clinical illustrations are not intended to highlight adolescent psychopathology in general. They do show, however, a typical course which adolescent development may take after it has come to a critical impasse, and in this sense, of course, the cases do represent psychopathology typical of and restricted to the adolescent period.

Since the boy and the girl follow different paths of emotional development, it stands to reason that deviate development must be represented by a male and a female syndrome.

1. Prolonged Adolescence in the Male*

The term "prolonged adolescence" was introduced by Bernfeld (1923). The object of his investigation at that time was prolonged male adoles-

---

* This section is based on an article that first appeared in somewhat different form in *The American Journal of Orthopsychiatry*, October, 1954.

cence as a social phenomenon observed in European youth movements after the First World War. Members of these groups presented a strong predilection for intellectualization and sexual repression, thus delaying the consolidation of the adolescent conflict. The designation of prolonged adolescence has come to have over the years broader connotations, with the result that the psychological specificity of the term has been lost. We are forced to say that "prolonged adolescence" is a descriptive and collective term which comprises conditions of heterogeneous dynamic constellations of which I have selected one for a more detailed discussion.

My observations were made on American middle-class young men, roughly between eighteen and twenty-two, who usually attend college or have at any rate some professional aspirations; this fact more often than not makes them financially dependent on their families during these years. The clinical picture which I shall sketch in the following has been observed with enough frequency to encourage the presentation of a synoptic summary.

The term *prolonged adolescence* as used here refers to a static perseveration in the adolescent position which under normal circumstances is of a transitory nature. A maturational phase which is intended to be left behind after it has accomplished its task becomes a way of life. Instead of the progressive push which normally carries the adolescent into adulthood, prolonged adolescence arrests this forward motion with the result that the adolescent crisis is never abandoned but kept open indefinitely. In fact, the adolescent crisis is adhered to with persistence, desperation and anxiousness. An admixture of satisfaction with this state of turmoil is never absent. The observer of such individuals senses quickly the superficial reassurance which is derived from a condition which keeps the adolescent crisis open. The fervent clinging to the adolescent unsettledness of all of life's issues renders any progression to adulthood an achievement which is hardly worth the price. This dilemma leads to the contriving of ingenious ways to combine childhood gratifications with adult prerogatives. The adolescent strives to bypass the finality of choices which are exacted at the close of adolescence.

Living in the twilight of an arrested transition renders the adolescent self-conscious and ashamed. When he tries to remain solitary he becomes restless and confused. This inability to be alone forces him to join groups. Company rescues him from daydreaming and autoerotic preoccupation. Friendships with boys are transient or unstable; homosexual involvement is a constant threat. When he becomes attached to a girl he clings to her with devoted and dependent faithfulness. Seemingly he is capable of intimacy and finds sexual relations satisfying; on closer examination these so-called "sexual relations" appear to be of the forepleasure type, such as kissing, fondling, body closeness, pleasure in nakedness, and mutual masturbation. This love relationship is by no means of sexual character only; the sharing of interests, of ideas and ideals, plays an important role. This intensive need to share involves an extreme egocentricity and demandingness which reveals the infantile nature of this relationship. The girl chosen is always a fitting challenge to the partner's incestuous attachment because she offers traits which are strikingly different or similar to the significant family member, be it mother or sister. The type of girl chosen is usually condemned by the boy's family. It appears as if the adolescent through the choice of his love object makes a convulsive effort to extricate himself from an infantile involvement. This battle of emancipation is fought with his girl friend as his comrade-in-arms and often continues for a long period of time; I have also seen such a relationship develop into a congenial marriage in cases where therapy intervened at this impasse in the separation struggle from the family.

Exalted self-expectations are dominant in the lives of these young men. In one way or another they have as children shown some promising talent; most of them are rather gifted and intelligent. Under the influence of parental ambition and narcissistic overevaluation these children came to expect fabulous achievements from themselves. Fame and greatness, passion and wealth, adventure and excitement figure vividly in their fantasies. The first failures in a career which supposedly would be foolproof come as crushing blows. At no point does the young man lose the recognition of the fact that failure is staring him in the face. He is annoyed, he is irritated and anxious; but he neither tries to maintain a lifeless phantasmagoria nor does he regress to childhood positions; he does not seek relief either in asocial acting out or in retaliatory passivity. The initiative for taking purposeful action is not lost; in fact, the imminent danger of surrender mobilizes all existing inner resources in order to ward off the final and decisive stages of the struggle. The lives of these adolescents never look quite empty and stale; only upon closer scrutiny one realizes how lost they are in the void of uncertainty and self-doubt. In order to escape from narcissistic impoverishment they rally desperately to continued attempts at "making good"; again, upon closer scrutiny these efforts appear slipshod and of phoney expediency. In all this turmoil the critical faculty of self-observation is never entirely lost and is in effect rather easily elicited if the proper cue is forthcoming in therapy. The well-known schizophrenic-like state of adolescence is not part of this clinical picture.

If we ignore for the moment the many similarities which the foregoing synoptic sketch shares with the general picture of adolescence, we will see more clearly the essential difference which sets off these cases from other forms of adolescent reaction. The difference is a remarkable resistivity against the regressive pull in conjunction with a persistent avoidance of any consolidation of the adolescent process. These are the dominant features of the specific condition called prolonged adolescence. Conversely, we might say that prolonged adolescence is the expression of an inner necessity to keep the adolescent crisis open.

The foregoing clinical synopsis needs to be complemented at this point by dynamic considerations. From "The Transformations of Puberty" (Freud, 1905, b) we learn that with the advent of sexual maturity at puberty a novel distribution of emphasis in sexual experience is introduced which permits the differentiation between fore- and end-pleasure, and which stimulates a rearrangement of instinctual aims. The biological innovation at puberty necessitates a hierarchical rearrangement of the multitudinous childhood positions—modes of gratification and of tension resolution as well as identifications—which, for various reasons, have remained indispensable to personality functioning and demand continued expression. It is a well-known fact that the pregenital drives manifest themselves again as soon as puberty has appeared. The urgency for a definitive hierarchical organization of drives gains momentum with advancing adolescence and provides the maturational push which allows no respite on the way to maturity. However, the hierarchical organization is not restricted to the sexual drives; it applies to ego functions as well. This may be illustrated by magical thinking, an archaic ego function; if magical thinking assumes dominance in adolescence it disrupts the unity of the ego and consequently disorganizes its capacity of reality testing. However, should magical thinking be subordinated to the realm of fantasy and find an outlet in creative experience, then the ego can retain its unity; in this case we can say that fantasy-oriented and reality-directed ideation become distinct and mutually exclusive. This process of differentiation widens the conflict-free sphere of the ego.

The adolescent process can be considered closed when a hierarchical and relatively inflexible organization of genital and pregenital drives has been attained, and when ego functions have acquired a significant resistivity against regression. Obviously, sublimation and defenses play their part in this process. Prolonged adolescence, if it is to be regarded as an indefinite respite on the way to adulthood, results, like any excessive perseveration on a developmental stage, in the deformation of personality attributes. In sharp contrast to differentiating processes which are essential for adolescent ego synthesis, it appears that prolonged adolescence is characterized by a failure at the hierarchical organization of drives and ego functions.

During prolonged adolescence, ego functions—thinking, memory, judgment, concentration, observation—become impaired from two sources: namely, from an inundation by sexual and aggressive drives, and by an ascendancy of archaic ego functions and primitive defenses. The adolescent falls back on the earliest modes of tension management; this reveals that the latency period has effected only meager progress in ego development. Let me illustrate this situation with a typical example: should studying create in the adolescent a tension which can only be relieved by recourse to autoerotic forms of discharge—masturbation, sleep, eating—or should studying be associated habitually with absorbing fantasies, then the tension span indispensable for the comprehension and mastery of a problem cannot be sustained and any effort at studying is bound to result in failure. In normal adolescence these *modi operandi* are transient and are eventually relinquished; but in prolonged adolescence this relinquishment is not only not sought but is avoided and counteracted.

The question now arises as to the economic factors which prevent the young men in prolonged adolescence from resorting to any even if abortive settlement of the adolescent crisis. In the study of this group of adolescent young men it became apparent that they had a typical childhood constellation in common. They all were regarded by both parents, or more emphatically by the mother, as destined to do great things in life. For reasons related to their own personality formation, their mothers were prone to bestow on their child fantasies of success, with complete disregard for the child's sex, capacities, and interests.

This situation is epitomized by the story of the pregnant woman who proudly replies to a friend who comments on her condition, "Yes, I am carrying my son, the doctor." Children who tend to live out the fantasies of their parents expect that life will unfold according to mother's or father's promises. Prolonged adolescence averts a crisis which must end in the crushing realization that the world outside the family fails to recognize the role which the child has tried to play for the first two decades of his life. Whenever his sources of identity are overwhelmingly external, the individual loses his sense of identity if he is removed from his environment; wherever he is, he follows the schema of infantile identity maintenance which says, "I am what others believe me to be." This is precisely what happens when these adolescents attempt the rupture of their emotional ties. They suddenly realize that this move is accompanied by a narcissistic impoverishment which they are unable to tolerate. Therefore, they continue to live in the self-image which their mothers, fathers, or sisters have created for them.

One might say of these young men that their great future lies behind them when they reach the threshold of manhood; nothing that reality has to offer can compete with that easy sense of elation and uniqueness which the child experienced when he was showered with maternal admiration and confidence. Both mother and child for reasons of their own persistently overlook the child's early failures, inhibitions, nervous habits, or feminine exhibitionistic traits. The sanction of the parent nullifies the significance of failure; the child comes to substitute narcissistic aggrandizement for mastery of reality. Fantasy never becomes distinctly separated from reality-directed thinking. The adolescent's sense of time is affected by his constant substitution of the past for the future, and in addition by his vague belief that a lucky break can accomplish what ordinarily takes a man years to achieve.

In the early lives of these young men we are not surprised to find startling deviations from the typical process of identification. As children they always lack assertiveness and self-criticism; they placidly accept the exalted position into which their mothers place them. Consequently, they develop a submissive, feminine, and narcissistic self-sufficiency which often makes them charming and attractive young boys. As young men these adolescents feel at home in the company of women, but are ill at ease, fearful, and inhibited in their dealings with men. In identifying with the mother these boys relinquish early the competition with the father and consequently passive strivings are always on the verge of breaking through. As adolescents they either treat their fathers with affectionate admiration, or with pity and contempt; here also they borrow their mothers' attitudes. It is not surprising that the adolescent revolt, when it appears, is directed toward the mother exclusively. Bernfeld (1923) emphasized the role of feminine identification in one type of prolonged adolescence which he has termed "genius-like adolescence" (*genialische Pubertät*). An example of the syndrome described here but rooted in and articulated on a different cultural milieu, that of Soviet society, can be found in "Oleg: A Member of the Soviet 'Golden Youth'" (Beier and Bauer, 1955). This Soviet adolescent's search for a "dual security" stalemated his adolescent development; the etiological factors appear similar to the ones of prolonged adolescence.

The basic identification with the mother creates a crisis for the growing boy when puberty confronts him with the urgent problem of sexual identity. This dilemma was expressed by an older male adolescent, who said, "There is one thing one should know and be sure of and that is whether one is a man or a woman." When the conflict of bisexuality which is part of normal adolescence presses, in adolescence proper, for a final settlement, prolonged adolescence circumvents it by a perseveration in the bisexual position. In fact, this position becomes libidinized and any abandonment of it is resisted rather than sought. The gratifications thus obtainable play into the need for limitless possibilities in life, and simultaneously assuage castration anxiety by perpetuating the ambiguity of sexual identity. This ambiguity is significantly reflected in the adolescent's vocational or educational floundering, ineffectualness or failure; and a progression to late adolescence is blocked.

For the narcissistic child there is always an easily accessible escape from conflictual tension at hand; he circumvents conflict by denial and/or self-aggrandizement. In fact, the child does not experience the nature of conflict but rather anger and rage due to narcissistic slight. When a child who has used exclusively narcissistic defenses approaches adolescence, it is not surprising that the typical conflicts of this age are indeed beyond the realm of his conscious experience. An adolescent of this type becomes apprehensive when he realizes that he falls short of his exaggerated self-expectations; he avidly seeks encouragement, to which he then reacts with elation in terms of his accustomed avoidance of conflictual tension. Prolonged adolescence presents a paradoxical picture: there is no conflict to deal with because there is no conflict experienced. These adolescents have to be helped in reaching the conflict of adolescence proper before the consolidation phase of late adolescence can be entered.

Adolescence proves for these boys a hopeful new development. Anna Freud (1936) pointed out the fact that sexual maturation at puberty ushers in an ascendancy of masculinity in the passive feminine boy which temporarily pushes passive strivings into the background; thus a condition is created which is more favorable for a potentially progressive development. The drive toward emotional dissociation from oppressing family ties momentarily gains the upper hand, and the adolescent feels hopeful as long as the adolescent crisis continues to exist. The inability to relinquish childhood positions, in conjunction with the desire for independence and manly self-assertion outside the confines of the family combine to make the prolongation of adolescence the one and only solution which is within his reach. We have come to understand that the necessity for keeping the adolescent crisis open is a protective measure against two fatal alternatives: either regression and rupture with reality (psychotic solution) or repression and symptom formation (neurotic solution). In this dilemma the adolescent ego chooses to avoid either alternative, and instead to change its own nature; thus a way of life is created out of a transitory maturational phase. "It is always possible for the ego to avoid a rupture in any of its relations by deforming itself, submitting to forfeit something of its unity, or in the long run even to being gashed and rent" (Freud, 1924, a).

Ego restriction and ego regression bring the adolescent into disharmony with the demands of society, and hamper the executive functions of the ego. The resulting frustrations are neutralized by narcissistic overcompensations, such as inflated optimism and fantasy gratification; a powerful recourse for the maintenance of the narcissistic balance is derived from magical thinking which has not been relinquished and has never been firmly superseded by the reality principle. Intentions and potentialities easily take the place of achievement and mastery. An always present undercurrent of anxiousness is only partly dammed up by the interference of defensive measures; the overflow serves to stimulate intensified pseudo-actions, abortive efforts to transpose infantile fantasies into adult activities. To illustrate: a college student who had to prepare for an examination in Elementary Biology turned passionately to the study of the most erudite articles in the field, but neglected to study his textbook or his notes.

Conflictual anxiety, which during adolescence normally activates libidinal reorganization and repression, has negligible motivating power in prolonged adolescence to activate synthesizing processes. By the ego accommodations described the adolescent crisis is kept open. We can say that the structure of prolonged adolescence is similar to that of a character disorder: in both, the ego-restricting attitudes are not experienced as ego-alien. However, the rigidity of a character disorder is never present in prolonged adolescence; in fact, the adolescent process is kept in flux and is accessible to therapeutic intervention. It must not be overlooked that the perseveration in the adolescent position is feasible only within certain age limits. Eventually—in the early or middle twenties—prolonged adolescence must yield to a more organized and rigid settlement; the narcissistic character disorder describes best the general trend of the pathological development which prolonged adolescence will finally take.

The dynamic and economic conditions of prolonged adolescence are opportune for therapeutic intervention. Personality development is still fluid and possesses a high degree of plasticity; in addition, the resistive position which the ego maintains on two fronts, namely, against progression and against regression, reveals considerable strength which can be utilized in therapeutic work. It is true that when young men of this type apply for help, they come with the hope of restoring a narcissistic and relatively tension-free existence, as well as to facilitate, as if by magic, the fulfillment of their contradictory drives—for example, self-assertion and submissiveness. However, what gives them the final push to seek therapy is the narcissistic frustration caused by recurrent disappointment or failure in vocational, educational, or social pursuits. Prominent in this picture are the disappointment over the glaring incompatibility between self-image and reality achievement, and an anxious urgency in finding a hasty way out of the intolerable state of narcissistic despair. But we look in vain for conflictual anxiety as an indicator of an intrapsychic struggle. This constellation involves a search for a solution essentially external; therefore, constant demands are made in therapy for sweeping interpretations, a revelation of the pathogenic childhood experience, suggestion or advice, a formula, or a trick. Whenever such a request is fulfilled the adolescent feels momentarily better, he is more hopeful and he is happier. This reaction is in conformity with the accustomed maintenance of self-esteem as established in childhood.

The fact that tension is not structured and organized in terms of psychic conflict points to the direction into which initial therapy has to move, namely, to bring about the experience of conflict; in other words, therapy has to help the young man to reach the conflict of adolescence proper. Toward this end two therapeutic intentions prevail: 1) to increase tension tolerance; 2) to expose the narcissistic defenses. This therapeutic endeavor makes it imperative for the therapist to abstain from any so-called "deep" or instinct interpretations, since such activity by the therapist would be exploited in the service of the narcissistic defense system; the adolescent's reaction could be paraphrased by saying, "Ah—now I know why—so this problem is settled." Furthermore, it is imperative that the therapist divest himself of all forms of the imputed omniscience and magical powers which are so reassuring to this type of adolescent. In doing this the therapist directly opposes himself to the maternal figure who provided narcissistic gratification by letting the child share in her greatness. It is most irritating to the adolescent when the therapist replies to his anxious questioning with an "I don't know"; but on the other hand the patient respects his courage, honesty, and incorruptibility. We must not forget that the adolescent retains a readiness to identify with an adult who possesses those personality attributes in which he desires to share. The therapist's aim is to replace infantile sharing and merging by identification; or, to put it differently, to replace the search for external sources of self-esteem (rescue fantasy) by the discovery of one's own resourcefulness. In fact, exploring and testing, validating and differentiating this resourcefulness in daily life constitute a large part of the therapeutic endeavor.

During this phase of work it becomes apparent that the adolescent welcomes the therapist's looking through the façade of his pretentiousness and arrogance. To illustrate: A man of twenty had attended a lecture and related all the stupid questions people had asked the lecturer. When the therapist inquired as to the question he himself had asked, he replied with complete composure: "None. What has that to do with it?" When the therapist insisted on the pertinence of this inquiry in the light of the critical attack on his fellow listeners, the patient became flustered and confessed to a total ignorance of the subject matter, which supposedly was in the field of his special interest. He volunteered the fact that his sophisticated and educated conversations were based entirely on ideas he had skillfully picked up from other people. He had not read a book since his first year in high school, but had cleverly managed to get the reputation of being a well-read student. This case excerpt illustrates the exposure of a narcissistic defense; whether the relinquishment of reading was related to a childhood conflict did not concern us at this stage of therapy, when the focus was on the disruption of the narcissistic defense system and the exposure of the ego to tension and conflict.

Whenever stereotyped ego attitudes are relinquished, new attempts at mastery are tried which are summarized under the general term of experimentation. Experimentation involves the testing of reality, of the self and of the interaction of both. In this sense, experimentation and progressive differentiation of the self-image go hand in hand and bring about a more effective functioning. Increasingly adequate mastery becomes a new source—we might say, a legitimate one—of narcissistic gratification. Consequently, the maintenance of the narcissistic balance becomes progressively determined by self-regulatory processes instead of being kept totally dependent on external influences.

During this phase of therapy, the life experience of the adolescent usually becomes enriched by purposeful experimentation; the scope of autonomous ego functions becomes enlarged, while the infantile strivings gradually acquire an ego-dystonic quality and become isolated from the rest of the ego. Reality achievement and greater tension tolerance make this progress possible. Concomitantly, the pathogenic determinants become more focused and an organized neurotic disturbance takes shape: the patient experiences conflict and anxiety. A decision as to the discontinuance of therapy depends on the balance between the affective mobility gained by the first phase of therapy and the unyielding strength of fixations not affected by it. Should it become evident that the forces which originally accounted for the condition of prolonged adolescence continue unremittingly to assert themselves, then despite an often impressive improvement in functioning, a progression to maturity remains an illusory expectation, and psychoanalysis must carry the therapeutic work to completion. In other cases, the first phase of therapy effects the relinquishment of the narcissistic defenses of prolonged adolescence, and mobilizes as well as channels the affective resourcefulness of the adolescent to a point from which he can carry forward the adolescent process and bring it unaided to a close.

2. *Pseudoheterosexuality in the Delinquent Girl**

The study of the psychodynamics of delinquency has always been prone to general and over-all formulations. Prevalent ideas in the field of human behavior and its motivation have a tendency to be used for its solution. In fact, etiological determinants change with prevalent psychoanalytic research; the instinct-gratification theory as well as the theory of the missing superego have been left way behind, and considerations of ego pathology have moved into the foreground.

What puzzles us most in the delinquent is his incapacity to internalize conflict, or rather, the ingenious way in which he circumvents symptom formation by experiencing an endopsychic tension as a conflict with the outside world. The exclusive use of alloplastic, antisocial solutions is a feature of delinquency which sets it apart from other forms of adaptive failures. It stands in clear contrast to the psychoneurotic or to the psychotic solution, the former representing an autoplastic and the latter an autistic adaptation.

Delinquency by definition refers to a personality disturbance which manifests itself in open conflict with society. This fact alone has pushed the social aspect of the problem into the forefront, and has stimulated sociological research which in turn has thrown light on those environmental conditions which are significantly related to delinquent behavior. The study of delinquency has by necessity always been multidisciplinary, and it should not be claimed by any one discipline as its exclusive domain of inquiry. However, I shall restrict myself here to the discussion of some predisposing psychodynamic factors as they can be reconstructed from the overt delinquent behavior and supported by the historical data in the case.

It has always been my opinion that male and female delinquency follow separate paths, indeed are essentially different. Cases of male and female delinquency give the impression that female delinquency stands in close proximity to the perversions; the same cannot be said with regard to male delinquency. The girl's delinquency repertoire is far more limited in scope and variety than the boy's; furthermore it lacks significantly in destructive aggressive acts against persons and property, and also does not show the boy's imposter-like adventuring. The girl's

---

* This material appeared in different form in the *Psychoanalytic Study of the Child*, Vol. XII, 1957.

wayward behavior is restricted to stealing of the kleptomanic type; to vagrancy; to provocative, impudent behavior in public; and to frank sexual waywardness. Of course, these offenses are shared by the boy offender; they constitute, however, only a fraction of his transgressions. In the girl, it seems, delinquency is an overt sexual act; or, to be more correct, it is a sexual acting out.

This disparity develops because in female delinquents the infantile instinctual organization which has never been abandoned breaks through with the onset of puberty and finds a bodily outlet in genital activity. The pregenital instinctual aims which dominate the delinquent behavior of the girl relate her delinquency to the perversions. An adolescent boy who is caught in an ambivalence conflict with his father may defend himself against both castration fear and castration wish by getting drunk, by destroying property, or by stealing a car and wrecking it; often his actions are an attempt at a progressive development even if abortive (Neauks and Winokur, 1957). The boy's typical delinquent activities contain elements of a keen interest in reality; furthermore he is fascinated with the struggle waged between himself and people, social institutions, and the world of nature. In contrast to this, an adolescent girl who possesses an equal propensity to acting out will take revenge on her mother by whom she feels rejected by seeking sexual relations. Girls of this type have told me of persistent fantasies during sex play or coitus such as: "If mother knew, it would kill her"; or "You see (mother), I have somebody too." Aichhorn (1949), in a paper on sex delinquent girls, considers that the predisposing condition outweighs any environmental factor. With reference to the rampant juvenile prostitution in Vienna after World War II he states that his observations led him to "believe that one of the causes of their [young prostitutes'] behavior was a certain emotional constellation. Milieu and deprivation were only secondary factors." Perhaps delinquent girls who have been classified as psychopaths might be viewed as cases of perversion. Schmideberg (1956) pursues similar trends of thought. She contrasts the neurotic and the perverse reaction or symptom, and emphasizes the fact that the former represents an autoplastic and the latter an alloplastic adaptation. She continues: "In a certain sense the neurotic symptom is of a more social kind, while the perverse is more antisocial. Thus there is a rather close connection between the sexual perversions and delinquent behaviour, which is by definition antisocial." The impulsivity which is equally strong in acting-out behavior and in the perversions is well known. Without generalizing about delinquency per se, I would stress that the identity of delinquency and perversion corresponds exceedingly well with the clinical picture of female delinquency, while it constitutes only one special variant in the diverse and far more heterogeneous etiology of male delinquency.

Why are male and female delinquency differently structured? I can answer this best by discussing certain aspects of the developmental schedule of early childhood. The developmental foci selected represent also potential points of fixation which can lead the adolescent boy or girl into totally different crisis situations.

1. All infants perceive the mother in early life as the "active mother." The characteristic antithesis at this period of life is "active" and "passive" (Mack Brunswick, 1940). The archaic mother is always active, the child is passive and receptive in relation to her. Normally an identification with the active mother brings the early phase of primal passivity to an end. A bifurcation in the psychosexual development of boy and girl is already foreshadowed at this juncture. The girl turns gradually toward passivity, while the boy's first turn toward activity becomes absorbed later in the identification which the boy normally forms with his father.

The early identification with the active mother leads the girl via the phallic phase into an initial active (negative) oedipal position as a typical step in her development. When the girl turns her love needs to the father, there always exists the danger that her passive strivings toward him will reawaken early oral dependency; a return to this primal passivity will preclude the successful advancement to femininity. Whenever an unduly strong father attachment marks the girl's oedipal situation, we can always suspect behind it the precursor of an unduly deep and lasting attachment to the preoedipal mother. Only when it is possible for the girl to abandon her passive tie to the mother and to advance to a passive (positive) oedipal position can she be spared the fatal regression to the preoedipal mother.

2. The first love object of every child is the mother. The girl eventually abandons this first love object, and seeks her sense of completeness as well as fulfillment in her femininity by turning toward the father; this turn always follows a disappointment in the mother. The sex of the boy's love object never changes; for this reason his development is more direct and less complicated than that of the girl.

In contradistinction to the boy, the girl's oedipal situation is never brought to an abrupt decline. The following words by Freud (1933) are relevant: "The girl remains in the oedipal situation for an indefinite period, she only abandons it late in life, and then incompletely." Therefore the female's superego is not as rigid and harsh as the male's; it consolidates only gradually and remains less tyrannical and less absolute. In the girl the oedipal situation continues to be part of her emotional life throughout the latency period. Is this fact perhaps responsible for her ready turn to heterosexuality early in puberty? At any rate, we observe in female adolescence a regressive pull which exerts its influence in the direction of a return to the preoedipal mother. This regressive pull, determined in its strength by the existent fixation, is reacted against by the exercise of excessive independence, hyperactivity, and a forceful turn toward the other sex. This impasse is dramatically displayed at adolescence in the girl's frantic attachment to boys as the attempt to resist regression. A regression will result for boy and girl alike in a passive dependency with an irrational overevaluation of the mother or mother representative.

3. The question has often been asked why preadolescence in boy and in girl is so markedly different; why the boy approaches his heterosexuality which is ushered in by puberty via a prolonged perseverance in preadolescence with a lengthy and often elaborate recapitulation of pregenital impulses; nothing of comparable scope can be observed in the preadolescent girl. There is no doubt that social milieu has an accelerating or retarding influence on adolescent development, and consequently a meaningful comparison of developmental patterns can only be made between boys and girls from a similar milieu.

Preadolescence as a phase marked by heterogeneous libidinal aims in boy and girl gives cause to severe tensions in children of this age. The girl approaches heterosexuality more directly and speedily than the boy. The relative value of masturbation as a bodily outlet of sexual tension for boy and girl may play a role in the girl's ready turn toward heterosexuality. However, I think that earlier events in the girl's life far outweigh any such consideration. The observable difference in preadolescent behavior is foreshadowed by the massive repression of pregenitality which the girl has to establish before she can move into the oedipal phase; in fact, this repression is a prerequisite for the normal development of femininity. The girl turns away from the mother, or, to be more precise, withdraws from her the narcissistic libido which was the basis for the comforting overevaluation of her and transfers this overevaluation to the father. All this is well known. I therefore hasten to make the point that the girl, in turning away from the mother, represses those instinctual drives which were intimately related to her care and bodily ministrations, namely the total scope of pregenitality. The return to these modes of gratification at puberty constitutes the basis for correlating female delinquency and perversion; regression and fixation always appear as necessary and complementary conditions.

It seems, then, that the girl who in her adolescence cannot maintain the repression of her pregenitality will encounter difficulties in her progressive development. A fixation on the preoedipal mother and a return to the gratifications of this period often result in acting-out behavior which has as the central theme "baby and mother" and the re-creation of a union in which mother and child are confused. Adolescent unmarried mothers and their attitudes toward their babies offer ample opportunity to study this problem.

In contrast to the girl's, the boy's situation is totally different. Since he preserves the same love object throughout his childhood, he is not confronted with the necessity to repress pregenitality equal in summary sweep to the girl. Mack Brunswick (1940), in her classical paper on the "Preoedipal Phase of Libido Development," states: "One of the greatest differences between the sexes is the enormous extent to which infantile sexuality is repressed in the girl. Except in profound neurotic states no man resorts to any similar repression of his infantile sexuality."

The adolescent boy who returns to pregenital drive satisfactions during transient regressive episodes is still in relative consonance with his progressive sex-appropriate development; certainly he is not in any fatal opposition to it. Behavior disturbances caused by these regressive movements are not necessarily as damaging to his emotional development as they are for the girl. "Paradoxically, the girl's mother relation is more persistent, and often more intense and dangerous, than the boy's. The inhibition she encounters when she turns toward reality brings her back to her mother for a period marked by heightened and more infantile love demands" (Deutsch, 1944).

4. It follows that there are basically two types of female delinquents: one has regressed to the preoedipal mother, and the other clings desperately to a foothold on the oedipal stage. The central relationship problem of both is the mother. These two types of adolescent delinquents commit offenses which look alike and are equal before the law, but which are essentially different as to dynamics and structure. In one

case we have a regressive solution; while in the other an oedipal struggle prevails which has never reached any degree of internalization nor settlement.

Theoretical considerations tend to support the thesis that female delinquency is often precipitated by the strong regressive pull to the pre-oedipal mother and the panic which the surrender implies. As we can readily see there are two solutions available to the girl who is faced with an oedipal failure or disappointment which she is unable to surmount. She either regresses in her object relationship to the mother, or she maintains an illusory oedipal situation with the sole aim of resisting regression. This defensive struggle is manifested by the compulsive need to create in reality a relationship in which she is needed and wanted by a sexual partner. These constellations represent the paradigmatic preconditions for female delinquency.

5. It is my impression that this second type of delinquent girl has not only experienced an oedipal defeat at the hands of a—literally or figuratively—distant, cruel or absent father, but, in addition, she has also witnessed her mother's dissatisfaction with her husband; mother and daughter share their disappointment, and a strong and highly ambivalent bond continues to exist between them. Under these circumstances no satisfactory identification with the mother can be achieved; instead, a hostile or negative identification forges a destructive and indestructible relationship between mother and daughter. Young adolescent girls of this type quite consciously fantasy that if only they could be in their mother's place the father would show his true self, that he would be transfigured by their love into the man of their oedipal wishes. In real life such delinquent girls promiscuously choose sexual partners who possess glaring personality defects which are denied or tolerated with masochistic submissiveness.

In more general terms we may say that her delinquent behavior is motivated by the girl's need for the constant possession of a partner who serves her to surmount in fantasy an oedipal impasse—but more important than this, to take revenge on the mother who had hated, rejected, or ridiculed the father. Furthermore, we observe the delinquent girl's desire to be sexually needed, wanted, and used. Spiteful and revengeful fantasies about the mother abound; in fact, the sex act itself is dominated by such fantasies, with the result that no sexual pleasure is ever obtained. We look in vain for these girls to wish for a baby; if pregnancy occurs, it is an act of revenge or competition which is reflected in the attitude to the infant: "It might just as well be given away."

6. Female delinquency based on regression to the preoedipal mother presents an entirely different dynamic picture. Helene Deutsch (1944) called our attention to the girl's dissolution of passive dependency on the mother as a precondition for the normal development of femininity; these "severance actions" are typical for early adolescence. Deutsch continues: "A prepuberal attempt at liberation from the mother that has failed or was too weak can inhibit future psychologic growth and leave a definitely infantile imprint on the woman's entire personality."

The delinquent girl who has failed in her liberation from the mother protects herself against regression by a wild display of pseudoheterosexuality. She has no relationship to nor interest in her sexual partner; in fact, her hostility to the male is severe. This was illustrated by a dream of a thirteen-year-old girl who accused her mother of not loving her, and who spitefully engaged in sexual relations with teenage boys; in the dream, she relates, she had 365 babies, one a day for a year from one boy, whom she shot after this was accomplished. The male only served her to gratify her insatiable oral needs. Consciously she was almost obsessed by the wish for a baby which, in its make-believe childishness, was reminiscent of a little girl's wish for a doll.

Behavior which at first sight seems to represent the recrudescence of oedipal wishes thus proves on careful scrutiny to be related to earlier fixation points lying in the pregenital phases of libidinal development where severe deprivation or overstimulation or both had been experienced.

The pseudoheterosexuality of this type of delinquent girl serves as a defense against the regressive pull to the preoedipal mother, that is, against homosexuality. A fourteen-year-old girl, when asked why she needed ten boy friends at once, answered with righteous indignation: "I have to do this; if I didn't have so many boy friends they would say I am a lesbian." This same girl was preoccupied with the idea of getting married. She related these fantasies to the social worker in order to elicit her protective interference. When the worker showed indifference to her marriage plans, she burst into tears, and accused the worker, "You push me! I don't want to get married!" Here we can see clearly how the heterosexual acting out receives its urgency or its decisive push from the frustrated need to be loved by the mother. This girl's preoccupation with marriage masked her longing for the preoedipal mother and found substitute gratification in the guise of heterosexual pseudo love.

An acute disappointment in the mother is frequently the decisive precipitating factor in illegitimacy. By proxy the mother-child unit becomes re-established, but under the most foreboding circumstances for the child. Unwed mothers of this type can find satisfaction in motherhood only as long as the infant is dependent on them; they turn against the child as soon as independent strivings assert themselves. Infantilization of the child is the result.

7. One more possibility is open to the girl who is fixated on her mother, and that is, identification with the father. This resolution of the oedipal conflict is often caused by a painful rejection by the father. The girl who thus assumes the masculine role watches jealously over her mother and defies any man who wants to possess her. We usually refer to this constellation as penis envy; this factor does not deserve the overwhelming importance which was once awarded to it in the etiology of female delinquency. Of course, its role in kleptomania cannot be denied, and the preponderance of this symptom in women does testify to its etiological significance; however, the dynamic factor of penis envy cannot be separated from the underlying accusation of the mother that her seemingly willful withholding of expected gratification has prevented the child from overcoming his oral greed. ". . . in accord with the oral origin of the regulation of self-regard by external supplies, the penis or fecal symbol that was obtained by robbing, stealing, or trickery . . . is in the final analysis always thought of in all these forms as having been acquired orally by swallowing" (Fenichel, 1939).

These theoretical considerations are exemplified in the following case abstract, which concerns Nancy, a young adolescent girl. The treatment aspect of the case is not made part of the record here; it is the clinical record, or the language of behavior, to which we must lend our ear in order to verify those ideas which were voiced above.

When Nancy was thirteen years old she presented the family, the school authorities, and the court with a problem of sexual delinquency; her stealing was known only to her mother. At home Nancy was uncontrollable and loudmouthed; she used obscene language, cursed her parents, and had her own way disregarding any adult interference. "The names Nancy calls me are so sexy," were the mother's repeated complaints. Despite this seeming independence Nancy never failed to report her sexual exploits to her mother, or at least to hint at them sufficiently so they would rouse her mother's curiosity, anger, guilt, and solicitude. With glee she showed her mother stories she had written consisting mostly of obscene language. Nancy was an avid reader of "dirty sex books"; she stole money from her mother for their purchase. Nancy's mother was willing to give her the money, but Nancy explained to the social worker that this was not what she wanted; "I wanted to *take* the money and not have it *given* to me."

Nancy blamed her mother angrily for not having been firm with her when she was a little girl: "Mother should have known that I acted up in order to get her attention and to have adults fuss over me." She would never marry a husband who says only "Dearie, dearie," but a man who slapped her when she was wrong. The criticism implied in this remark was obviously directed against her weak father. She did not blame him for being a man of no education, who earned a modest income as a butcher, but for his indifference and his ineffectual role in the family. Nancy grew up in a small apartment in a crowded city neighborhood. Nancy's family wanted for her the "finer things in life" and found ways and means to pay for them; thus Nancy had lessons in dancing, acrobatics, and elocution; with puberty all these activities came to an end.

Nancy was preoccupied with sex to the exclusion of almost everything else. This interest reached abnormal proportions soon after menarche at age eleven. She boasted of her many boyfriends, of having sexual relations, and of asking her peers at school to join her "sex club." Nancy only liked "bad boys" who stole, lied, and had a criminal record, boys who "know how to get around a girl." She herself wanted to steal and smoke, but she did not accompany the boys on their delinquent excursions because she "might get caught." Nancy puzzled over why she could always get a fellow if another girl was after him but not otherwise. She had established a position of respect among the girls because she would challenge them quickly to a fist fight; "I have to show them that I am not afraid of them."

Nancy admitted to the social worker that she desired sexual relations but denied having ever given in to her desire; she said that she used her body only to attract boys and get their attention. She was, however, observed being intimate with several boys on a rooftop and was found there "dazed, disheveled, and wet." It was at this time that the case was taken to court; Nancy was put on probation under the condition that she receive treatment. In the light of the evidence Nancy did not deny any longer to the social worker that she had sexual relations, but she now expressed her hope to have a baby. She explained that she engaged in sexual relations to take revenge on her mother. She, Nancy, would keep the baby and marry the boy. Her mother, she was convinced, did not want her and, in fact, had never wanted her. At this time Nancy had a dream in which she had sexual relations with teenage boys; in the dream she had 365 babies, one a day for a year from one boy whom she shot after this was accomplished.

Nancy daydreamed a great deal; her fantasies concerned marriage and she was consumed by the wish for a baby. She was afraid of not being attractive to boys and never getting married. Physically, Nancy was well-developed for her age, but she was dissatisfied with her own body, especially her skin, hair, height, eyes (glasses), and ears (the lobes were attached to the sides of her face). At home she was extremely modest and never allowed her mother to see her naked. Nancy could think of only one reason for all her troubles, disappointments, and anxieties—her mother; she was to be "blamed." She accused the mother of taking her friends—boys and girls— away from her, of begrudging her the happiness she found in having friends, of putting a lock on the phone to cut her off from the world. Nancy said she needed girl friends, close friends who would become her blood sisters; she and Sally scratched their initials into each other's arms with a razor blade as proof of their eternal friendship. The mother scolded Nancy when she showed her the scars; to the daughter this was another demonstration of her mother's not wanting her to have any close girlfriends. In disappoint- ment she tried to run away from home, but the tie to her mother always proved to be too strong; before long she returned.

Despite her vehement rejection of her mother Nancy nevertheless needed her presence at every turn. She would, for instance, insist that her mother accompany her on her visits to the social worker. Being at a loss about a summer job, Nancy thought that her mother should take a job as a camp counselor and she would assist her as junior counselor. Nancy was totally unaware of her mother's unfitness for such a job, nor was she able to assess reasonably her own abilities.

If mother, Nancy continued her accusations, had only had more babies, not just one child and a girl at that, Nancy was sure that her life would have taken a different turn. During the first interview with the social worker, who inquired sympathetically about Nancy's purpose for seeing her, she preserved a long sullen silence; then suddenly began to cry. In her first words she expressed her overwhelming need to be loved; she said: "As an only child I have always been so lonesome." She had always wanted a baby brother or sister and begged her mother to have one. She had a dream in which she was taking care of babies; they were really her girlfriend's babies. Nancy's mother remarked in the dream, "It's a shame that such cute chil- dren have no proper mother to take care of them; let's adopt them." In the dream Nancy was overjoyed and ran to her social worker to tell her that they were adopting babies. The worker replied that it would cost a lot of money, and Nancy answered: "But don't you know we are loaded?" After waking from this dream Nancy asked her mother to take in a foster child. "The child," Nancy said, "will have to be a boy as I only know how to diaper boys." She fancied herself having a summer job taking care of chil- dren, in a family, way out in the country. When she was a little older, at fourteen, she actually took a summer job with children as a helper in the nursery school of a community center. There she was a child among chil- dren, an older sister who helped the little ones with their play. Nancy al- ways liked to babysit; she loved to hold a baby in her arms, especially if it was very young. When her cousin became pregnant Nancy looked forward to taking care of the baby, but added: "I will babysit free for three months, that's fun; but later I shall get paid."

Nancy attached herself during these years of sexual preoccupation to a young pregnant woman of twenty who had married at the age of sixteen, had had three children, and lived an erratic and promiscuous life. Nancy vicariously shared this woman's sex life and motherhood; she took care of the children during their mother's absence from her home. This necessitated staying overnight when this young woman did not return for a day or two; consequently, Nancy became a truant. Once she brought the three children to her own home to take care of them while her woman friend was off on a sexual escapade and had not been heard from for three days. Nancy emphatically sided with her girlfriend against the husband with whom, Nancy said, she was once in love. She also protested violently her mother's accusations against her friend, commenting to the social worker: "My mother has a mind like a sewer." Nancy knew that she understood her girl friend; she knew that she was unhappy because her father had died early in her life and she never loved her mother. "It's no use," Nancy said, "arguing with mother," and summed it up by saying: "My mother and I just don't understand each other." After these fights, Nancy suddenly became afraid that the aggravation she had caused might kill her mother who suffered from high blood pressure.

Nancy found a temporary haven, albeit a dangerous one, in the home of this married girlfriend. She felt safe in the close friendship with this pregnant mother who knew how to attract men and get many babies. Nancy also relished the jealous anger of her own mother who disapproved of this friendship. Nancy felt she possessed a girlfriend-mother with whom she could share everything. During this time Nancy withdrew from the girls of her own age, feeling that they had nothing in common any longer. An embarrassing testimony of the fact that she had outgrown her peers was her response to a group of girls discussing clothes; to the question, "What kind of clothes do you like best?" Nancy blurted, "Maternity clothes." Such incidents drew Nancy more deeply into the make-believe family life with her girlfriend. Nancy loved this woman, and said to the worker, "I can't get her out of my mind."

In her relationship to the social worker Nancy fluctuated between closeness and distance; this instability is well expressed by her own words: "When I think of coming to the office, I don't want to come; but when I am here, I am glad, and I feel like talking." She finally admitted that she would like to be confidential with the social worker, but gave her a warning by confessing that she really was a "compulsive liar." She suggested to the worker that they both should reveal to each other the secrets of their lives; then they could learn from each other. The need for intimacy which exerted its emotional pull toward the social worker was conversely responsible for her repeated running away from her.

Nancy finally came to repudiate the "crude, rough stuff of the teenagers" and her fancy moved into the direction of acting. Here she drew on the interests and playful activities of her latency years. Wild and childish daydreams of meeting movie actors, fainting in front of them, and being discovered as the new star eventually gave way to a more sober approach to the study of acting. From acting Nancy expected to "become a lady"; by this she meant to be gentle, to speak gently, to act gently; then, she was sure, people would like her.

Nancy clung to her acting all through her adolescence; in fact, at sixteen she achieved a modest degree of recognition in summer stock productions. The stage had become the legitimate territory where her impulsiveness was allowed expression in many directions and where her exhibitionistic needs were slowly tamed by the aesthetic code of acting itself. By this time Nancy had become somewhat of a prude; she was a good mixer with her peers but only to promote her self-interest in dramatic productions. As good a manipulator as her mother always had been, Nancy now became narcissistically related to her environment and learned how to exploit others. The interest in acting became Nancy's identity, around which her personality integration took shape. The core of this identity hails back to the "finer things in life" which Nancy's mother had always wanted for her daughter. In adolescence Nancy reverted to these imposed aspirations which were instilled in the child by lessons in the performing arts during the latency years. It was precisely this artistic endeavor which served in adolescence as an avenue for sublimation of the unresolved fixation to the mother. The vocational identity rescued Nancy from regression and delinquency, but it also prevented a progression to mature object finding; after all, it was still the mother whose desire she continued to gratify by her artistic activity. When reminded once at the age of sixteen of her wish for babies, she snapped back in disgust, "Babies is kid stuff."

It hardly seems necessary to point out those aspects of this case which illustrate the etiological importance of the preoedipal mother fixation in Nancy's delinquent behavior. Her pseudoheterosexuality was clearly a defense against the return to the preoedipal mother and against homosexuality. The only safe relationshop which Nancy found was a *folie à deux* with a pregnant mother-girlfriend; this attachment and transient identification rendered the sexual acting out temporarily expendable. However, an advance in her emotional development was precluded until a turn to a sublimated endeavor, that of becoming an actress, had firmly taken possession of her. This ego ideal—adolescent and probably transient—resulted in a relatively more stable self-representation, and opened the way to adolescent experimentation and to ego-integrative processes.

Nancy's delinquent behavior can only be understood in conjunction with the personality disturbance of her mother. Upon closer inspection of the family pathology we recognize—quoting Johnson and Szurek (1952)—"the unwitting employment of the child to act out for the parent his own poorly integrated and forbidden impulses."

From the analysis of adults who also happen to be parents we know about their delinquent, perverse, and deviant unconscious fantasies, and we also know how often the parent is identified with his child and the instinctual life of the child's various ages. However, many children of such parents show no tendency toward acting out the delinquent, perverse, and deviant unconscious strivings of their parents; in fact, many demonstrate in this respect a resistivity which Nancy totally lacked. Children normally seek in their environment compensatory experiences which will to some degree make up for the deficiencies which exist in the emotional diet of the family. This is especially true for children of the latency period; but it is also true of younger children who establish meaningful relationships with older siblings, neighbors, relatives, family friends, teachers, and others. In constrast, children like Nancy are totally unable to supplement their emotional experiences in their broader environment, but continue to live their impoverished social life in the narrow confines of their family.

It seems, then, that a special kind of interaction between parent and child must be at work in order to prevent the child from establishing progressively his more or less independent life. This special quality of the parent-child relationship lies in a sadomasochistic pattern which has permeated not only the instinctual life of the child but has adversely affected his ego development as well. Primal ambivalence rooted in the biting stage of oral organization constitutes a nucleus for a lasting pattern of interaction between mother and child; this is carried like a leitmotiv through all the stages of psychosexual development. The polarities of love-hate, giving-taking, submission-domination continue to exist in an ambivalent reciprocal dependency of mother and child. The sadomasochistic modality gradually inundates all interaction between child and environment; it eventually influences ego development via the introjection of an ambivalent object. As a consequence, inhibitory functions are poorly developed and tension tolerance is low. The stimulus hunger of these children represents the lasting expression of their oral greed. Is, perhaps, Nancy's impulsive behavior an essential aspect of an all-pervasive sadomasochistic drive organization? Szurek (1954) pointed out that "two factors, the libidinous fixations and the internalization of the parents' attitudes, determine which impulses of the child became ego-syntonic and which are repressed. To the extent that these factors interfere with the child's satisfactory experience in any developmental phase, the internalized attitudes are revengefully (i.e., sadistically) caricatured and the libidinous impulses are masochistically distorted, *i.e.*, the libidinous energy of both the id and the superego is fused with the rage and anxiety consequent to the repeated thwarting." The case of Nancy is of interest in the light of these considerations. Therefore, we shall now turn to her early life in search of those experiences which played a primary and predisposing role in terms of the sadomasochistic fixation on the preoedipal mother, and of the eventual adaptive failure at puberty.

Nancy was an only child, born two years after marriage. She was wanted by her mother who desired to have many children. The husband intended to wait ten years; his wife, unable to bear this delay, applied for a foster child but was turned down in her request. Soon after she became pregnant.

Nancy was breast fed for six months; at four months the infant started to bite the nipple, causing the mother considerable pain. Despite the mother's protestations the doctor insisted that the mother continue to nurse; two months later, when nursing had become an ordeal, she was permitted to take the baby off the breast. For two months mother and child were engaged in a battle over sucking and biting, over offering and withholding the nipple. A lasting effect of this period can be recognized in Nancy's persistent refusal to drink milk. Thumb sucking started at the age of three months; it was forcibly suppressed by the use of gloves. We can assume that the infant obtained insufficient stimulation and gratification from nursing at an early age. The child started to talk at about one year and walked well at sixteen months.

When Nancy entered kindergarten she vomited daily before going to school; this symptom disappeared after several weeks of enforced attendance. The teacher then noticed that the child ignored her presence in a way that suggested defective hearing. Tests proved this assumption to be incorrect. When Nancy started the first grade she had temper tantrums in school and tried to run away. Her mother waylaid her and returned her forcibly to the classroom; after a few weeks her running away ceased for good. From this time on her conduct in school was a constant cause for complaint. All through her latency years Nancy was "stubborn, quick-tempered, a grumbler, and a complainer." Nancy slept in the parental bedroom until the age of eight. At that time she was given a room of her own. She then started to have nightmares and would come to her parents' room. No disciplinary action kept her from disturbing her parent's sleep; then, when Nancy refused to return to her room, the mother made her sit up all one night on a chair in her parents' bedroom.

After this ordeal the child surrendered, stayed in her own room, and did not complain any longer about having nightmares. Nancy knew very few children and played with them but rarely; she preferred to stay in the company of her mother. She had "imaginary companions" all through her early childhood and very likely during her latency years; in her early adolescence she still used to talk to herself in bed and forbade the mother to listen in. The mother was just as curious about her daughter's private life as Nancy was about hers. With reference to Nancy's lack of friends the mother remarked, "Nancy wants too much love."

Two complementary factors in the early mother-child interaction seem to have predisposed Nancy and her mother to a lasting ambivalent attachment. The mother expected to have babies in order to gratify her own infantile needs, while Nancy—perhaps endowed with an unusually strong oral drive—made demands on the mother she was not capable of fulfilling. This battle over self-interests which were not reciprocally tolerated continued without letup and without settlement up to the time of Nancy's puberty. Her submissiveness to the mother's cruel discipline, and her surrender of symptoms at the cost of masochistic gratification reveal the progressive integration of a sadomasochistic object relationship which precluded the development of any successful individuation; on the contrary, it resulted in the child's close, symbiotic entanglement with the archaic mother.

Nancy's attempts at separation in early childhood and puberty are apparent in her creation of "imaginary companions" and in her attachment to the mother-girlfriend at the age of thirteen. These attempts at liberation were unsuccessful; pseudoheterosexuality was the only avenue open to this impulsive-driven girl as a way to gratify her oral greed, to take revenge on the "selfish" mother, and to protect herself against homosexuality. Nancy's delinquent behavior thus goes back to the predisposing antecedents residing in the second (sadistic) oral phase. The circle is closed.

APPENDIX

Chronological Bibliography of the Psychoanalytic Literature on Adolescence

1905

Freud, S., "Fragment of an Analysis of a Case of Hysteria" ("Dora"), *Standard Edition*, Vol. VII, The Hogarth Press, London, 1953.

——, "The Transformations of Puberty," third essay in "Three Essays on the Theory of Sexuality," *Standard Edition*, Vol. VII, The Hogarth Press, London, 1953.

1912

Die Onanie (On Masturbation), 14 Beiträge zu einer Diskussion der Wiener Psychoanalytischen Vereinigung, J. F. Bergmann, Wiesbaden, 1912. "Introduction" and "Concluding Remarks," by S. Freud in *Standard Edition*, Vol. XII, The Hogarth Press, London, 1958; "On Masturbation" by V.

246

Tausk in *Psychoanalytic Study of the Child*, Vol. VI, International Universities Press, Inc., New York, 1951.

1914

Freud, S., "Some Reflections on Schoolboy Psychology," *Standard Edition*, Vol. XIII, The Hogarth Press, London, 1955.

1919

Hug-Hellmuth, H. von, *A Young Girl's Diary*, Seltzer, New York, 1921 (first published in German, 1919). "Preface" by S. Freud in *Standard Edition*, Vol. XIV, The Hogarth Press, London, 1957.

1922

Bernfeld, S., *Vom Gemeinschaftsleben der Jugend* (Concerning Community Life of Youth), Internationaler Psychoanalytischer Verlag, Wien, 1922.

Jones, E., "Some Problems of Adolescence," in *Papers on Psycho-analysis*, The William & Wilkins Co., Baltimore, 1948.

1923

Bernfeld, S., "Über eine typische Form der männlichen Pubertät" (A Typical Form of Male Puberty), *Imago*, Vol. IX (1923).

1924

Bernfeld, S., *Vom dichterischen Schaffen der Jugend* (Concerning the Poetic Creativeness of Youth), Internationaler Psychoanalytischer Verlag, Wien, 1924.

Harnik, J., "The Various Developments Undergone by Narcissism in Men and Women," *International Journal of Psycho-analysis*, Vol. V (1924).

1925

Aichorn, A., *Wayward Youth*, The Viking Press, Inc., New York, 1948 (first published in German, 1925).

1927

Bernfeld, S., "Die heutige Psychologie der Pubertät" (Present-day Psychology of Puberty), *Imago*, Vol. XIII (1927).

1928

Federn, P., "Die Wiener Diskussion aus dem Jahre 1912" (The Viennese Discussion [on Masturbation] of 1912), *Zeitschrift für psychoanalytische Pädagogik*, Vol. II (1928).

"Onanie" Sonderheft (Masturbation; Special Issue), *Zeitschrift für psychoanalytische Pädagogik*, Vol. II (1928).

Read, C. S., *The Struggle of Male Adolescence*, Allen & Unwin, London, 1928.

1929

Bernfeld, S., "Der soziale Ort und seine Bedeutung für Neurose, Verwahr-losung und Pädagogik" (The Social Environment and Its Significance for Neurosis, Delinquency and Education), *Imago,* Vol. XV (1929).

Williams, F. E., *Adolescence,* Farrar and Rinehart, New York, 1930.

1931

Bernfeld, S., *Trieb und Tradition im Jugendalter; kulturspychologische Studien an Tagebüchern* (Instinct and Tradition in Youth; Studies in Cultural Psychology Based on Diaries), J. A. Barth, Leipzig, 1931.

"Menstruation" Sonderheft (Menstruation; Special Issue), *Zeitschrift für psychoanalytische Pädagogik,* Vol. V (1931).

1932

Chadwick, M., *The Psychological Effects of Menstruation,* Nervous and Mental Disease Publishing Co., New York and Washington, 1932.

———, *Adolescent Girlhood,* Allen & Unwin, London, 1932.

Klein, M., "The Technique of Analysis in Puberty," in *The Psycho-analysis of Children,* Chap. 5, The Hogarth Press, London, 1949.

Meng, H., "Über Pubertät und Pubertätsaufklärung" (On Puberty and En-lightenment in Puberty), *Zeitschrift für psychoanalytische Pädagogik,* Vol. VI (1932).

1933

Buxbaum, E., "Angstäusserungen von Schulmädchen im Pubertätsalter" (Anxiety Manifestations of Schoolgirls During Puberty), *Zeitschrift für psychoanalytische Pädagogik,* Vol. VII (1933).

1934

Balint, M., "Der Onanie—Abgewöhnungskampf in der Pubertät" (The Struggle against Masturbation during Puberty), *Zeitschrift für psycho-analytische Pädagogik,* Vol. VIII (1934).

1935

Bernfeld, S., "Über die einfache männliche Pubertät" (Simple Male Pu-berty), *Zeitschrift für psychoanalytische Pädagogik,* Vol. IX (1935).

Horney, D., "Personality Changes in Female Adolescents," *American Journal of Orthopsychiatry,* Vol. XIX (1935).

Landauer, K., "Die Ichorganisation in der Pubertät" (Ego Organization in Puberty), *Zeitschrift für psychoanalytische Pädagogik,* Vol. IX (1935).

"Psychoanalyse und Pubertät" Sonderheft (Phychoanalysis and Puberty; Special Issue), *Zeitschrift für psychoanalytische Pädagogik,* Vol. IX (1935).

Redl, F., " 'Pansexualismus' und Pubertät" ("Pansexuality" and Puberty), *Zeitschrift für psychoanalytische Pädagogik,* Vol. IX (1935).

"Verzeichnis der psychoanalytischen Literatur über Pubertät" (Listing of the Psychoanalytic Literature on Puberty), *Zeitschrift für psychoanalytische Pädagogik,* Vol. IX (1935).

248

Zulliger, H., "Über Hochstapler und Verwahrloste" (About Imposters and Delinquents), *Zeitschrift für psychoanalytische Pädagogik*, Vol. IX (1935).

1936

Freud, A., "The Ego and the Id at Puberty" and "Instinctual Anxiety during Puberty," in *The Ego and the Mechanisms of Defence*, Chaps. XI and XII, The Hogarth Press, London, 1937.

Freud, S., "A Disturbance of Memory on the Acropolis," *Standard Edition*, Vol. V, The Hogarth Press, London, 1950.

1937

Katan, A., "The Role of 'Displacement' in Agoraphobia," *International Journal of Psycho-analysis*, Vol. XXXII (1951) (first published in *Internationale Zeitschrift für Psychoanalyse*, Vol. XXIII [1937]).

1938

Bernfeld, S., "Types of Adolescence," *Psychoanalytic Quarterly*, Vol. VII (1938).

1939

Hartmann, H., *Ego Psychology and the Problem of Adaptation*, International Universities Press, Inc., New York, 1958 (first published in German in *Internationale Zeitschrift für Psychoanalyse und Imago*, Vol. XXVI [1939]).

Zachry, C., "Contributions of Psychoanalysis to the Education of the Adolescent," *Psychoanalytic Quarterly*, Vol. VIII (1939).

1941

Friedlander, K., "Children's Books and Their Function in Latency and Puberty," *American Imago*, Vol. III (1942) (first published in German in *Internationale Zeitschrift für Psychoanalyse und Imago*, Vol. XXVI [1941]).

1942

Gitelson, M., "Direct Psychotherapy in Adolescence," *American Journal of Orthopsychiatry*, Vol. XII (1942).

Lander, J., "The Pubertal Struggle against the Instincts," *American Journal of Orthopsychiatry*, Vol. XII (1942).

1944

Deutsch, H., *Psychology of Women*, Vol. I, Grune & Stratton, Inc., New York, 1944.

Johnson, A. M., and Fishback, D., "Analysis of a Disturbed Adolescent Girl and Collaborative Psychiatric Treatment of the Mother," *American Journal of Orthopsychiatry*, Vol. XIV (1944).

1945

Buxbaum, E., "Transference and Group Formation in Children and Adolescents," *Psychoanalytic Study of the Child*, Vol. I, International Universities Press, Inc., New York, 1945.

Fenichel, O., *The Psychoanalytic Theory of Neurosis*, W. W. Norton and Company, Inc., New York, 1945.

Hacker, F. J., and Geleerd, E. R., "Freedom and Authority in Adolescence," *American Journal of Orthopsychiatry*, Vol. XV (1945).

Redl, F., "The Psychology of Gang Formation and the Treatment of Juvenile Delinquents," *Psychoanalytic Study of the Child*, Vol. I, International Universities Press, Inc., New York, 1945.

1946

Blos, P., "Psychological Counseling of College Students," *American Journal of Orthopsychiatry*, Vol. XVI (1946).

Erikson, E. H., "Ego Development and Historical Change," *Psychoanalytic Study of the Child*, Vol. II, International Universities Press, Inc., New York, 1946.

Hartmann, H., Kris, E., and Loewenstein, R. M., "Comments on the Formation of Psychic Structure," *Psychoanalytic Study of the Child*, Vol. II, International Universities Press, Inc., New York, 1946.

Hoffer, W., "Diaries of Adolescent Schizophrenics," *Psychoanalytic Study of the Child*, Vol. II, International Universities Press, Inc., New York, 1946.

Maenchen, A., "A Case of Superego Disintegration," *Psychoanalytic Study of the Child*, Vol. II, International Universities Press, Inc., New York, 1946.

1947

Friedlander, K., *The Psycho-analytical Approach to Juvenile Delinquency*, International Universities Press, Inc., New York, 1947.

1948

Gitelson, M., "Character Synthesis: The Psychotherapeutic Problem of Adolescence," *American Journal of Orthopsychiatry*, Vol. XVIII (1948).

1949

Aichorn, A., "Some Remarks on the Psychic Structure and Social Care of a Certain Type of Female Juvenile Delinquent," *Psychoanalytic Study of the Child*, Vol. III–IV, International Universities Press, Inc., New York, 1949.

Eissler, K, R., "Some Problems of Delinquency," in *Searchlights on Delinquency*, ed. Eissler, K. R., International Universities Press, Inc., New York, 1949.

Johnson, A. M., "Sanctions for Superego Lacunae of Adolescents," in *Searchlights on Delinquency*, ed. Eissler, K. R., International Universities Press, Inc., New York, 1949.

Wittels, F., "The Ego of the Adolescent," in *Searchlights on Delinquency*, ed. Eissler, K. R., International Universities Press, Inc., New York, 1949.

1950

Beres, D. and Obers, S. J., "The Effects of Extreme Deprivation in Infancy on Psychic Structure in Adolescence: A Study in Ego Development," *Psychoanalytic Study of the Child,* Vol. V, International Universities Press, Inc., New York, 1950.

Eissler, K. R., "Ego-Psychological Implications of the Psychoanalytic Treatment of Delinquents," *Psychoanalytic Study of the Child,* Vol. V, International Universities Press, Inc., New York, 1950.

Erikson, E. H., *Childhood and Society,* W. W. Norton & Company, Inc., New York, 1950.

Greenacre, P., "The Prepuberty Trauma in Girls," *Psychoanalytic Quarterly,* Vol. XIX (1950) (reprinted in *Trauma, Growth and Personality,* W. W. Norton & Company, Inc., New York, 1952).

Lample-de Groot, J., "On Masturbation and Its Influence on General Development," *Psychoanalytic Study of the Child,* Vol. V, International Universities Press, Inc., New York, 1950.

Reich, A., "On the Termination of Analysis," *International Journal of Psycho-analysis,* Vol. XXXI (1950).

1951

Arlow, J. A., "A Psychoanalytic Study of a Religious Initiation Rite, Bar Mitzvah," *Psychoanalytic Study of the Child,* Vol. VI, International Universities Press, Inc., New York, 1951.

Erikson, E. H., "Sex Differences in the Play Configurations of Preadolescents," *American Journal of Orthopsychiatry,* Vol. XXI (1951).

Reich, A., "The Discussion of 1912 on Masturbation and Our Present-Day Views," *Psychoanalytic Study of the Child,* Vol. VI, International Universities Press, Inc., New York, 1951.

Spiegel, L. A., "A Review of Contributions to a Psychoanalytic Theory of Adolescence: Individual Aspects," *Psychoanalytic Study of the Child,* Vol. VI, International Universities Press, Inc., New York, 1951.

1953

Blos, P., "The Contribution of Psychoanalysis to the Treatment of Adolescents," in *Psychoanalysis and Social Work,* ed. Heiman, M., International Universities Press, Inc., New York, 1953.

Keiser, S., "A Manifest Oedipus Complex in an Adolescent Girl," *Psychoanalytic Study of the Child,* Vol. VIII, International Universities Press, Inc., New York, 1953.

1954

Bettelheim, B., *Symbolic Wounds,* The Free Press, Glencoe, 1954.

Blos, P., "Prolonged Adolescence: The Formulation of a Syndrome and Its Therapeutic Implications," *American Journal of Orthopsychiatry,* Vol. XXIV (1954).

Joselyn, I., "The Ego in Adolescence," *American Journal of Orthopsychiatry*, Vol. XXIV (1954).

1955

Fraiberg, S., "Some Considerations in the Introduction to Therapy in Puberty," *Psychoanalytic Study of the Child*, Vol. X, International Universities Press, Inc., New York, 1955.

1956

Erikson, E. H., "The Problem of Ego Identity," *Journal of the American Psychoanalytic Association*, Vol. IV (1956) (reprinted in *Identity and the Life Cycle*, International Universities Press, Inc., New York, 1959).

Male, P., "Etude Psychanalytique de l'Adolescence," in *La Psychanalyse d'Aujourd'hui*, ed. Nacht, S., Vol. I, Presses Universitaires, Paris, 1956.

Wolfenstein, M., "Analysis of a Juvenile Poem," *Psychoanalytic Study of the Child*, Vol. XI, International Universities Press, Inc., New York, 1956.

1957

Blos, P., "Preoedipal Factors in the Etiology of Female Delinquency," *Psychoanalytic Study of the Child*, Vol. XII, International Universities Press, Inc., New York, 1957.

Geleerd, E. R., "Some Aspects of Psychoanalytic Technique in Adolescents," *Psychoanalytic Study of the Child*, Vol, XII, International Universities Press, Inc., New York, 1957.

Lample-de Groot, J., "On Defense and Development: Normal and Pathological," *Psychoanalytic Study of the Child*, Vol. XII, International Universities Press, Inc., New York, 1957.

Noshpitz, J. D., "Opening Phase in the Psychotherapy of Adolescents with Character Disorders," *Bulletin of the Menninger Clinic*, Vol. XXI (1957).

Root, N., "A Neurosis in Adolescence," *Psychoanalytic Study of the Child*, Vol. XII, International Universities Press, Inc., New York, 1957.

1958

Adatto, C. P., "Ego Reintegration Observed in Analysis of Late Adolescents," *International Journal of Psycho-analysis*, Vol. XXXIX (1958).

Blos, P., "Preadolescent Drive Organization," *Journal of the American Psychoanalytic Association*, Vol. VI (1958).

Buxbaum, E., "The Psychology of Adolescence" (panel report), *Journal of the American Psychoanalytic Association*, Vol. VI (1958).

Erikson, E. H., *Young Man Luther*, W. W. Norton & Company, Inc., New York, 1958.

Freud, A., "Adolescence," *Psychoanalytic Study of the Child*, Vol. XIII, International Universities Press, Inc., New York, 1958.

Loomie, L. S., Rosen, V. H., and Stein, M. H., "Ernst Kris and the Gifted Adolescent Project," *Psychoanalytic Study of the Child*, Vol. XIII, International Universities Press, Inc., New York, 1958.

252

Pearson, G. H. J., *Adolescence and the Conflict of Generations,* W. W. Norton & Company, Inc., New York, 1958.

Spiegel, L. A., "Comments on the Psychoanalytic Psychology of Adolescence," *Psychoanalytic Study of the Child,* Vol. XIII, International Universities Press, Inc., New York, 1958.

1959

Gardner, G. E.. "Psychiatric Problems of Adolescence," in *American Handbook of Psychiatry,* ed. Arieti, S., Basic Books, Inc., New York, 1959.

Solnit, A. J., "The Vicissitudes of Ego Development in Adolescence" (panel report), *Journal of the American Psychoanalytic Association,* Vol. VII (1959).

1960

Lample-de Groot, J., "On Adolescence," *Psychoanalytic Study of the Child,* Vol. XV, International Universities Press, Inc., New York, 1960.

Levy, K., "Simultaneous Analysis of a Mother and Her Adolescent Daughter: The Mother's Contribution to the Loosening of the Infantile Object Tie," with an Introduction by Anna Freud, *Psychoanalytic Study of the Child,* Vol. XV, International Universities Press, Inc., New York, 1960.

1961

Fountain, G., "Adolescent into Adult: An Inquiry," *Journal of the American Psychoanalytic Association,* Vol. IX (1961).

Geleerd, E. R., "Some Aspects of Ego Vicissitudes in Adolescence," *Journal of the American Psychoanalytic Association,* Vol. IX (1961).

Harley, M., "Some Observations on the Relationship between Genitality and Structural Development at Adolescence," *Journal of the American Psychoanalytic Association,* Vol. IX (1961).

Lorand, S., and Schneer, H. I., eds., *Adolescents, Psychoanalytic Approach to Problems and Therapy,* Paul B. Heober, Inc., New York, 1961.

Spiegel, L. A., "Disorder and Consolidation," *Journal of the American Psychoanalytic Association,* Vol. IX (1961).

References*

Abegg, W. (1954), *Aus Tagebüchern und Briefen junger Menschen* (From Diaries and Letters of Young People), Ernest Reinhard, Basel.

Adatto, C. P. (1958), "Ego Reintegration Observed in Analysis of Late Adolescents," *International Journal of Psycho-analysis*, Vol. XXXIX.

Aichhorn, A. (1949), "Some Remarks on the Psychic Structure and Social Care of a Certain Type of Female Juvenile Delinquent," in *Psycho-analytic Study of the Child*, Vol. III–IV, International Universities Press, Inc., New York.

Aiken, Conrad (1952), *Ushant*, Duell, Sloan & Pearce, Inc., New York.

Alexander, F. (1929), "The Psychoanalysis of the Total Personality," *Nervous and Mental Disease Monographs*, No. 52, New York.

---

* If no translation of a foreign language title is given here, it can be found in the Chronological Bibliography.

Alpert, A. (1941), "The Latency Period," *American Journal of Orthopsychiatry*, Vol. XI.

Anderson, Sherwood [1919], *Winesburg, Ohio*, The Viking Press, Inc.

Arlow, J. A. (1953), "Masturbation and Symptom Formation," *Journal of the American Psychoanalytic Association*, Vol. I.

Balint, A. (1939), "Love for the Mother and Mother Love," reprinted in Balint, M., *Primary Love and Psycho-analytic Technique*, Liveright Publishing Corp., New York, 1953.

Barker, George (1951), *The Dead Seagull*, Farrar, Straus & Young, New York.

Beier, H. and Bauer, R. A. (1955), "Oleg: A Member of the Soviet 'Golden Youth'," *Journal of Abnormal and Social Psychology*, Vol. 51, No. 1.

Benedek, T. (1956, a), "Toward the Biology of the Depressive Constellation," *Journal of the American Psychoanalytic Association*, Vol. IV.

Benedek, T. (1956, b), "Psychobiological Aspects of Mothering," *American Journal of Orthopsychiatry*, Vol. XXVI.

Benedek, T. (1959, a), "Sexual Functions in Women and Their Disturbance," in *American Handbook of Psychiatry*, ed. Avieto, S., Vol. I. Basic Books, Inc., New York.

Benedek, T. (1959, b), "Parenthood as a Developmental Phase," *Journal of the American Psychoanalytic Association*, Vol. VII.

Beres, D. and Obers, S. J. (1950), "The Effects of Extreme Deprivation in Infancy on Psychic Structure in Adolescence: A Study in Ego Development," *Psychoanalytic Study of the Child*, Vol. V, International Universities Press, Inc., New York.

Bernfeld, S. (1923), "*Über eine typische Form der männlichen Pubertät*," *Imago*, Vol. IX.

Bernfeld, S. (1924), *Vom dichterischen Schaffen der Jugend*, Internationaler Psychoanalytischer Verlag, Wien.

Bernfeld, S. (1927), "*Die heutige Psychologie der Pubertät*," *Imago*, Vol. XIII (translation of quoted passage by P. Blos).

Bernfeld, S. (1929), "*Der soziale Ort und seine Bedeutung für Neurose, Verwahrlosung und Pädagogik*," *Imago*, Vol. XV (translation of quoted passage by P. Blos).

Bernfeld, S. (1931), "*Trieb und Tradition im Jugendalter; kulturpsychologische Studien an Tagebüchern*" (Instinct and Tradition in Youth; Studies in Cultural Psychology Based on Diaries), T. A. Barth, Leipzig.

Bernfeld, S. (1935), "*Über die einfache männliche Pubertät*," *Zeitschrift für psychoanalytische Pädagogik*, Vol. IX.

Berto, G. (1948), *The Sky Is Red*, trans. Davidson, A., New Directions, New York.

Bettelheim, B. (1954), *Symbolic Wounds*, The Free Press, Glencoe.

Bibring, G. (1953), "On the Passing of the Oedipus Complex in a Matriarchal Family Setting," in *Drives, Affects and Behavior*, ed. Loewenstein, R. M., International Universities Press, Inc., New York.

Blos, P. (1941), *The Adolescent Personality*, Appleton-Century-Crofts, Inc., New York.

Blos, P. (1954), "Prolonged Adolescence: The Formulation of a Syndrome and Its Therapeutic Implications," *American Journal of Orthopsychiatry,* Vol. XXIV.

Blos, P. (1960), "Comments on the Psychological Consequences of Cryptorchism: A Clinical Study." *Psychoanalytic Study of the Child,* Vol. XV, International Universities Press, Inc., New York.

Bornstein, B. (1951), "On Latency," *Psychoanalytic Study of the Child,* Vol. VI, International Universities Press, Inc., New York.

Bornstein, B. (1953), "Masturbation in the Latency Period," *Psychoanalytic Study of the Child,* Vol. VIII, International Universities Press, Inc., New York.

Braatöy, T. (1934), *Männer zwischen 15 und 25 Jahren* (Men between 15 and 25 Years of Age), Fabritius and Sønner, Oslo.

Brierley, M. (1951), *Trends in Psychoanalysis,* The Hogarth Press, London.

Buxbaum, E. (1951), "A Contribution to the Psychoanalytic Knowledge of the Latency Period," *American Journal of Orthopsychiatry,* Vol. XXI.

Church, Richard (1956), *Over the Bridge,* E. P. Dutton & Co., Inc., New York.

Conrad, Joseph (1900), *Lord Jim,* Doubleday, Page, & Co., Inc., Garden City, New York, 1923.

Deutsch, H. (1944), *Psychology of Women,* Vol. I, Grune & Stratton, New York.

Deutsch, H. (1954), "The Imposter," *Psychoanalytic Quarterly,* Vol. XXIII.

Dostoevsky, Fyodor (1879–1880), *The Brothers Karamazov,* Garden City, 1949.

Erikson, E. H. (1946), "Ego Development and Historical Change," *Psychoanalytic Study of the Child,* Vol. II, International Universities Press, Inc., New York.

Erikson, E. H. (1950), *Childhood and Society,* W. W. Norton & Co., Inc., New York.

Erikson, E. H. (1951), "Sex Differences in the Play Configurations of Preadolescents," *American Journal of Orthopsychiatry,* Vol. XXI.

Erikson, E. H. (1956), "The Problem of Ego Identity," *Journal of the American Psychoanalytic Association,* Vol. IV.

Erikson, E. H. (1958), *Young Man Luther,* W. W. Norton & Co., Inc., New York.

Federn, P. (1929), "Ego as Subject and Object in Narcissism," in *Ego Psychology and the Psychoses,* Basic Books, Inc., New York, 1952.

Fenichel, O. (1939), "Trophy and Triumph," *Collected Papers,* Vol. II, W. W. Norton & Co., Inc., New York, 1954.

Fenichel, O. (1945, a), "Neurotic Acting Out," *Collected Papers,* Vol. II, W. W. Norton & Co., Inc., New York, 1954.

Fenichel, O. (1945, b), *The Psychoanalytic Theory of Neurosis,* W. W. Norton & Co., Inc., New York.

256

Frank, Anne (1947), *The Diary of a Young Girl*, Doubleday & Co., Inc., Garden City, New York, 1952.

Freud, A. (1936), *The Ego and the Mechanisms of Defence*, International Universities Press Inc., New York, 1946.

Freud, A. (1949), "Certain Types and Stages of Social Maladjustment," in *Searchlights on Delinquency*, ed. Eissler, K. R., International Universities Press, Inc., New York.

Freud, A. (1951), "A Connection between the States of Negativism and of Emotional Surrender (*Hörigkeit*)," [paper read at the International Psychoanalytic Congress, Amsterdam, August, 1951], summary in *International Journal of Psycho-analysis*, Vol. XXXIII, 1952, p. 265.

Freud, A. (1952), "Mutual Influences in the Development of Ego and Id," *Psychoanalytic Study of the Child*, Vol. VII, International Universities Press, Inc., New York.

Freud, A. (1954), "Psychoanalysis and Education," *Psychoanalytic Study of the Child*, Vol. IX, International Universities Press, Inc., New York.

Freud, A. (1958, a), "Adolescence," *Psychoanalytic Study of the Child*, Vol. XIII, International Universities Press, Inc., New York.

Freud, A. (1958, b), "Child Observation and Prediction," *Psychoanalytic Study of the Child*, Vol. XIII, International Universities Press, Inc., New York.

Freud, S. (1898), "Sexuality in the Aetiology of the Neuroses," *Collected Papers*, Vol. I, The Hogarth Press, London, 1949.

Freud, S. (1905, a), "Fragment of an Analysis of a Case of Hysteria," *Standard Edition*, The Hogarth Press, London, 1953.

Freud, S. (1905, b), "Three Essays on the Theory of Sexuality," *Standard Edition*, Vol. VII, The Hogarth Press, London, 1953.

Freud, S. (1908), "Hysterical Phantasies and Their Relation to Bisexuality," *Standard Edition*, Vol. IX, The Hogarth Press, London, 1959.

Freud, S. (1909, a), "A Case of Obsessional Neurosis," *Standard Edition*, Vol. X, The Hogarth Press, London, 1955.

Freud, S. (1909, b), "Family Romances," *Standard Edition*, Vol. IX, The Hogarth Press, London, 1959.

Freud, S. (1910), "Contributions to the Psychology of Love," *Collected Papers*, Vol. IV, The Hogarth Press, London, 1949.

Freud, S. (1914), "On Narcissism: An Introduction," *Standard Edition*, Vol. XIV, The Hogarth Press, London, 1957.

Freud, S. (1915), "Instincts and Their Vicissitudes," *Collected Papers*, Vol. IV, The Hogarth Press, London, 1949.

Freud, S. (1920), "The Psychogenesis of a Case of Homosexuality in a Woman," *Standard Edition*, Vol. XVIII, The Hogarth Press, London, 1955.

Freud, S. (1921), "Mass Psychology and the Psychoanalysis of the Ego," *Standard Edition*, Vol. XVIII, The Hogarth Press, London, 1955.

Freud, S. (1923, a), "The Ego and the Id," Standard Edition, Vol. XIX, The Hogarth Press, London, 1961.

Freud, S. (1923, b), "The Infantile Genital Organization of the Libido," *Collected Papers*, Vol. II, The Hogarth Press, London, 1949.

Freud, S. (1924, a), "Neurosis and Psychosis," *Collected Papers*, Vol. II, The Hogarth Press, London, 1949.

Freud, S. (1924, b), "The Passing of the Oedipus-Complex," *Collected Papers*, Vol. II, The Hogarth Press, London, 1949.

Freud, S. (1925), "Some Psychological Consequences of the Anatomical Distinction between the Sexes," *Collected Papers*, Vol. V, The Hogarth Press, London, 1950.

Freud, S. (1926), "Inhibitions, Symptoms and Anxiety," *Standard Edition*, Vol. XX, The Hogarth Press, London, 1959.

Freud, S. (1928), "Dostoevski and Parricide," Collected Papers, Vol. V, The Hogarth Press, London, 1950.

Freud, S. (1930), "Civilization and Its Discontents," *Standard Edition*, Vol. XXI, The Hogarth Press, London, 1961.

Freud, S. (1931), "Female Sexuality," *Collected Papers*, Vol. V, The Hogarth Press, London, 1950.

Freud, S. (1933), *New Introductory Lectures on Psychoanalysis*, W. W. Norton & Co., Inc., New York, 1933.

Freud, S. (1936), "A Disturbance of Memory on the Acropolis," *Collected Papers*, Vol. V, The Hogarth Press, London, 1950.

Freud, S. (1937), "Analysis, Terminable and Interminable," *Collected Papers*, Vol. V, The Hogarth Press, London, 1950.

Freud, S. (1938), *An Outline of Psychoanalysis*, W. W. Norton & Co., Inc., New York, 1949.

Freud, S. (1939), "Moses, His People and Monotheistic Religion," in *Moses and Monotheism*, Alfred A. Knopf, New York, 1939.

Friedlander, K. (1942), "Children's Books and Their Function in Latency and Puberty," *American Imago*, Vol. III.

Fries, M. E. (1958), "Review of the Literature on the Latency Period," *Journal of the Hillside Hospital*, Vol. VII.

Gallagher, J. R. (1960), "General Principles in Clinical Care of Adolescent Patients," *Pediatric Clinics of North America*, Vol. VII, No. 1, W. B. Saunders Co., Philadelphia.

Gesell, A., Ilg, F. L., and Ames, L. B. (1956), *Youth*, Harper and Brothers, New York.

Gitelson, M. (1943), "Character Synthesis: The Psychotherapeutic Problem of Adolescence," *American Journal of Orthopsychiatry*, Vol. XVIII.

Glover, E. (1956), "Psycho-analysis and Criminology: A Political Survey," *International Journal of Psycho-analysis*, Vol. XXXVII.

Golan, J., Ed. (1954), *The Diary of a Boy* [Diary notes and letters of an Israeli boy (age 13–18)], The Kibuts Artsi, Hashomer Hazair, Publishing House, Merhavia (in Hebrew).

Greenacre, P. (1948), "Anatomical Structure and Super-ego," in *Trauma, Growth and Personality*, W. W. Norton & Co., Inc., New York, 1952.

258

Greenacre, P. (1950, a), "Special Problems of Early Female Sexual Development," in *Trauma, Growth and Personality*, W. W. Norton & Co., Inc., New York, 1952.

Greenacre, P. (1950, b), "The Prepuberty Trauma in Girls," in *Trauma, Growth and Personality*, W. W. Norton & Co., Inc., New York, 1952.

Greenacre, P. (1954), "Problems of Infantile Neurosis, A Discussion," *Psychoanalytic Study of the Child*, Vol. IX, International Universities Press, Inc., New York.

Greenacre, P. (1958), "Early Physical Determinants in the Development of the Sense of Identity," *Journal of the American Psychoanalytic Association*, Vol. VI.

Greenson, R. (1954), "The Struggle against Identification," *Journal of the American Psychoanalytic Association*, Vol. II.

Greulich, W. W. et al. (1942), "Somatic and Endocrine Studies of Pubertal and Adolescent Boys," *Society for Research in Child Development*, Vol. VII, No. 3. National Research Council, Washington, D.C.

Grinker, R. R. (1955), "Growth Inertia and Shame," *International Journal of Psycho-analysis*, Vol. XXXVI.

Grinker, R. R. (1957), "On Identification," *International Journal of Psycho-analysis*, Vol. XXXVIII.

Harnik, J. (1924), "The Various Developments Undergone by Narcissism in Men and Women," *International Journal of Psycho-analysis*, Vol. V.

Hartmann, H. (1939, a), *Ego Psychology and the Problem of Adaptation*, International Universities Press, Inc., New York, 1959.

Hartmann, H. (1939, b), "Psychoanalysis and the Concept of Health," *International Journal of Psycho-analysis*, Vol. XX.

Hartmann, H. (1944), "Psychoanalysis and Sociology," in *Psychoanalysis Today*, ed. Lorand, S., International Universities Press, Inc., New York.

Hartmann, H., Kris, E. and Loewenstein, R. M. (1946), "Comments on the Formation of Psychic Structure," *Psychoanalytic Study of the Child*, Vol. II, International Universities Press, Inc., New York.

Hartmann, H. (1947), "Rational and Irrational Action," in *Psychoanalysis and the Social Sciences*, ed. Roheim, G., Vol. I, International Universities Press, Inc., New York.

Hartmann, H. (1950, a), "Psychoanalysis and Developmental Psychology," *Psychoanalytic Study of the Child*, Vol. V, International Universities Press, Inc., New York.

Hartmann, H. (1950, b), "Psychoanalytic Theory of the Ego," *Psychoanalytic Study of the Child*, Vol. V, International Universities Press, Inc., New York.

Hartmann, H. (1956), "Notes on the Reality Principle," *Psychoanalytic Study of the Child*, Vol. XI, International Universities Press, Inc., New York.

Hoffer, W. (1954), "Defensive Process and Defensive Organization: Their Place in Psycho-analytic Technique," *International Journal of Psycho-analysis*, Vol. XXXV.

Horney, K. (1935), "Personality Changes in Female Adolescents," *American Journal of Orthopsychiatry*, Vol. V.

Hug-Hellmuth, H. von (1919), *A Young Girl's Diary*, "Foreword" by S. Freud, Seltzer, New York, 1921.

Inhelder, B. and Piaget, J. (1958), *The Growth of Logical Thinking*, Basic Books, Inc., New York.

Jacobson, E. (1950), "The Wish for a Child in Boys," *Psychoanalytic Study of the Child*, Vol. V, International Universities Press, Inc., New York.

Jacobson, E. (1953), "Contribution to the Metapsychology of Cyclothymic Depression," in *Affective Disorders*, ed. Greenacre, P., International Universities Press, Inc., New York.

Jacobson, E. (1954), "The Self and the Object World," *Psychoanalytic Study of the Child*, Vol. IX, International Universities Press, Inc., New York.

Jacobson, E. (1957), "On Normal and Pathological Moods," *Psychoanalytic Study of the Child*, Vol. XII, International Universities Press, Inc., New York.

Johnson, A. M. and Szurek, S. A. (1952), "The Genesis of Antisocial Acting Out in Children and Adults," *Psychoanalytic Quarterly*, Vol. XXI.

Jones, E. (1913), "The Phantasy of the Reversal of Generations," *Papers on Psychoanalysis*, The Williams and Wilkins Co., Baltimore, 1948.

Jones, E. (1955), *The Life and Work of Sigmund Freud*, Vol. II, Basic Books, Inc., New York.

Josselyn, I. (1954), "The Ego in Adolescence," *American Journal of Orthopsychiatry*, Vol. XXIV.

Joyce, James (1916), *A Portrait of the Artist as a Young Man*, The Viking Press, Inc.

Katan, A. (1937), "The Role of 'Displacement' in Agraphobia," *International Journal of Psycho-analysis*, Vol. XXXII, 1951.

Kinsey, A. C., et al. (1948), *Sexual Behavior in the Human Male*, W. B. Saunders Co., Philadelphia.

Kris, E. (1939), "Laughter as an Expressive Process," *Psychoanalytic Explorations in Art*, International Universities Press, Inc., New York, 1952.

Kris, E. (1950), "On Preconscious Mental Processes," *Psychoanalytic Explorations in Art*, International Universities Press, Inc., New York, 1952.

Kris, M. (1957), "The Use of Prediction in a Longitudinal Study," *Psychoanalytic Study of the Child*, Vol. XII, International Universities Press, Inc., New York.

Lampl-de Groot, J. (1950), "On Masturbation and Its Influence on General Development," *Psychoanalytic Study of the Child*, Vol. V, International Universities Press, Inc., New York.

Lampl-de Groot, J. (1957), "On Defense and Development: Normal and Pathological," *Psychoanalytic Study of the Child*, Vol. XII, International Universities Press, Inc., New York.

Landauer, K. (1935), "Die Ichorganisation in der Pubertät," Zeitschrift für psychoanalytische Pädagogik, Vol. IX (translation of quoted passage by P. Blos).

Loomie, L. S., Rosen, V. H., and Stein, M. H. (1958), "Ernst Kris and the Gifted Adolescent Project," Psychoanalytic Study of the Child, Vol. XIII, International Universities Press, Inc., New York.

Mack Brunswick, R. (1940), "The Preoedipal Phase of the Libido Development," in The Psychoanalytic Reader, ed. Fleiss, R., International Universities Press, Inc., New York, 1948.

Mann, Thomas (1914), "Tonio Kröger," in Stories of Three Decades, Alfred A. Knopf, Inc., New York, 1936.

Mead, M. (1959), "Cultural Contexts of Puberty and Adolescence," Bulletin of the Philadelphia Association for Psychoanalysis, Vol. 9.

More, D. M. (1953), "Developmental Concordance and Discordance During Puberty and Early Adolescence," Monograph, Society for Research in Child Development, Vol. XVIII, No. 1, National Research Council, Washington, D.C.

Neauks, J. C., and Winokur, G. (1957), "The Hot-Rod Driver," Bulletin of the Menninger Clinic, Vol. XXI.

Parsons, T. (1950), "Psychoanalysis and the Social Structure," Psychoanalytic Quarterly, Vol. XIX.

Pearson, G. H. J. (1958), Adolescence and the Conflict of Generations, W. W. Norton & Co., Inc., New York.

Peller, L. (1954), "Libidinal Phases, Ego Development, and Play," Psychoanalytic Study of the Child, Vol. IX, International Universities Press, Inc., New York.

Peller, L. (1958), "Reading and Daydreaming in Latency," Journal of the American Psychoanalytic Association, Vol. VI.

Peto, A. (1959), "Body Image and Archaic Thinking," International Journal of Psycho-analysis, Vol. XL.

Pratolini, V. (1951), A Hero of Our Time, trans. Mosbacher, E., Prentice-Hall, Inc., Englewood Cliffs, N.J.

Redl, Fritz (1942), "Group Emotion and Leadership," Psychiatry, Vol. V.

Reich, A. (1951), "The Discussion of 1912 on Masturbation and Our Present-Day Views," Psychoanalytic Study of the Child, Vol. VI, International Universities Press, Inc., New York.

Root, N. (1957), "A Neurosis in Adolescence," Psychoanalytic Study of the Child, Vol. XII, International Universities Press, Inc., New York.

Sachs, Hanns (1929), "One of the Motive Factors in the Formation of the Superego in Women," International Journal of Psycho-analysis, Vol. X.

Schilder, P. (1935), The Image and Appearance of the Human Body, International Universities Press, Inc., New York, 1950.

Schmideberg, M. (1956), "Delinquent Acts as Perversions and Fetishes," International Journal of Psycho-analysis, Vol. XXXVII.

Sharpe, E. F. (1940), "An Examination of Metaphor," The Psychoanalytic

Reader, ed. Fliess, R., International Universities Press, Inc., New York, 1948.

Shuttleworth, F. K. (1938), "The Adolescent Period: A Graphic and Pictorial Atlas," Monograph, Society for Research in Child Development, Vol. III, No. 3, National Research Council, Washington, D.C.

Solnit, A. J. (1959), "The Vicissitudes of Ego Development in Adolescence," panel report, *Journal of the American Psychoanalytic Association,* Vol. VII.

Spiegel, L. A. (1958), "Comments on the Psychoanalytic Psychology of Adolescence," *Psychoanalytic Study of the Child,* Vol. XIII, International Universities Press, Inc., New York.

Spiegel, L. A. (1959), "The Self and Perception," *Psychoanalytic Study of the Child,* Vol. XIV, International Universities Press, Inc., New York.

Spitz, R. (1957), *No and Yes,* International Universities Press, Inc., New York.

Stolz, H. R. and Stolz, L. M. (1951), *Somatic Development of Adolescent Boys,* The Macmillan Co., New York.

Stone, C. P. and Baker, R. G. (1939), "The Attitudes and Interests of Premenarchial and Postmenarchial Girls," *Journal of Genetic Psychology,* Vol. 54.

Stuart, H. (1946), "Normal Growth and Development during Adolescence, *New England Journal of Medicine,* May, 1946.

Szurek, S. A. (1954), "Concerning the Sexual Disorders of Parents and Their Children," *Journal of Nervous and Mental Diseases,* Vol. CXX.

Tausk, V. (1912), "On Masturbation," *Psychoanalytic Study of the Child,* Vol. VI, International Universities Press, Inc., New York, 1951.

Van der Leeuw, P. J. (1958), "On the Preoedipal Phase of the Male," *International Journal of Psycho-analysis,* Vol. XXXIX.

Van Waters, M. (1930), "Adolescence," *Encyclopaedia of the Social Sciences,* Vol. I, New York.

Waelder, R. (1936), "The Principle of Multiple Function," *Psychoanalytic Quarterly,* Vol. V.

Warren, A. (1945), *Gerald Manley Hopkins,* New Directions, New York.

Weiss, E. (1950), *Principles of Psychodynamics,* Grune and Stratton, New York.

Werner, H. (1940), *Comparative Psychology of Mental Development,* Follett Publishing Co., Chicago, 1948.

Winnicott, D. W. (1953), "Transitional Objects and Transitional Phenomena," *International Journal of Psycho-analysis,* Vol. XXXIV.

Wittels, F. (1949), "The Ego of the Adolescent," in *Searchlights on Delinquency,* ed. Eissler, K. R., International Universities Press, Inc., New York.

Wolf, K. M. (1945), "Edouard Pichon: Le Development de l'Enfant et de l'Adolescent," *Psychoanalytic Study of the Child,* Vol. I, International Universities Press, Inc., New York.

Wolfenstein, M. (1955), "Mad Laughter in a Six Year Old," *Psycho-*

262

analytic *Study of the Child*, Vol. X, International Universities Press, Inc., New York.

Wolfenstein, M. (1956), "Analysis of a Juvenile Poem," *Psychoanalytic Study of the Child*, Vol. XI, International Universities Press, Inc., New York.

Woolf, Virginia (1928), *Orlando*, Penguin Books, 1946.

Index

Abegg, W., 95
Abraham, K., 143
Acne, 8, 36
Acting out, 76, 107, 125, 167, 213, 234
  in preadolescence, 67
Action language, 183
Adaptation, 181, 205
  to puberty, 2
Adatto, C. P., 140
Adolescence, abbreviated, 219
  case histories, 34–51, 59
  vs. childhood, 11
  definitions of, 1–14
  early, 75–87
  and ego, 170–197
  genetic considerations, 17–34
  genital phase, 22

late, 127–148
miscarried, 143
phallic phase, 22
phases of, 52–158
phenomenology, 206
prolonged, 12, 90, 130, 153, 219–229
proper, 87–128
protracted, 218
simulated, 219
terminal stage, 11
traumatic, 219
typical, 218
Adolescent behavior, problems of, 56, 68, 83, 106, 208, 213, 234
Adopted child, 213
Adulthood, 148, 157
Advanced puberty, 72

PB 1047-9 SB
21A
B-5

PB 1047-9 SB
314
D-3

136.7354
B656o

136.7354
B656o

Southern Methodist Univ.   br
136.7354B656O

3   2177   00887   7068